P9-DFV-621

DISCARDED

MEDIA POWER

Robert Stein

MEDIA POWER

WHO IS SHAPING YOUR PICTURE OF THE WORLD?

HOUGHTON MIFFLIN COMPANY BOSTON

19 72

144115

FIRST PRINTING C

COPYRIGHT © 1972 BY ROBERT STEIN
ALL RIGHTS RESERVED. NO PART OF THIS WORK MAY BE REPRODUCED
OR TRANSMITTED IN ANY FORM BY ANY MEANS, ELECTRONIC OR MECHANICAL,
INCLUDING PHOTOCOPYING AND RECORDING, OR BY ANY INFORMATION
STORAGE OR RETRIEVAL SYSTEM, WITHOUT PERMISSION
IN WRITING FROM THE PUBLISHER.
ISBN: 0-395-14006-4
LIBRARY OF CONGRESS CATALOG CARD NUMBER: 72-108692
PRINTED IN THE UNITED STATES OF AMERICA

To Gregory, Keith, and Clifford,
who are the good news in my life

Acknowledgments

WRITING A BOOK is like any other act of indecent exposure:
You may enjoy doing it, but you have the uneasy feeling that
sooner or later you will be punished for it. To whatever extent these pages expose my ignorance or incomprehension to
criticism, the eventual punishment will surely have been lessened by the efforts of a number of friends and colleagues
who read this manuscript and/or discussed with me the main
ideas in it. Among them, I especially want to thank Robert
Lescher, Byron Dobell, Irving Rosenthal, Edward Fitzgerald, Alfred Balk, Louis Cowan, Helen Markel and Herbert
Rowland.

While I have drawn on many written sources, and have so
indicated throughout, a few books and publications deserve
particular mention, not only for their value to me but as
sources for those readers who may want to pursue some of
the questions raised herein: *Public Opinion* by Walter Lippmann (New York: Free Press paperback edition, 1965); *The
Image: A Guide to Pseudo-Events in America* by Daniel J.
Boorstin (New York: Atheneum, 1962; Harper and Row,
1964); *Understanding Media* by Marshall McLuhan (New
York: McGraw-Hill, 1964); *The Golden Web: A History of
Broadcasting in the United States 1933–1953* by Erik Barnouw (New York: Oxford University Press, 1968); *The Im-*

age Empire: A History of Broadcasting in the United States from 1953 by Erik Barnouw (New York: Oxford University Press, 1970); *Mass Culture and Mass Media*, the Spring 1960 issue of *Daedalus*, the *Journal of the American Academy of Arts and Science*, with particular emphasis on the contribution of Randall Jarrell, "A Sad Heart at the Supermarket"; and all issues of the *Columbia Journalism Review* from Volume 1, Number 1 (Spring 1962) to date, published by the Graduate School of Journalism, Columbia University, New York. Beyond that, I can only refer readers to the lifework and spirit of A. J. Liebling, which continue to be the constant reference points for anyone who attempts to look at American journalism with a critical eye.

R. S.

Contents

Introduction

THE SUBJECT of this book is the picture of the world that you and I carry around in our heads: who puts it there, why, how and under what conditions.

Beyond our limited daily experience, it is television, radio, newspapers, magazines and books — the media — that furnish our consciousness with the people, places and events that we agree to call reality. But reality, in a literal sense, is what happens to three and a half billion people all over the world twenty-four hours a day. Out of that teeming experience, the media can only give us, in words and pictures, a representation of tiny fragments that are deemed significant or suggestive.

In the past, our picture of the world was largely shaped by the established institutions of the society. Most vital information was, at least for a time, the exclusive property of government officials, military men and business leaders. News, with rare exceptions, was what they wanted us to know. Throughout most of its history, journalism was limited to mediating between the public and those who held power. Like education, journalism was concerned with describing and cataloguing our condition rather than questioning and changing it, and, like education, journalism operated largely within the received values of the society.

Now, in little more than a generation, technology has changed this situation. In making it possible for the media to give us more words and pictures than ever before and to give them to us instantaneously, television and transistors have, at the same time, loosened the grip of authority on our consciousness. In an era of instant and almost universal communication, such control is hardly possible. When something dramatic happens in Vietnam, the streets of an American city or on a college campus, the President of the United States and the man in the street learn about it almost simultaneously.

Both the President and the man in the street have had trouble adjusting to this new situation, but the most severe dislocations have taken place among media people themselves — reporters, editors, publishers and broadcasters. After 200 years of fixed tradition and accepted practice, American journalists are now facing a new situation: If knowledge is power, it is no longer concentrated in the hands of the powerful. From thousands of sources every day, information bypasses those in authority and flows directly to the media, and, in the case of television, not just information but experience: the raw sights and sounds of conflict and pain. As substantial control over what we know has passed from established institutions, a new force has emerged in American life: Media Power. By shaping our picture of the world on an almost minute-to-minute basis, the media now largely determine what we think, how we feel and what we do about our social and political environment.

Media Power may seem a strange phrase in a time when its counterparts designate minorities seeking more control over their lives: Black Power, Red Power, Youth Power,

Woman Power, Consumer Power. Yet, I have chosen the phrase because of, rather than despite, a basic irony: Far from grasping for power, people in the media keep insisting they have none. As they plead the neutrality of their enterprise, critics from all sides accuse them of distortion and deceit. Conventional politicians insist, with some justice, that the media, by making such groups visible, have given birth to and sustain the activities of college rebels, black militants, environmentalists, consumer advocates and the women's movement, among others. The groups seeking political power complain, with some justice, that the media, by holding on to the standards of the past, make it possible for conventional politicians to retain considerable control over the society. There is only one proposition to which these contesting forces agree: The media have a new kind of power over us all.

The result has been internal upheaval — reporters' revolts and challenges by the New Journalism and the underground press — and external attacks by both the public and politicians — Spiro Agnew's polemics, legal and legislative inquiries into the Pentagon Papers and "The Selling of the Pentagon," complaints about Presidential domination of television, arguments over equal time and access to broadcast outlets. The underlying issue in all of these debates has been Media Power. Both the journalists and their critics are struggling to understand why and how the "mirrors of the society" have begun to manufacture rather than reflect new cultural and political images. Meanwhile, each group accuses the other of bad faith, while trying to cope with a force that neither has fully defined or analyzed.

The purpose of this book is to explore Media Power — how it has come into existence, almost imperceptibly, over the past generation, how the people who exercise it have largely failed to recognize the nature of their new problems and possibilities, how the present conflicts suggest the new values and standards that are needed for the future. The opening chapters deal with the enormous increase in the amount and kind of information we receive ("The World Ends Tomorrow, Details after This Message"), the complicated impact of the new media (McLuhan and Agnew) and the difficulties of practicing journalism in a corporate atmosphere amid social change (Cowardice, Stupidity, Guilt — One Flight Up), followed by an examination of how traditional processes and forms have been transformed: celebrity-making (Publicity Saints and Disposable Celebrities), inside stories (The Truth as Property) and the death of mass magazines (They Must Know What They're Doing or They Wouldn't Be Where They Are). The passing of the old has been accompanied by the birth of the New Journalism (Who's Afraid of Tom Wolfe?) and the underground press (Action-Painting the News) as well as turmoil in the established media (The Newsroom Revolt). Future technology promises even more drastic change (Old Banality in New Boxes), a fact that makes even more urgent the painful reordering of journalistic values and practices that is just barely beginning (Two Cheers for Freedom of Expression).

The difficulties of writing about journalism are similar to the difficulties of practicing it. Human life has to be reduced to words, and, in the process, much of the richness, contradiction and complexity of people and events is lost. Each of us, trapped in his own skin, with his own way of seeing things, can use words only to suggest the truth, as he sees it, out of many possible truths. Reporters and editors have to live with this awareness and, at the same time, trust their observation, instincts, experience and judgment to make the best choices they can. They have to reject the comforts of both omniscience and impotence. So it must be in writing about them and their work. If there are any tendencies toward easy generalization or hand-wringing in this book, they represent my shortcomings, not my intentions.

Of the two, the temptation toward easy generalization is greater. In a time when people are surfeited with information and starved for understanding, there are rewards for those observers who, on any complex subject, are willing to rush in and package their astonishment and disgust. Such writers, someone once observed, have systematically exposed the fact that society is organized. It is not enough to expose the fact that large media organizations suffer from the problems of large organizations and that the people who work in them are human and subject to human weakness and imperfection. What *is* important, it seems to me, is to look behind the various stereotypes projected by journalists themselves and their critics, particularly since both groups tend toward self-righteous rhetoric that places all evil and error outside themselves. In attempting to explore the implications of Media Power, I hope to put these stereotypes into a different context, one that may contribute toward turning a shouting match into a more useful debate.

Although the intention of this book is hardly autobiographical, it does draw on my experience and, inescapably, my prejudices. The reader has a right to know something of both. Over the past twenty-five years, I have worked as a copy boy on a large newspaper, college publicity man, part-time journalism teacher, free-lance writer and reporter, editor of two national magazines, book publisher and a corporate executive assigned, among other things, to study future communications technology such as cable television and satellite transmission. Most of my working life has been spent as an

editor of popular magazines. Like all editors and writers, I
have been conducting my own education at the expense of
both the readers and owners of the publications I edited.
There has hardly been a day of my working life that I have
not wished I knew more about all those subjects that seemed
so remote in college and graduate school. This is a common
enough condition. Most of the legendary editors of the past
were largely self-educated, i.e., under-educated. Most of
them were proud of it. They considered their curiosity and
common sense uncontaminated by abstract considerations.
But ignorance is no virtue in an age of intercontinental mis-
siles, lunar exploration and social upheaval.

This book was written over several years in which I did
not have to meet deadlines but, as a publishing executive,
worked with and worried over the problems of those who
did. During that time, I searched my experience, discussed
and argued over the most troubling questions with friends
and colleagues in publishing and broadcasting, read and re-
read everything pertinent from Tocqueville and Walter
Lippmann to McLuhan and Abbie Hoffman, and, above all,
tried to examine the outpourings of all the media, printed
and electronic, with both an open mind and an awareness of
the pressures faced by those who produce our newspapers,
magazines, books and radio and television news.

All of this has led to my concern over Media Power. In an
age of instant and pervasive communication, those who decide what we see, hear and read — whether they want to or
not, whether they admit it or not — are sitting astride a great
source of power over our lives.

Under the circumstances, publishers and broadcasters
cannot sustain their traditional modesty about being simple
businessmen when they are criticized for doing too little on

the public's behalf, and their platitudes about objective reporting when they are criticized for doing too much. The profit sheet and the First Amendment will no longer serve to shelter them from the responsibilities they now possess.

On their part, the critics will have to realize that it is as futile to lament the effects of Media Power as it is to bewail the destructive potential of nuclear fission. Neither will be disinvented. Both require sophistication and social responsibility. If old-line generals are inviting disaster by treating the H-bomb as an enormous cannonball, old-line politicians are doing no less by approaching today's media as a huge megaphone.

Perhaps the most disturbing symptom of our condition is the growing hostility on the part of millions of men and women who live within a social reality made by the media toward the few thousand who shape that reality for them. More and more, each group tends to see the other abstractly rather than as a collection of people who live, love, work and suffer in a confusing and contradictory world.

To keep the new technology, and the power it has generated, from dividing or enslaving us, we must agree on its implications and uses. Without a conscious moral and philosophical base, the danger for all persuasions of journalism is the same. And it may be that the poet W. H. Auden has expressed it most clearly:

"Cocktail-party chatter and journalism in the pejorative sense are two aspects of the same disease, what the Bible calls Idle Words for which at Judgment Day God will hold us accountable. Since the chatterer has nothing he really wishes to say, and the journalist nothing he really wishes to write, it is of no consequence to either what words they actually use. In consequence, it is not long before they forget the exact meanings of words and their precise grammatical relations and, presently, without knowing it, are talking and writing nonsense."

If we are not to be engulfed by nonsense — or worse — it is time for journalists and the people they serve to think carefully and talk frankly about what they wish to say to each other.

MEDIA POWER

1

"The World
Ends Tomorrow,
Details after
This Message"

SOON AFTER he became President, Richard Nixon developed the habit of starting each working day by scanning the contents of a loose-leaf binder marked "For the President's Eyes Only." The document is a summary of news and comment from dozens of newspapers, magazines, specialized journals and newsletters as well as the three major television networks, based on hours of reading, watching and sifting by at least half a dozen White House employees. The need for such exertions was explained by Ronald L. Ziegler, the White House press secretary: "It is important for the President to be informed and aware, but not consumed by the news."

Nixon's predecessor, Lyndon Johnson, personally monitored all the wire-service tickers and watched the NBC, CBS and ABC evening news programs simultaneously. (Once, when I admired the quality of color on his three television sets, I was told that a technician came into the Oval Office early every morning to adjust them for perfect reception.) Johnson's predecessor, John F. Kennedy, had taken a speed-reading course so that he could devour scores of newspapers and magazines every week. With modern communications, Nixon, Johnson and Kennedy had access to more direct intelligence from all over the world than previous Presidents. Their at-

tention to the media reflects much more than a desire for
information or a nervous checking of their own political pulses.
In consuming the news so avidly, and trying to avoid being
consumed by it, they were recognizing a critical change that
has overtaken all of us.

The effects of that change have been felt by those who
oppose the government as well as those who control it. Even
their metaphors are similar. Allan Katzman, a founder of
the *East Village Other*, an underground newspaper, has
written: "When we reach across to twist the dials of our set
or touch the black encrustation of alphabet soup called words
that appear daily on cheap paper, how can we say where we
end and it begins? When we bite into the first morning's bit
of toasted bread and stare at our everyday reality of digest-
ible events, who's to say we are not more addicted to this
mental feast than we are to breakfast? And who's to say that
the thing being devoured and the devourer are not one and
the same, that we are not fodder for a greater feast called
Media?" At every level of American life, there seems to be
the same sense of being overwhelmed and threatened, rather
than simply informed, by the news — of being controlled by
Media Power.

In Truman's and Eisenhower's time, most of us still lived
inside our private reality. Distant events might eventually
affect our daily lives, but the Bomb, the Korean war and the
black ghettos were abstractions. News was something that
happened to other people. But television, transistors, satellites and a proliferation of print changed that. The Cuban
missile crisis, the war in Vietnam and the urban riots of the
1960s were not abstractions. They happened in our living
rooms. The wall between private and social reality had
cracked, and news would never be the same again.

No President can now govern without a constant awareness of the sense of the world being imparted to the American people. That sense of the world is a political fact. In the past, a President's decision, such as Nixon's sending of troops into Cambodia in the spring of 1970, might lead to phone calls, telegrams and letters to the White House: words. In 1970, it brought on campus demonstrations that led to the closing down of more than 200 colleges and universities, marches and mass meetings in large cities and an influx of protesters to Washington itself. It culminated in the killing of four students at Kent State and the beating of peace-marchers by construction workers in New York. News is no longer restricted to words. Neither is the response to it, which often comes in the form of what one social psychologist has called "body rhetoric." The media are no longer simply mirrors for society, if indeed they ever were, but are directly implicated in what happens and why.

This realization has led to bitter criticism of reporters, editors, publishers and broadcasters. Both the attackers and defenders have spent their time arguing about the judgment and motives of those who report the news. The result has been a simplistic and misleading debate. The critics are in the position of blaming traffic jams and accidents on reckless drivers, while the journalists keep insisting that they are obeying all the traditional rules of the road. Neither side seems willing to acknowledge that there are many more vehicles than ever before, some of radically new design, and that the old roads and ways of driving may no longer serve to keep the traffic moving safely and smoothly toward a predetermined destination.

Fifty years ago, Walter Lippmann examined all the available research and found that the average man spent about fifteen minutes a day on newspaper reading. Allowing for

magazines, newsreels and public meetings, Lippmann concluded that "the time each day is small when any of us is
directly exposed to information from our unseen environment." Today, the unseen environment is with us much of
the time.

Consider a day in the life of a more or less typical suburban
man. The first sounds he hears on awakening come from the
alarm clock-radio. He may be lulled by a few strands of
music before the arrival of those hourly "swatches of news"
(as Eric Sevareid has described them), the main purpose of
which is to assure him that nothing catastrophic has happened
overnight: The Bomb has not been dropped, there has been
no major disaster in his own community. As he gropes his
way out of the shower, he switches the bathroom radio to
the all-news station, which accompanies his shaving with a
stream of disjointed reports from Vietnam, Washington, the
mediators of whichever strikes are current or imminent, a
critic of the play that opened last night and the helicopter
that is checking traffic conditions. Returning to the bedroom
to dress, he finds that his wife has turned on the television
set. He strips the wrapping from his clean shirt to the ac-
companiment of an interview with a birth control expert,
who is extrapolating the populations of India and China for
1990. At breakfast downstairs, his children are listening to
the chatter of a pop-music station, whose time checks will
keep them from missing the school bus. When he turns the
ignition key in his car, the local radio station will leap
up to assure him that his commuter train is running on time
and to report last night's school board meeting, the town
council's latest deliberations on business-district parking and
the descriptions of all the lost dogs in the area. He parks at
the station and, before boarding the train, buys the morning

newspaper, which will occupy him all the way into the city
with everything from front-page crises to a sour review of
last night's television special. (In a recent year, the *New
York Times* published 74 million words, the equivalent of
800 fair-sized books, or more than two books a day. No wonder, in its advertising to attract new readers, the *Times* had
adopted the slogan: "You don't have to read it all, but it's
nice to know that it's all there.")

At his office, no matter what his business or profession, our
suburban man will spend a good part of his day absorbing
information: reading letters, memos, reports, trade or professional journals. For the train ride home, he will pick up
the afternoon paper — a potpourri of warmed-over news
and overheated columnists — and perhaps a newsmagazine,
which, in the name of sifting the week's events, swells the
flood with its own outpouring of omniscience. He will arrive
in time to join his wife for what Richard Rovere has described as "the daily cocktail-time spectacle of death and
atrocity" on the early evening television news. After dinner,
if he does not join his family in escaping into televised entertainment, he will face a pile of unread mail, which may in-
clude:

One or more mass magazines (*Life, Reader's Digest*) that
re-package the accumulation of daily and hourly news into
trends and issues;

A political-cultural magazine or two (*Harper's, The
Atlantic, The New Yorker, Saturday Review, New Republic,
National Review*) which will offer up reports and viewpoints
on problems and developments that television, radio, the
newspapers and larger magazines may have overlooked;

The latest selection of his book club, which more than likely
will be the memoirs of a former public figure, explaining the

errors and distortions in all the information published about important past events, including a rebuttal of most of the previous memoirs of that period by other insiders;

And perhaps a newsletter or two, expensive weekly bulletins of inside information on every conceivable subject that confidently sweep aside everything else he has heard and read in pithy little paragraphs of totally unsupported assertion.

By the time he finds himself dozing off before the eleven o'clock television news, the well-informed man may very well feel like one of those Strasbourg geese that is constantly being force-fed, not for its own nutrition but for the ulterior motives of those who do the feeding.

This obviously exaggerated "typical" day barely touches a growing spectrum of publications and broadcasts: specialized magazines that engage our attention on the basis of some particular personal or professional interest; 30,000 new book titles a year in hardcover, augmented by millions of copies of paperbacks from the reservoir of the past; television documentaries and talk shows; educational television's nightly efforts toward mass improvement; telephone discussions on radio between uninformed listeners and aggressively ignorant announcers; and a multitude of bulletins, journals and reprints that are stuffed into the mailbox by organizations of all kinds.

Still the flood grows. Technology keeps opening new sluiceways: cable television, which offers residents of some communities additional channels of news and other information; commercial space satellites that will eventually transmit directly to the home as many as a hundred channels; video cassettes, which promise a staggering choice of packaged electronic entertainment and information; and, eventually, print-out units, connected from computers to television sets, that will make it possible to receive a continuous stream of printed information along with the twenty-four-hour flow of pictures and sound.

How is all this affecting the nervous systems of men and women who only a generation ago were exposed to the smallest fraction of the words and images now pouring in on them? And how is it changing not only their perception of the world but their feelings about that world and their responses to it?

As far back as 1959, in a symposium on "Mass Culture and Mass Media" sponsored by the American Academy of Arts and Sciences, Ernest van den Haag warned: "Of course we have more communication and mobility than ever before. But isn't it possible that less is communicated? We have all the opportunities in the world to see, hear and read more than ever before. Is there any independent indication to show that we experience and understand more? Does not the constant slick assault on our senses and minds produce monotony and indifference and prevent experience? Does not the discontinuity of most people's lives unsettle and sometimes undo them?"

Discontinuity is enhanced, if not caused, by the arbitrary amount of news we receive. What we get, which is determined, not by what we need to know, but by the size of newspapers and magazines and the length of television and radio news programs, damages our sense of proportion. Particularly on radio and television, every item — from a major disaster to a minor pronouncement by a politician — receives roughly the same attention and emphasis. (It would not be surprising some day to hear an announcer begin the hourly news this way: "The world ends tomorrow, details after this message.") Every newspaper and magazine starts with the requirement of filling a predetermined number of pages, regardless of what has actually happened in the preceding day, week or month. As a result, every form of journalism gives distorted emphasis to events, because the standard is not the importance of those events in our lives, but only their place in an inflexible quota of news.

Under these conditions, our attention span seems to be growing progressively shorter. What happens to the sensibilities of human beings who are given thirty seconds to take in the fact that 10,000 people a day are starving to death in Biafra before turning their attention to the next item on the evening news? In 1968, *The New Yorker* commented on the pictures of starving Biafran children that had been published in *Life*: "One cannot allow the plight of those children to be made into a newsy event, something of passing interest. The child with the senile features, swollen joints and faded hair of kwashiorkor must not be put in his place — a little metaphor for injustice between a review of 'Futz' and a story about one of the Presidential campaigns. Unless we are stirred to action by his photograph, his expression of deprivation and hope will within a few weeks be buried beneath the weight of other news and other issues of *Life*. The real child, too, will probably be buried. Once again a larger response is called for: the telegram, the ample check or, if you are President, as many jets and as many thousands of tons of protein as are needed. The child must not be lost as soon as we turn the page." But the page *will* be turned just as the television news will inexorably be swallowed up by the next cheerful commercial.

This constant bombardment of news does not allow us to reflect on any of it. To fill the vacuum, an increasing number of columnists and commentators are on hand to stuff us with ready-made reflections, but we do not have the time or tranquillity to sort out and absorb these judgments, either.

We become aware of these effects only in their absence.

Most of us have had the experience of being isolated from all sources of news for short periods, usually during vacations. At first, there is some anxiety about being out of touch. We miss the news in much the same way a cigarette smoker or drug user craves the object of his addiction. But, after a few days of withdrawal symptoms, we find a kind of repose in not monitoring the world's convulsions in almost continuous detail. And when we return to our media-filled lives, rested and relaxed, there is always a mild astonishment at how little of importance we have missed.

The unspoken premise of science and technology, Lewis Mumford has pointed out, is that constantly increasing production of goods and knowledge is a desirable condition. The result, in many areas of our lives, is "deprivation by surfeit." In the rapidly increasing production and consumption of news, we appear to be reaching that point. As we learn more and more of what is happening in the world, we seem less and less capable of understanding what it means. "Because of our concentration on speed and productivity," Mumford has written of the society as a whole, "we have ignored the need for evaluation, correction, selection and social assimilation." Journalism as an industry is as vulnerable to that criticism as the manufacture of automobiles and appliances.

Knowledge is power, but, paradoxically, the surfeit of information being produced daily also seems to be contributing to a sense of powerlessness in the country. The young, who complain bitterly of that condition, have responded by plunging in and thrashing about in the flood of media events in an attempt to divert its course. Older people express their anxiety differently. Some have withdrawn into a sullen mistrust of all news. Others, more sophisticated, have used journalism to convert real problems into less threatening abstractions. Exposed to endless information and analysis about any issue — race and poverty, for example — they can indefinitely postpone individual commitment and action. Drenched in conflicting points of view and interpretation, they can substitute cocktail-party commentary for personal involvement. On almost any important question, they can read enough books and articles and watch enough television panels and documentaries to make amateur social critics of themselves; in that event, it seems petty and futile to take any small, concrete steps in their own lives and communities to implement their views. It is much more convenient to analyze than act.

This curious substitution of observation for involvement could be seen as long ago as the period following John F. Kennedy's appeal for Senate ratification of the limited nuclear test-ban treaty in the summer of 1963. Substantial numbers of Americans had been expressing their support of the treaty through various peace organizations in letters, advertisements and meetings. Yet, after millions watched the President's televised speech in which he asked citizens to write to him and their Senators to urge ratification of what he described as the first step of a "thousand-mile journey" to peace — the crucial point at which individual concern could be translated into political action — relatively few letters were written. Several weeks later, when I asked him about the response, President Kennedy answered with some bemusement, "We received two thousand letters. A few weeks before that, there were five thousand letters asking for one of the puppies that had been born at the White House."

Since then, Richard Nixon has discovered and identified the Silent Majority. But their silence may be less the result

of a political attitude than a helpless feeling about the picture
of the world they have been getting.

The highest levels of affluence and education ever achieved
by a mass society have created an unforeseen situation. More
people than ever are free from total concern with their immediate survival and well-being to ask questions about the
meaning of what is happening to them and the world in which
they live. At the same time, technology has provided the
means of giving them the largest possible choice of printed
and electronic answers. But much of what they read, see and
hear only adds to the general clamor and confusion. In our
society, any widespread human desire — even a desire for
understanding — is, by definition, a market, and the standards of the market emphasize not what people want or need
but what they will buy.

The sale of information is one of America's biggest busi-
nesses — and one of its most unusual. It is the only business in which the customer either gets the product for nothing,
as with radio and television, or for much less than it costs to
make, as with newspapers and magazines. What is sold for
profit is a by-product: the attention of the customer. In effect,
that becomes the media's main order of business — manufacturing attention and delivering it to advertisers.

This is a peculiar kind of enterprise to operate under the
protection of a Constitutional Amendment, which was written at a time when readers, not advertisers, provided the
main financial support of the press. The resulting ambiguity
underlies much of the turmoil that now surrounds the media.
On the simplest level, publishers and broadcasters are free to
exploit their audiences in any way they can, as long as they
hold their attention long enough to deliver the advertiser's

message. But life is never that simple. The result is less often outright venality than divided loyalty and disorientation.

In 1922, in a now classic book, *Public Opinion,* Walter Lippmann pointed out that "the community applies one ethical measure to the press and another to trade or manufacture. Ethically a newspaper is judged as if it were a church or a school. But if you try to compare it with these you fail; the taxpayer pays for the public school, the private school is endowed or supported by tuition fees, there are subsidies and collections for the church. You cannot compare journalism with law, medicine or engineering, for in every one of these professions the consumer pays for the service . . . The citizen will pay for his telephone, his railroad rides, his motor car, his entertainment. But he does not pay openly for his news." If the drug companies were paying our doctor bills, we might look with suspicion on the prescriptions we were given for our aches and pains. Yet, in the absence of a Hippocratic oath for journalists, we expect them to protect us from quackery of all kinds, including their own. What should be surprising is, not that they occasionally fail in this responsibility, but how often, against their own selfish interests, they succeed in fulfilling it.

As the media multiply, the more difficult problems arise from their relationship to one another in a free and competitive society. Each newspaper, each news broadcast is produced as though no other sources of information exist. As a result, we are bombarded with repetitive and fragmentary reports that compete for our attention at the expense of comprehension and coherence. Each reporter and editor is under pressure to be first to tell us what is new rather than what is important and why — to break a story rather than help us understand it. Even in magazines, where deadlines allow for selection and evaluation, competition places a premium on

novelty rather than depth, on the cover line that catches our
eye rather than the article that sorts out our confusions.

No such problem exists where there is centralized control
of all sources of information. As we congratulate ourselves
on freedom from such control, we fail to ask whether the only
alternative is chaos. But the questions cannot be evaded indefinitely. Technology and social change keep posing choices.
Our failure to choose may become the choice we will have to
live with.

The past decade has provided ample clues to what the
alternatives will be. But nowhere in the society — in government, the universities, the think tanks or the media themselves — has any concerted effort been undertaken to for-
mulate the basic questions and consider possible answers.
We have been subjected to the self-serving analyses of the
McLuhans, the Marcuses, the Agnews and the National Association of Broadcasters. But none of these matches the needs
of the society with the daily reality of working journalists.

For the past twenty-five years I have spent most of my
waking hours with men and women who, in one way or another, feed the communications machines — writers and
reporters; magazine, newspaper and book editors; television
and radio commentators and producers. Among them are
some of the most serious and responsible people to be found
in our society; others have the ethics and moral aspirations
associated with used-car dealers. What they have in common
is that their working lives involve the constant pressure of
deadlines and competition, the unremitting necessity of
getting favorable responses to what they produce from vast
numbers of unseen people and the corroding knowledge
that, no matter how hard they work, they can never see
enough or know enough to offer more than the most tenuous
reports on a complex, equivocal world.

In every area of our lives, we encounter accelerating change. Journalists are charged with the incredibly difficult task of reporting all these changes and giving them some measure of coherence. It is not surprising that the important social change that they seem to have treated most superficially is the one closest to home — the change in their own power and possibilities.

2

McLuhan and Agnew

The 1960s produced two media prophets: H. Marshall McLuhan and Spiro T. Agnew. Early in the decade, McLuhan appeared in a cloud of metaphor and literary allusion to inform us that "The medium is the message." Late in 1969, Agnew arrived to announce, in the blunter language of politics, that the message is the message and the media had better deliver it properly or else. Between them, McLuhan and Agnew had managed to mark the boundaries of our confusion about news and reality.

Something *has* been happening to our sense of reality and, as a result, to our responses to it. Over the past generation, television and transistors have been taking apart our perceptions of the external world and putting them together again in ways that are still not clear. McLuhan, who has more to tell us about these changes than anyone else, has managed to obscure his insights by wrapping them in an apocalyptic grand theory that insists on reinterpreting all of human history and that leads to a mindless celebration of much that is now bedeviling us. Agnew has evoked a more classic form of mindless response, the kind that looks for black magic to explain every human frustration: If the crops fail, find the witches who are responsible and burn them. Media people, defensive as always, have devoted more time to denouncing the former professor of English literature and the former Maryland supermarket manager than to dealing with the underlying conditions that have brought so much attention to their pronouncements.

One basic change in our sense of the outer world, as compared to a generation ago, is that we are getting much more news of it and we are getting it much faster. But this is only the obvious difference. It is not simply what television and all-news radio give us (immediacy) but what they deprive us of (distance) that is changing our picture of what lies beyond our own experience. News on the printed page always came to us with most of the sting removed — by the lapse of time between an event and publication, by the abstract nature of words, by the reassuring context of other headlines and stories. But we no longer get our news from newspapers. When anything important happens, we experience it immediately, directly and with total involvement. John Kennedy's death came to us, not in an impersonal headline, but from the stricken face and shaking voice of a network newscaster; within minutes on that Friday afternoon, we were at Parkland Hospital and Love Field. By Sunday, the familiar word-and-picture machinery had taken over, and we were wrapped in the relatively safe distance of a media event until suddenly Lee Harvey Oswald's blood was splattered over our television screens.

In order to build his larger theory, McLuhan insists on defining television as an "electric extension of our central nervous system." It is not necessary to accept his theory to accommodate his observation: We are living among the first people in history to experience distant crises with their nervous systems rather than their minds. We see Oswald's face as the bullet strikes. We hear an announcer urging the men struggling for Sirhan's gun to break his thumb. We watch our men dying and killing in Vietnam and the faces of Chicago policemen as they batter the heads of young men and women protesting the war. In the past, words and frozen pictures shielded us from the raw impact of such reality. Now, television and transistors make it inescapable. It is not so much the selection of news that comes to us this way, or even the commentary on it, that affects us so deeply, but the immediacy of transmission itself. We used to live in a world that seemed orderly by comparison to the one we live in today. How much of that apparent order was in the nature of the medium that brought the world to us rather than in the world itself?

Traditionally, the effect of printed journalism has been to reassure us that the world is manageable. A few years ago, *The New Yorker* observed: "One never encounters in the newspapers the luxuriant disorder of actuality. Events are pruned into paragraphs, docketed, and docked until they are free of all but typical qualities. The triumph of the news is that it so seldom appears to be really new, but merely a fresh instance of a familiar general occurrence."

By placing a safe distance between events and our nerve ends, newspapers always drained them of emotional content. The world may have seemed unruly, but everything that happened had happened before; one day's front page looked very much like another's; the world was under control. Even today, as they attempt to deal with the changes brought about by the competition of radio and television, newspapers still serve, however unintentionally, to reassure us in this way. During the Cuban missile crisis of 1962, I was away from home. After seeing President Kennedy make his somber announcement on a hotel-room television set, I followed the news on a car radio. On the third day, when I was able to get a copy of the *New York Times*, I realized that my anxiety had somewhat lessened despite the fact that the danger of nuclear war seemed greater than ever. Somehow the familiar typography and layout of a newspaper I was used to reading every morning gave comforting evidence that the world had not been jarred loose from its moorings.

This view of the newspaper as security blanket predates radio and television. Over the years, the social scientists have observed that newspaper reading has a ritual quality that goes well beyond the search for information. Almost fifty years ago, C. H. Cooley described the phenomenon of a man who would "sit down to his breakfast table, and, instead of conversing with his wife and children, hold before his face a screen on which is inscribed a world-wide gossip." He concluded that newspapers, rather than providing serious information and ideas, served primarily to give readers a sense of belonging to a community, an extension of the part played by verbal gossip among neighbors in an earlier time.

Since then, mass communications researchers have compiled a staggering body of literature, drawing heavily on Freud and his successors, to explain what happens between a reader and his newspaper. They have attempted to reconcile newspaper reading with the pleasure principle, but failed: If we seek pleasure and avoid pain, why do we voluntarily expose ourselves to so much news that threatens our comfort and peace of mind? Their failure may lie in dealing with the content rather than the psychological function of the newspaper. In a recent book entitled *The Play Theory of Mass Communications*, William Stephenson of the University of Missouri observed: "The commuter trains in New York City are full of men who sit, two by two, each absorbed in his own newspaper, all deadly silent. The reader is in a sense disinterested in what he is reading; he might look at the stock exchange prices to see how his recent purchase of shares is faring, but normally what he reads is entirely outside the immediate satisfactions of his needs or specific interests. Yet the reading creates a certain order, as in a child's playing, a brief grasp of the reader's own world." Professor Stephenson's conclusion is that the absorption of the reader — the "communications pleasure" he receives from being absorbed — is an end in itself, rather than a means toward affecting his ideas and attitudes.

After all the statistics and psychological terminology have been brought to bear, we are back very close to the proposition that "The medium is the message." Newspapers, by their nature, have always provided a framework of reassuring continuity to the chaotic world of events that surrounds us; even as they make us aware of the new threats and disturbances that are arising daily, they are at the same time neutralizing our anxiety over them. If Armageddon ever comes, what newspaper readers will miss most is seeing it confirmed in the next day's headlines, having it placed reassuringly in context by the analysis of Lippmann and Reston, and getting the inside story of how it happened from Jack Anderson or Evans and Novak. Or in still another of McLuhan's metaphors: "People don't actually read newspapers, they get into them every morning like a hot bath."

But now the media taps are wide open. In the world of communications satellites, we no longer step into a daily bath — we are plunged into an ocean of words and images. Immersion in the news, which used to be reassuring and relaxing, now leaves many of us exhausted and anxious. Advertising, in its venal little dramas, often gives us clues about social change: In 1969, a radio commercial portrayed a man who insists on hearing all the news in detail but is unable to cope with the anxiety it raises in him without a tranquilizing product.

If the receivers of news are in turmoil, so are the senders. They can see that the traditional forms of reporting are collapsing. All kinds of ominous public passions are breaking into the open, and they can no longer be comfortably contained by the stately marching paragraphs of the classic news story or the empty resonance of the conventional newsmagazine summary. Television news reflects most clearly the growing disharmony between journalism and reality. The newscasters are giving us traditional reporting; their bland faces and impersonal voices add up humanity's daily toll with the detachment of supermarket check-out clerks. But the war in Vietnam, the disorder in our cities, the turmoil on campuses break upon our consciousness in moving images that bypass the neutralizing effect of the words that accompany them. And it is those images, registering directly on our nerve ends, that are shaping our picture of reality — and making more and more of us uncomfortable.

Spiro Agnew's answer is that "a tiny, enclosed fraternity of privileged men" who manage televised journalism is giving us the wrong kind of news. But one of Agnew's own examples — the disorders during the 1968 Democratic Convention — does less to support his argument than to validate McLuhan's contention that the way in which we get news is more responsible for our discomfort than the selection and presentation of what we are getting. According to the Vice President, quoting Theodore H. White, "Television's intercutting of the film from the streets of Chicago with the current proceedings on the floor of the convention created the most striking and false political picture of 1968 — the nomination of a man for the American presidency by the brutality and violence of the merciless police." As it happened, Thomas Whiteside, a staff writer for *The New Yorker,* spent that week observing the activities of CBS, the network most heavily criticized for distorting its coverage of the violence in the streets. Afterward, Whiteside reviewed what CBS had actually shown and, writing in the *Columbia Journalism Review,* commented:

"The television sequences that CBS ran as its version of events on Wednesday night showed far less violence, and far less detail of what took place outside the Conrad Hilton, than reports that appeared in the daily press or those that were compiled by, say, *Time* or *Newsweek.* And even the still photographers, it seemed to me, provided far more detailed documentation of the violence than the CBS sequences that appeared on television did."

Whiteside listed eight incidents, reported by the press but not recorded by television cameras, that were part of the evidence that later prompted the Walker Report to the National Commission on the Causes and Prevention of Violence to characterize the events in the street as a "police riot." A month before the Vice President complained that television had presented a "false political picture," the Federal Communications Commission, after reviewing all the coverage, unanimously absolved the networks of any bias. Even Agnew's own source — Theodore White in *The Making of the President, 1968* — had criticized the *delayed* intercutting of the violence in the streets with the convention proceedings while pointing out that the delay was caused by Mayor Richard Daley's efforts to prevent live coverage outside the convention.

Unlike Agnew, I was in Chicago that week, not as a journalist but as an alternate delegate. If anything, the television cameras understated the atmosphere of repression inside the convention hall. The networks showed Sander Vanocur of NBC complaining of "gumshoes," Dan Rather of CBS being punched in the stomach and thrown to the ground by security men, and Mike Wallace of CBS being dragged off the floor during a scuffle. What they could not show was the continuing control of delegates as well as newsmen to suit Mayor Daley's political purposes. After the vote on the Vietnam plank, for example, when some of us attempted to join anti-war delegates in their protest, the police were stationed at all doors and refused us entry "for security reasons" to areas which our electronic badges entitled us to enter. For the first time in my life, I disobeyed a policeman's direct order and pushed my way through. During another such altercation, a Chicago police lieutenant shrugged at his own illegal actions. "You know who's running this convention," he explained.

As Whiteside pointed out, the newspapers and newsmagazines later documented the violence of that week in far more detail and with more vehement commentary than did the networks. But it was television, not the print media, that drew the angry reactions of Agnew as well as of Congressmen and other critics. The television images had registered in the pit of the American public's stomach. The printed words and frozen news photographs had been filtered through the distancing mechanism of the public mind.

At any given moment, Aldous Huxley contended, each of us is capable of "perceiving everything that is happening anywhere in the universe. The function of the brain is to protect us from being overwhelmed and confused by the mass of largely irrelevant and useless knowledge by shutting out most of what we should otherwise perceive and remember at any moment, and leaving only that very small and special selection which is likely to be practically useful." But we know very little about how this crucial process works in the case of printed words and pictures that can be sorted out by the brain at its own pace. And we know even less of how it deals with moving images that can bypass the brain and affect our emotions directly.

There is a particular irony in television's difficulties over its newly discovered power to arouse strong feelings with news coverage. For almost a quarter of a century, the medium has been used, in the words of Jack Gould of the *New York Times*, as "a cultural barbiturate" that "kills time efficiently and economically." Having profited handsomely from drugging millions nightly, the networks are now under attack for overstimulating them. Television people reacted to the Agnew polemic with typical self-justification in public but surprising self-doubt in private. CBS termed the speech an "unprecedented attempt by the Vice President of the United States to intimidate a news medium which depends for its existence upon government licenses," while NBC described it as "an appeal to prejudice." But below the corporate echelons, network newsmen were much less certain. One evening, I listened as an executive producer and two network correspondents privately examined their own political and social attitudes, wondering aloud if they were unwittingly guilty of distorting the news to suit their own prejudices. In attacking television journalists for being too liberal, the Vice President had succeeded in stimulating the kind of self-examination that others had been urging for years in accusing them of being too smug and conservative.

Television's dilemma over news can be traced to the early days of radio half a century ago. Unlike printing presses, broadcast frequencies are limited in number; thus, from the start, the new medium could be privately operated, but the channels were owned by the people and licensed by the gov-

ernment. In return for using the public airwaves, broadcasters were pledged to "serve the public interest, convenience or necessity."

At the start, serving and selling were not considered compatible. Addressing the first conference of broadcasters in
1922, Herbert Hoover, then Secretary of Commerce, declared: "It is inconceivable that we should allow so great a
possibility for service, for news, for entertainment, for education and for vital commercial purposes to be drowned in
advertising chatter." In 1930, William Paley of CBS told
a Senate Committee that, during a recent week on his network "the actual time taken for advertising mention was
seven-tenths of one per cent of all our time."

Within a few years, however, broadcasters found that
there were no real barriers to making immense profits by
serving advertisers rather than the public interest, convenience or necessity. By 1934, one third of network time was
sponsored. The next few years saw the emergence on radio
of all the forms that dominate television today — variety
shows, soap operas, talk programs, dramatic and comedy
series. Since news was not considered a salable commodity,
there was very little of it. In the early 1930s, the NBC news
operation consisted of one man placing long-distance telephone calls to people he had read about in the morning newspapers.

Over the past few years, I have been invited to take part
in a number of conferences and seminars on such subjects
as The Future of Broadcasting, Satellite Television and The
Public Interest. These meetings have been attended by
thoughtful men — former FCC chairmen and commission-
ers, leading executives of public and commercial television
organizations, professors of journalism, historians, some of

our most responsible politicians. The talk is always of diversity and openness, but there is never any serious questioning of the basic premise that broadcasting — by satellite, cable or some unknown future technology — will operate largely within the commercial framework established almost forty years ago by radio. Diversity invariably means selling concerts or bridge tournaments, through sponsors or directly, to audiences smaller than those reached by "Laugh-In." Public television generally means Establishment television, safe enough not to disturb the academic figures and business leaders who populate the boards of trustees. When the question arises of access to broadcasting by groups who have nothing to sell but ideas — innovative educators, religious and political groups, organized minorities — there are always reservations that resolve themselves into one central fear: Can we trust people who want power as readily as we can trust people who want only money?

In the early history of radio, it was this basic American concern that allowed the medium to be taken over by businessmen. At first, the Federal Radio Commission, later renamed the Federal Communications Commission, attempted to set standards of public service. But, in practice, license renewals were denied rarely and only for the most flagrant violations — one station owner was defrocked for repeatedly promoting goat-gland rejuvenation operations on the air. To determine public service in the positive sense, however, has proved to be an insoluble problem; our politicians and our people have simply refused to entrust any individuals or small groups with the power to define the public interest on a continuing basis. This reluctance seems to reflect something deeper in the American character than simply our belief in profit-making as one of life's highest values: a mis-

WF-R S.R. HI. LIB.

trust of political power so profound as to prefer risking the waste of our social and cultural assets rather than see them used in any way, no matter how remote the danger, that might threaten our political freedom. As a result, every effort to define and put into effect standards of public service has resolved itself into a struggle to curb the worst commercial abuses. If the result has been that no individuals or small groups have been able to harness American broadcasting to their own political purposes, the cost of preventing such a takeover has been high: Eternal banality, not vigilance, may be the real price of liberty.

Under these conditions, it should not be surprising that it was neither David Sarnoff of NBC nor William Paley of CBS who was responsible for the emergence of broadcasting as a news medium. It was Adolf Hitler who provided the audience. In March of 1938, Edward R. Murrow and CBS correspondents in European capitals broadcast on-the-spot reports of the German annexation of Austria and, in September, H. V. Kaltenborn was on the air continually during an eighteen-day period, interpreting bulletins on the Czechoslovakian crisis that led to Hitler's victory at Munich. From then on, as World War II approached, news became an indispensable part of broadcasting, and sponsors began inserting their pitches for soap and toothpaste between reports of death and devastation all over the world.

After World War II, television came to us, not as a newborn medium, but fully clothed in the traditions and practices of radio. The new medium was owned and regulated by the same people who owned and regulated the old. The disembodied voices that had been bringing us the world's agonies suddenly became flesh, but the voices and the agonies did not change. The only difference was that we could see the little pieces of paper from which the newscasters had always been reading to us.

"It is not true to say that television journalism *is* show business," former NBC correspondent Robert MacNeil wrote in 1968. "It is true that its destiny is ultimately in the hands of men who make their livings in show business and advertising." In his book *The People Machine,* MacNeil observed that "people at the network level above the news department . . . look upon news as another commodity, which sells or does not sell, attracts audiences or does not . . . There is, however, one factor which distinguishes news from almost everything else the networks transmit: it earns prestige."

More than prestige, news allows television to wrap around all of its activities the protection of the First Amendment of the Constitution whenever the networks sense any threat to their freedom to earn one of the largest annual returns on tangible assets of any industry in the United States. Over the years, in my mail as a magazine editor and book publisher, I have received a steady stream of tastefully printed little brochures reproducing speeches by Messrs. Paley, Stanton, Sarnoff Sr., Sarnoff Jr. and other network executives, their arms figuratively draped around the shoulders of magazine, newspaper and book people, glowingly celebrating our common services to Freedom of Information and the Public Interest. (The level of sincerity of these efforts has always been measured for me by a former magazine editor I know, who has earned a living writing some of these speeches for both Stanton and Sarnoff as well as an occasional attack by a publisher on the shallowness of television.) It is safe to assume that Congressmen, governors, univer-

sity presidents and other Opinion Leaders are on the same
mailing lists.

Almost everyone in American life to some extent tries to
have it both ways — profits *and* prestige — but even so, it
does take remarkable gall on the part of the purveyors of
"The Beverly Hillbillies," "Laugh-In," "Hee-Haw," "Ho-
gan's Heroes," "The Secret Storm" and The Every-Night-of-
the-Week Movie to keep presenting themselves as the defenders of our intellectual freedom. It is one of the wonders
of American society that television news is as good as it is,
considering the conditions under which television journalists labor:

Their medium is primarily in the business of selling
entertainment to advertisers. News, by network bookkeeping, is relatively unprofitable. Try to imagine what newspapers would be like if they were to produce each page to the
requirements of advertisers, most of whom want to reach
people who like comic strips and gossip columns, and who
suspect that news provides a poor climate for their messages.

In addition to its deficiencies as a moneymaker, news
has the tiresome habit of involving someone's point of view,
which may annoy people who do not agree, some of them
in high places. Network executives prefer programs that do
not ruffle anyone; news always upsets someone. Not so with
entertainment: Those who don't like hilarious comedies
about World War II prison camps, run by funny Nazis,
hardly ever complain — they simply don't watch.

By its nature, television is at its best with news you can
see. It is not good with facts and figures, ideas or subtleties.
Television can only show us people talking about legislation,
foreign policy, strikes, trials, government budgets and disarmament proposals — it can rarely help us understand the
issues involved. When anything complicated is happening,

the cameras are reduced to recording harried-looking people entering and leaving meeting rooms, while brushing aside the questions of men who shove microphones in their faces.

Television news must have pictures. If there are no pictures of what is important, it will show pictures of what is trivial. The cumbersome camera and lighting equipment often dictates which pictures are possible. In any disorder at night, for example, the cameras will be drawn to fires because, as one television journalist has pointed out, "a fire is its own source of light." The premium is on action: Cameramen in Vietnam were under pressure to "shoot bloody" if their film was to be used, and, in any crowd scene at home, it is invariably the most turbulent fringe incident that finds its way to the screen. In this sense, there is justice in Agnew's charge that "the labor crisis settled at the negotiating table is nothing compared to the confrontation that results in a strike — or better yet, violence along the picket lines." The need for drama influences rhetoric as well as action. A minister described a civil-rights meeting in Mississippi: "At dimly-lit open-air rallies each night, the speaker's face lights up in the glare of photofloods during those passages a cameraman thinks most likely to win ten seconds of network time. The lights go off abruptly when the cameraman's interest flags, leaving the speaker blinking in the dark, and undoubtedly fishing for another and even more startling statement to bring the lights back on."

As a corollary to its enslavement to pictures, television news must be sparing in its use of words. The major network programs in half an hour use fewer words than you find every morning on the front page of the *New York Times*. Each swatch of news comes floating past us without background or context. Is it any wonder that we are confused about the politics of Vietnam when the only continuing impression we can absorb is the flow of bloody images night after night?

Finally, and perhaps most significant of all, television by nature is a self-annihilating medium. A newscast exists in its own moment in time, and then it is gone forever. As a result, competition is total and controlling. A reader can look at both *Time* and *Newsweek*, the *New York Times* and the *Daily News*, or any number of books, magazines and newspapers he chooses. But in most cases, he can watch only CBS *or* NBC *or* ABC each weekday night. A magazine or newspaper editor is free to publish an article that only a fraction of his readers may appreciate. The television producer has no such freedom. Each time he risks boring or confusing his audience, he is risking everything. The viewer who turns to another channel or turns off the set is lost to the entire program. As a magazine editor, I was always haunted by this murderous fact of television life. It sets severe limits on the scope of television news and, in the case of news documentaries, it is nearly fatal. To inform people by television about such subjects as war, racism, poverty or the pollution of the environment means riveting their attention against the competition of comedy, vaudeville, old movies or whatever is on the other channels. In a medium that lives or dies by the size of its audience at any given moment, how do you do it? The answer is that, for the most part, you can't. The fact that television has dealt with important but difficult subjects to any extent at all under these circumstances is a tribute to the ingenuity and persistence of the men and women in its news departments.

Over the years, the disdain of newspaper and magazine people for television reporters has slowly changed, in many cases, to admiration for their skill under difficult working conditions. In the early days, newspaper reporters, resenting television's parasitical use of their skills during press conferences, would sometimes deliberately insert profanity into their questions to make them unusable on the air. But such childishness is now rare. There is even some understanding that there can be different kinds of news. "The newspaperman," one network correspondent has explained, "considers pictures an annoying necessity for us, but we consider them simply part of the medium, and the source of much of its impact. Being condescending toward us for our reliance on pictures is like knocking a newspaper article for not being a book, or a movie for not being a novel. Our coverage just gives another aspect of the news. It's only part of the news, but sometimes it's an important part."

How important it can be we have learned, not from the one-minute movies that make up the evening news programs, but from those cataclysmic moments when television *is* the news, when it draws us into an experience that takes over our lives in a way that no newspaper story or newsmagazine summary can duplicate. Our most vivid demonstration of that possibility came during those four days in November 1963 following the murder of John F. Kennedy. Instead of coating our senses as usual with trivia, television drew us into an experience as emotionally charged as a death in the family. Since then, there have been other times when television has broken through the bounds of journalism and, in varying degrees, become the reality of our lives: during the urban riots in the summer of 1967, the aftermath of Martin Luther King, Jr.'s assassination in April 1968, the death watch and funeral of Robert Kennedy that June, the Democratic convention in August and the first landing on the moon in July 1969. Those events exist for us not as dimly remembered words and photographs we saw in newspapers and magazines but as living images that have become part of our own experience: In my own memory, John Kennedy's funeral is as *real* as anything that happened to me in combat during World War II.

This power cannot be understood, let alone exercised, in the terms of traditional journalism. In moments of crisis, television is more than journalism; it is a direct line to the nation's nervous system. At such times, journalistic conventions are hopelessly inadequate. Journalism demands of its practitioners the kind of detachment that is almost impossible to achieve at the moment John Kennedy's widow emerges from the plane that is carrying her husband's body or the moment Robert Kennedy's blood is oozing out on a hotel kitchen floor or the moment uniformed men are clubbing children in the streets of Chicago. The problem is not only in what reporters say at such times — for the most part, they are reduced to sonorous banalities — but what the producers decide to show us. The buttons they press to release one image rather than another are directly connected to our emotional responses, and there are no rules or ideologies that can tell them which images are appropriate, fair or useful. At such times, their power over us is immense and we have to trust their instincts to serve rather than exploit our feelings.

Their dilemma was dramatized for me in an incident the morning Robert Kennedy died in a Los Angeles hospital. In an effort to respond to the shock that had enveloped us all, a local New York television station decided to ask people who had known Kennedy, however slightly, to come to the studio and talk about his life and its meaning — a kind of public wake. As I sat numb in the studio before taking part, I became involved with the interviewer in one of those slippery discussions about objectivity and journalistic responsibility. "We have to be objective," the interviewer insisted. "We have to be responsible," I insisted. A hopeless exchange between people who earn their living by communicating with other people. After we went on camera, the talk about Kennedy was suddenly interrupted for a live showing of a press conference being held in Los Angeles by Mayor Sam Yorty. While Kennedy's body was still on its way home, Yorty, one of his most bitter enemies, was gratuitously offering "evidence" that Sirhan's car had been seen at pro-Communist meetings and, in general, prejudicing the case against Kennedy's murderer in an outrageous demagogic display. I asked my interviewer if he were going to comment on Yorty's conference when the camera was back on us. No, that wouldn't be objective. Would I be allowed, as a professional journalist, to offer my reactions? No, that wouldn't be objective, either. I left the studio. The next day, I read that commentators on both NBC and CBS had managed to convey their distaste for Yorty's performance.

Unlike newspaper reporters, who had the opportunity to evaluate the content of Yorty's conference and, for the most part, reported it as a minor embarrassment, television producers had no way of knowing in advance what he would say; under the circumstances, they had to turn their cameras on him. There are no textbook answers to situations like this, but I fear for the society that would allow politicians like Yorty to abuse their access to the American people during moments of crisis and for journalists who would feel impotent to point out the abuse.

In the short time that television has held such power, the people who control the networks have not only failed to develop a set of principles for using it — they have not even begun to understand its nature and dimensions. Nor have the critics. Most newspaper coverage of television is sup-

plied by hacks who rewrite network press releases. Even the
minority of responsible critics — such as John O'Connor of
the *New York Times* and Lawrence Laurent of the Washington *Post* — seem to be swamped in the constant struggle to
make sense of the content and practices of the medium. The
result is that even the best criticism is almost as impersonal
and faceless as television itself. Outside of McLuhan, who
keeps disappearing into the thickets of his own private vision, hardly anyone has attempted to deal with the medium
itself rather than its outpourings. One of the few has been
Michael Arlen, struggling through his pieces in *The New
Yorker* to find some connection between his humanity (as
well as ours) and the machinery that has us in its grip:

> It's not so much that people don't get "content" from television,
> or that the content isn't important. They do — movies, informa-
> tion, spy shows, good, bad, indifferent — and the content is ter-
> ribly important, unless, of course, one chooses to compress the
> sum of all one's energy and will into one of those McLuhanesque
> shrugs. But what people really and mostly receive from tele-
> vision, it would seem, is a sense of themselves — the same sort of
> sense, perhaps, that people once received by looking into the
> faces of their neighbors, when people still had neighbors, when
> neighbors still had faces and looked back. On the surface, tele-
> vision now gives us isolated facts. Some fun. Even, now and
> then, a tiny morsel of the world. But what it mostly gives us is
> some *other* world, the world we dream we live in. It tells us
> nothing, almost *nothing* about how life is and how we are . . .

How now, Spiro Agnew? One can almost hear the Vice
President dismissing such notions as the vaporings of "im-
pudent snobs who characterize themselves as intellectuals."
By his lights, the problem is simply that the medium is in the
hands of the wrong people — producers and commentators
who live and work in New York and Washington, "draw

their political and social views from the same sources" and "talk constantly to one another, thereby providing artificial reinforcement to their shared viewpoints." Supporting Agnew in his contention, Frank J. Shakespeare, Jr., director of the United States Information Agency and a former CBS executive, has suggested that the simple remedy is to hire more correspondents and commentators who are conservative rather than liberal. "The overwhelming number of people who go into the creative side of television and news side of television," Shakespeare has noted, "tend by their instincts to be liberally oriented." As a result, he told an audience of radio and television news directors, "out of fifty or one hundred men that you hire purely on the basis of ability you are going to end up with tremendous numbers on one side of the ideological fence rather than the other." In the same speech, Shakespeare noted that most people who go into business tend to be conservative, but he sounded no alarm about the ultimate control of the networks by businessmen, most of whom are on *that* side of the ideological fence.

Ideological fences. After the dislocations of American society in the 1960s, it is almost quaint to find public figures who still see the country divided into herds labeled liberal and conservative, grazing peacefully on their own sides of the ideological fences. At the same time that Agnew and Shakespeare were attacking television people for being too liberal, the New Left was attacking them for being reactionary: A report on broadcast journalism emanating from Columbia University pointed out that young dissidents "had, over the year, expressed time and again suspicion and dislike for the television press. At the disruptions at San Francisco State, Berkeley and Harvard, television newsmen were singled out for hostile comment and physical violence."

Excoriated by our highest elected officials; physically at-

tacked by both young radicals and Chicago policemen;
limited in scope by the fears and venality of their own executives; harnessed to a medium that devours pictures, resists
ideas and requires them to compete for attention on a murderous basis — in the face of all these disabilities, how do
television journalists manage to do their jobs with so much
competence and such occasional distinction? The answer
here, as elsewhere in the media and in the society as a whole,
comes down to individual talent and integrity. In a poll
after the Agnew speech, three fourths of the 92 Congressmen
responding agreed with the Vice President's criticism of television; asked to select the "most fair" commentators, they
included Eric Sevareid and Walter Cronkite. Yet it was
Sevareid who described the time of the Presidential ballot-
ing at the Democratic convention in Chicago as "the most
disgraceful night in American political history," and it was
Cronkite, after complaining about "thugs" on the floor, who
remarked: "It makes us want to pack up our cameras and go
home." The Congressional critics who agreed with the Vice
President in principle seem to have differing criteria for fairness in practice.

Working for ABC, Frank Reynolds, a talented man, has
earned the distinction of being publicly attacked by both a
Democratic President and a Republican Vice President:
During Lyndon Johnson's interview by network correspondents in late 1967, after Reynolds had asked a question that
suggested that the Administration might have done more
about the problems of the cities, 50 million people saw the
President of the United States badgering the ABC correspondent for *his* views: "What is your answer to it, Frank?"
The question was put several times in the kind of soft-voiced
bullying that revealed more about Lyndon Johnson than any
of his answers during the program. (In characteristic John-

son fashion, the President, who edited other segments from the tape, let this exchange stand, but several weeks later, on his whirlwind trip around the world, indirectly expressed some regret by going out of his way to invite Reynolds, a Catholic, to pose for a picture with himself and Pope Paul.) Two years later, in The Speech, Spiro Agnew singled out Reynolds for "slander" against Richard Nixon during the 1968 campaign. In 1971, Reynolds was removed as co-anchorman of ABC's evening news, reportedly after pressure from the White House. Throughout, Reynolds had been guilty only of questioning the actions and motives of politicians. To such complaints, Eric Sevareid once responded: "I shall defer any full flowering of sympathy with officials who feel badly treated by the press until that marvelous day when I awake to see public officials complain that this newspaper or that commentator has bestowed greater praise upon them than they deserve, which, indeed, happens frequently."

Sevareid's comment brings to mind one of the first public officials to associate himself with Agnew's critique of television, the Secretary of Housing and Urban Development, George Romney. In a speech the following day, the former Governor of Michigan said: "The new culture, which has only contempt for anything from the past, is dominating the networks from Washington to New York. As the Vice President suggests, we can all do something about this by lending our support to those principles and views that will strengthen the nation."

Ironically, Romney's own career was enhanced by the helpless good will rather than the contempt of those who serve the media. Throughout 1966 and 1967, the Governor of Michigan was considered the leading contender for the Republican nomination for President in 1968. During this period, he was a source of deep frustration for reporters and

editors, many of whom admired his resistance to Goldwater
in 1964 and his generally liberal Republicanism, but were
dismayed by his inability, in public and private, to rise above
the level of platitude on any subject. Even by the generous
standards of politics, which invite comparison to Richard
Nixon and Nelson Rockefeller, George Romney was clearly
no intellectual giant. At one private luncheon, I watched
him lull a group of sympathetic editors into total boredom;
when Mrs. Romney, who was with him, ventured an opinion,
it fairly crackled with interest by comparison.

During this time, I heard any number of reporters, television correspondents and politicians discuss the gap between
the growing popularity of the genial former automobile
salesman and his qualifications for the most demanding job
in the world, coupled with their own reluctance to comment
on it. Finally, after a series of confusing statements about
the war, Romney blurted out that he had been a victim of
"brainwashing" on his trip to Vietnam. That gaffe was the
first public evidence of what media people had known for a
long time but had scrupulously avoided communicating by
what Agnew later described as their way of editorializing:
"a raised eyebrow, an inflection of the voice, a caustic remark dropped in the middle of a broadcast." When Romney
finally removed himself during the New Hampshire primary
campaign, after playing reveille on a trumpet and falling
out of a snowmobile, he was still receiving straight-faced
journalistic attention as a leading contender for the Presidency. If such forbearance is the mark of the media that he
joined Agnew in assailing, Romney at least has reason to be
grateful. No television commentator ever made as pointed a
public comment on his campaign as did a fellow Republican
governor, James Rhodes of Ohio, who remarked: "Watching

George Romney run for the Presidency was like watching a duck try to make love to a football."

AGNEW: A small group of men, numbering perhaps no more than a dozen anchormen, commentators and executive producers . . . decide what 40 to 50 million Americans will learn of the day's events in the nation and the world. We cannot measure this power and influence by the traditional democratic standards, for these men can create national issues overnight.

McLUHAN: Current discussion of media programming seems to take the line that it is the hot-dog vendors at the ball game who decide what kind of ball game we are going to see.

AGNEW: The question is, Are we demanding enough of our television news presentation? Are the men of this medium demanding enough of themselves?

McLUHAN: We still cannot free ourselves of the delusion that it is how a medium is used that counts, rather than what it does to us and with us. This is the zombie stance of the technological idiot.

Juxtaposing these unrelated pronouncements by our two media prophets (McLuhan's direct comments on Agnew's speech were similar but much more arch), we can see the outlines of our dilemma about television and, by extension, all of the media today. In one sense, it is the classic argument: Do men control technology or does technology control men? Agnew, in expressing his resentment of the results, recognizes the vast power of the medium but insists that its effects can be reversed if we use it *correctly*. McLuhan argues that it does not matter how we use it — by its nature, television is changing our perceptions of our environment.

It takes the single-mindedness of an Agnew or a McLuhan to deny that both problems exist simultaneously and in complex interrelationship. Agnew's position, which is shared in principle by the radical young, has a wide appeal for those who have been confused and angered by what television has been showing them in recent years. And ironically, the media, particularly television, now find themselves the target of a national tendency they have played a large part in fostering: the belief that all problems have definable sources and solutions, and that the world is made up of heroes and villains. "Life is unfair," John F. Kennedy once remarked during a televised press conference. It was one of the few times a television audience has been exposed to the suggestion that we are all subject to contingencies that cannot be resolved before the final commercial. The networks, newspapers and mass magazines have all been dedicated to smoothing the rough edges of our lives. If problems existed, their sources were external; the answers were not to be found in our own imperfections and inner conflicts. In the post–World War II period, all our political difficulties could be traced to the machinations of international Communism rather than complex social forces that defied simple explanation; out of this myth, fostered by the media, Senator Joseph McCarthy and his rabble created an era of suspicion and hysteria. Two decades later, the same process was at work. But this time, the media managers found themselves replacing the alleged spies and traitors in government as the authors of our political and social turmoil.

This time, the accusations are coming from the Left as well as the Right. It is easy enough to understand Agnew's longing for a simpler time when only the rich, the powerful and the respectable were fit subjects for media attention. His counterparts on the Left substitute paranoia for nostalgia. They refuse, for example, to accept John Kennedy's murder as an irrational accident ("Life is unfair") rather than the product of a conspiracy with identifiable villains, abetted by media suppression of "the facts."

While condemning television, both the Establishment and the Revolutionaries have been relentless in their efforts to exploit it. In its first year, the Nixon Administration seemed to spend almost as much time producing pseudo-events for the home screen as running the country; even Agnew's speech attacking the networks was carefully timed and its subject leaked in advance in order to expropriate the time of all the major evening news programs. After noting that "use of television for major policy pronouncements by high public officials continued to increase throughout the year," the 1968–1969 Columbia University survey of broadcast journalism went on to point out:

In a parallel development, minorities and dissidents of all kinds were putting television to use as frequently as they could to get *their* message across. "The nonviolent demonstration," said one expert, "is the press conference for those who cannot otherwise command the attention of the media and their audiences." Leaders were accused of scheduling and rescheduling their demonstrations to suit the television producers' convenience and of canceling them altogether if the promise of coverage was withheld.

Television has provided instant access to mass emotions. It is not surprising that the first to exploit such an unprecedented opportunity would be those who have no doubts about their own moral superiority. But the ultimate contest for television's power is not between the Establishment and the Revolutionaries, but between those who would use it for confrontation or suppression, on the one hand, and those who see possibilities for enhancing human freedom and growth. Political pressures and commercial greed stand in the way of these possibilities, but there is some hope. For the time being, all we may be able to do is endorse the professionalism and probity of the men who mediate our encounters with Spiro Agnew, Richard Daley, Stokely Carmichael and Jerry Rubin: the network news directors and commentators. But in time, we will have to risk more. We will have to insist that television's power be used with the highest professional and *moral* standards, from day to day as well as in time of assassination or riots. How to accomplish that goal will require long and serious debate by all segments of American society, but first it will be necessary to disentangle the questions from both Agnew's rhetoric and McLuhan's metaphors. It is past time to begin.

3

Cowardice, Stupidity, Guilt— One Flight Up

AFTER YEARS of listening to shoptalk by writers, reporters, editors, publishers and television producers, I can identify one recurring theme: Cowardice, stupidity and moral guilt are all concentrated on the next level up in the organizations of those who are doing the talking; their own work is informed by unfailing tough-mindedness combined with idealism.

One job applicant, a man with twenty years' experience as a senior editor on a large national magazine, took me into his confidence about the editor-in-chief he was then still working for. "He really is a pompous ass," the senior editor told me. "He relishes his own editorial judgment so much that I always have to feed him two or three weak article ideas to turn down before I spring the one I really want to sell him." After I declined to hire him, this editor continued to serve the same pompous ass for some years before retiring to a nearby campus to instruct future journalists on how to maintain their integrity in a compromising commercial world.

There is an illusion, shared by campus Maoists and some members of the Nixon Administration, that Powerful Interests dictate what we see, read and hear. In the context of this comfortable myth, all we need to do is loosen the grip of these Sinister Forces in order to let Truth and Light prevail. On paper or in speeches, both versions occasionally seem plausible, even with diametrically opposed definitions of who the Powerful Interests are and what they are attempting to do.

All conspiratorial theories require blindness to the nature of large enterprises and the people who labor in them. Sooner or later, such illusions breed counter-illusions, in which organizations are stripped of all professional principles and purposes, to be reduced to cockpits of personal struggles for power. Gay Talese's book, *The Kingdom and the Power*, became a best seller precisely because, for the first time, it showed the *New York Times*, not as an impersonal monolith, but a place where people sweat, struggle and scheme. Talese's view was fascinating, as was the spate of books and articles detailing the comedy and pathos behind the scenes of *The Saturday Evening Post*'s final years. But such entertainments are just as incomplete as the bloodless analyses that define issues without taking into account people and their motives. What remains elusive is the complex dimension that results from the interplay of the personal and the professional in a large organization, and transcends them both. With the growth of chains and networks, and the merging of publishing and broadcasting enterprises, American journalism is produced today, for the most part, in the atmosphere of large organizations. In most cases, the underlying attitudes are shaped, not by the convictions and prejudices of one man or a small group of men, but by the policies and practices of large corporations. The new forms of control are difficult to analyze because they are so indirect, so diffuse and so pervasive. For the same reasons, they are difficult to evade or resist on the part of those who labor under them. It is simple enough to understand one man's autocratic behavior; those who work for him as reporters or editors have the choice of fighting back or finding a more congenial employer. In the huge journalistic corporations today, however, the controlling principles are seldom explicit and their sources are almost always invisible; fighting back is like flailing at smoke. Moreover, the inclination to resist is drained in most members of the organization by their own complicity, conscious or not, in its purposes and needs.

This description is incomplete if it suggests that what is produced results from a large degree of premeditation. What has been left out is the fact that an organization's most basic aims are its own growth and survival; that its managers have no fixed answers for meeting those goals; and that it is the nature of large organizations, even those with coherent and conscious working principles, that the people at the top find it impossible to control the day-to-day performance of those below, who act on their own vested interests, long-established habits, fears of criticism and subjective interpretation of company goals. Those who attack the media as though its work were the tightly controlled, conscious output of its management, fail to understand how much of what seems to be policy is determined by the practices of the dense bureaucracy through which material passes before it is published or aired.

Although, in terms of hierarchy, reporters stand on the bottom rung of the ladder, it is their perception that colors everything we ultimately see, read and hear. On the whole, reporters today are undoubtedly better educated, better trained and less venal than those of generations past. But, despite their elitist pretensions, reporters are subject to a universal human condition: In common with craftsmen of all kinds, only a few are brilliant and gifted beyond the average. The rest have the familiar mortal limitations that are determined by skill, intelligence and instincts toward comfort, approval and material rewards. It is the members of this majority who witness and report the day-to-day news, and about them we can entertain a general proposition: The stereotype of the past — the hard-boiled cynic with a press card — has been replaced by something more modern, the urbane reporter from Time Inc. or NBC or Associated Press who approaches every story armored in his own sophistication, knowing that what he sees and hears will be filtered upward through an organization little different in business operation and internal policies from IBM and General Motors. It is not what he consciously does but what he unconsciously accepts that informs the work of such a reporter. He approaches the larger society with the same curious blend of knowing skepticism about its people and unconscious acceptance of its principles that the average junior executive brings to his corporation.

Such reporters have not been given to boat-rocking, either in their own organizations or the fields of activity they cover. Their professional curiosity is more likely to operate within established limits they share with those who control the wealth and political power in the society. As their knowledge of complicated subjects grows, they move toward closer identification with those who work on the same problems in government, academic and business circles. One journalist put it this way: "Sometimes a reporter gets such a vested interest in his own expertise that, when he comes up against a genuine expert in the field, he finds himself not interviewing the man but nodding in agreement to show he's still in the club."

From the venial errors of pride and over-identification, it is easy to go on to more serious offenses in reporting. Clark R.

Mollenhoff, a Pulitzer Prize winner, in his 1964 William Allen White lecture at the University of Kansas, warned: "Specialists have been assigned to government agencies to develop more knowledgeable coverage. In too many cases these specialists have been converted into propagandists for the agencies they cover — a type of kept press . . . Certainly we need specialization, but there needs to be constant examination to assure that the specialists are not seduced by their sources. How much objectivity can one expect from a Pentagon reporter who shows up to cover a hearing accompanied by his wife and the wife of the Defense official who is under a critical investigation? Some social contact with high public figures is inevitable, but reporters and editors have an obligation to ask themselves if they have sacrificed independence for a White House dinner or a scuba diving party with the Secretary of Defense."

Ironically, five years later, Mollenhoff himself became a prize example of how the seductions of power can affect a journalist. After twenty-eight years as a relentless reporter, exposing scandals in the Eisenhower, Kennedy and Johnson Administrations, Mollenhoff startled his Washington colleagues in 1969 by accepting an appointment as deputy counsel to President Nixon. In the following months, he turned his investigative zeal to the purposes of the Administration in supporting the nomination of Judge Clement F. Haynsworth to the Supreme Court (on television, Mollenhoff accused two syndicated columnists of "the most despicable fraud" in opposing the appointment); collaborating with a Republican Congressman in an attack on the ethics of a close associate of Nixon's former Democratic opponent, Hubert Humphrey; and leaking to columnists details of the contention that CBS had "doctored" film of an incident in Vietnam that had embarrassed the Pentagon (an accusation that CBS convincingly rebutted on a later news program, with Walter Cronkite characterizing the episode as "a threat to all of us in the media"). The former reporter's encounter with official power may have been too heady for the Nixon Administration itself, for, less than a year after his appointment, Mollenhoff resigned to return to journalism.

Walter Lippmann has summed up the problem succinctly: "The most important forms of corruption in the modern journalist's world are the many guises and disguises of social-climbing on the pyramids of power."

If a reporter's perception can be influenced by the desire for intellectual approval and social acceptance by his sources, how far will he go, consciously or unconsciously, to please his own superiors, who hold the key to future promotions and salary increases? In 1937, Leo Rosten published a detailed study, "The Washington Correspondents"; in 1962, a parallel study was undertaken by William L. Rivers, a journalism professor and former Washington reporter. The following statement was proposed: "My orders are to be objective, but I *know* how my paper wants stories played." In 1937, more than 60 per cent of the correspondents applied this statement to themselves. In 1962, fewer than 10 per cent did. They were asked to respond to another statement: "In my experience I've had stories played down, cut or killed for 'policy' reasons." In 1937, more then 55 per cent answered "yes." In 1962, just over 7 per cent did.

"It should be obvious from all this," Dr. Rivers commented, "that most of the Washington correspondents believe that their superiors do not require slanted reporting. It is worth considering, however, whether this freedom is more apparent than real, as some social scientists believe . . . Can part of the reduction in home-office pressure be explained by the possibility that social controls have brought correspondents' reports more in line with superiors' policies?"

The definition of social controls need not be restricted to the reporter's relationship with his employers and his sources. His life as a college-educated, middle-class, white-collar, white American plays a large part in determining what he sees and what he misses in the confusing world he is paid to observe and describe. Behind the mounting pressure by government and private groups against the historic exclusion of minorities from journalism is the realization that much of the distortion in reporting of racial matters is unconscious rather than willful.

Perhaps the most potent social control has been the time-honored tradition of objective reporting. If journalism has served to deaden the public's responses to human suffering, it may be because it has anesthetized these responses in most reporters. All but the most extraordinary have been shielded from involvement not only by their roles in large organizations and in society as a whole but by professional standards that require them to be as detached about human pain as surgeons.

Item: The starving children of Biafra. After weeks of seeing the pictures and reading the reports, all carefully detailed and impersonally precise, I was startled one morning while shaving to hear a reporter on radio describing what he was seeing in a Biafran village. His voice was breaking with grief. A very unprofessional performance by journalistic standards, but it was only in that moment that the reality of Biafra finally penetrated my consciousness. All the objective words and pictures had failed to convey what that man's sobbing finally brought to me: Children, *real* children were dying before his eyes.

Item: The front-page pictures of a South Vietnamese officer firing a pistol held at a Vietcong prisoner's head. As readers, we are shocked — and move on to the next piece of news. But, at such moments, there are *men* behind the cameras and other men holding the pencils that record the caption material. For them that moment is not an abstraction. A man is being deliberately killed before their eyes, and their human reaction is to take pictures and take notes.

Even the best reporters learn to suppress their instinctive responses on the job. Malcolm Browne, who later won a Pulitzer Prize for his reporting from Vietnam, was the only Western correspondent on the scene in 1963 when a Buddhist monk burned himself to death on a Saigon street to protest the actions of the Diem regime. Browne's picture of this human sacrifice was published in newspapers around the world.

"I have been asked," Browne later wrote, "why I didn't try to do something to stop that suicide once I realized what was happening. Actually, I probably could have done nothing in any case . . . But frankly it never occurred to me to interfere. I have always felt that a newsman's duty is to observe and report the news, not to try to change it. This attitude may be subject to criticism, but that is how I reacted . . . and how I would react again."

Browne's answer, at the very least, reflects his awareness that a disturbing question exists. Until reporters and photographers themselves felt the weight of clubs wielded by Chicago police during the 1968 Democratic Convention, most of them were unfailingly cool and dispassionate in reporting the violence directed at protesters during other peace demonstrations. Since then, as we shall see, a new generation of journalists has arrived to ask sharp questions about traditional standards of detachment, in what has come to be

known as the Newsroom Revolt. Yet, until very recently, the
questions have not been asked.

Talking to the Radio-Television News Directors Association some time ago, Eric Sevareid described a network situation that has grown even worse in the intervening years:
"The most personal form of journalism ever known, in terms
of the immediate communicator and the immediate listener,
has become depersonalized in its processing stages, so many
are the people and the separate functions that become involved. Anyone who has ever tried to get a new program on
the air, especially a new television news or public-affairs
program, knows what I am talking about when I say that the
ultimate sensation . . . is the feeling of being bitten to death
by ducks."

Sevareid's former colleague, Howard K. Smith, as he moved
from one network to another in 1962, told an interviewer that
"if as many people listen to me on ABC as used to edit
my copy on CBS, we'll have a large audience to build on."

The men in the middle — on large newspapers, newsmagazines, wire services and network news staffs — share many of
the day-to-day problems of their counterparts in other
large bureaucracies: middle managers in industry, career officers in government, deans and department chairmen in
universities. They make dozens of decisions daily based on
their own professional instincts, often without any clear organizational policies or standards. Lacking guidelines, all but
the best are tempted to play it safe on most occasions. A reporter on a large metropolitan newspaper once explained to
me why, beyond the front page, so many stories in his paper
were treated at roughly the same length and headline size.
"The assistant managing editor makes most of these deci-

sions after his boss has gone home," he explained. "If he can't decide whether a story is worth big treatment or small, he always makes it medium. That way he can only be criticized for being one step away from being right if the managing editor second-guesses him the next day."

This kind of self-protection by organization men may be responsible for as much of what critics perceive as the venality and cowardice of the media as the conscious decisions of people at the top. "You never have to explain away something you didn't say" is an old political axiom. Its journalistic counterpart is that a department editor or deskman does not have to justify an editorial risk he did not take. His security can be threatened by approving a news item that might irritate or anger his superiors; it is not endangered by quashing one that might or might not have disturbed them. The cumulative effect is a fine screen that blocks all but the most homogenized material.

Change is the raw material of journalism. Reporters and editors spend their working hours trying to discover and explain what is new in every aspect of human behavior. The irony is that they do this work in organizations that, for the most part, resist change as passionately as any institution since the medieval church. It is in the bowels of the media that the real resistance to change resides — in the neat little assignment charts of sub-editors who every day send reporters to cover those places where news traditionally has been made (City Hall, the police precincts, the school board) and who feel threatened when news persists in breaking out in unlikely places; in the small minds of copy editors who want every article or news story to read like every other that has been published over the years; in the rituals of veteran television news directors who "know" that viewers will not follow one subject for more than thirty or forty seconds un-

less they are distracted by irrelevant film clips; in the practices of administrators who find it too difficult to judge young
editors and reporters by the quality of their work and all
too easy to judge them by the length of their hair and how
they dress; in the inflexibility of production managers whose
schedules are engraved on stone and who bend neither to
the urgency of events or the imaginations of their editors.

Human machinery, like any other kind, tends to grow slug-
gish after years of use. Its performance reflects its own capac-
ities and limitations more than it does the skill of those who
press the buttons.

In the good old days, Chicago newspapers regularly used to
cock a snoot at authority, civic and social . . . There is a tradition that can be traced to Wilbur F. Storey, the owner of the
Chicago *Times,* who proclaimed in June, 1861: "It is a newspaper's duty to print the news, and raise hell."
Such a stance would be inconceivable today. Chicago newspaper editors lunch with other distinguished leaders at the Tavern Club, raise families, speak softly and serve as university
trustees.

These are the opening sentences of an article about Chicago newspapers in the *Columbia Journalism Review.* The
point can be applied well beyond Chicago and well beyond
newspapers. Top-level editors, in publishing and broadcasting, lead the lives of substantial citizens. Their earn-
ings put them in the upper tax brackets; the power they wield
draws them together socially with the rich and powerful;
their sophistication brings them into the company of the intellectual and the gifted. For the most part, they are not the
same people as their readers and viewers. Often they are not
the same people they themselves were in the early years

of their working lives. As a man moves upward in management, he gradually drifts toward those who share his involvements and interests, on the job and off. Before he knows it, there is a serious gap between his own situation and that of the people for whom he is providing information and insights. The best editors are conscious of this gap and are constantly struggling to narrow it. Others accept it unthinkingly.

It is not always possible, especially for a busy man, to keep a firm line between professional judgments and personal circumstances. Most editors of national magazines and metropolitan newspapers have consumed a cocktail or a meal with the Richard Nixons and the Henry Fords of the world. Few have spent time in the company of the Eldridge Cleavers and the Cesar Chavezes. And no man, regardless of how fair or objective he may be, can escape the subtle influence of exposure to people as individuals rather than the fictional characters they become on television screens and the printed page.

An even more insidious form of corruption is the whole environment that envelops a successful editor. Twenty years ago, I was working as a junior editor and writing free-lance articles for other magazines. Shortly before he died, Fulton Oursler, a leading editor and best-selling author, invited me to lunch to discuss an article I had written. He began by asking me a number of questions about myself. Then he remarked wistfully: "I don't understand young writers these days. They seem so dissatisfied and pessimistic. Look around you, most people don't feel that way." Although he was speaking figuratively, his gesture prompted me to look around the elegant hotel dining room we were in. No, I thought, they don't feel that way — not *here*.

For the most part, media executives are not conscious of the extent to which they are separated from the people they serve. A few years ago, the late C. D. Jackson, then publisher of *Life*, while discounting accusations of moral flabbiness against the American people, remarked to an interviewer: "I have just come from a very luxurious business lunch in one of our private dining rooms upstairs where we had cocktails and a nice lunch, served by waiters in uniform with good china and good silver in a richly decorated room. Would I be any better an American if I had gone to a one-arm lunch room and had a hairshirt lunch because I didn't think it was right to have an expensive lunch at this particular moment in American history? I don't think so." At precisely the time the publisher of *Life* was defending his luxurious business lunch, a young writer and editor named Michael Harrington was completing a book entitled *The Other America* about the extent of hidden poverty in the United States. The book, which prompted President Kennedy and later President Johnson to undertake programs to relieve hunger and deprivation, was written by a young man whose journalistic experience had been limited to such publications as the *Catholic Worker* and *Dissent*. If the publisher and editors of *Life* had been spending less time in their private dining room and its equivalents, perhaps the persistence of widespread poverty in the country might not have escaped their attention.

The ideological isolation of those who manage large media organizations begins with their own privileged position in the society. It is compounded by the tendency of their subordinates to shelter them from disagreement and conflict. And it is further complicated by the self-serving flattery of almost everyone they encounter in public life. After a while, the editor-in-chief of a large newspaper or magazine is living

in a world that constantly confirms his own wisdom and re-
lieves him of any pressure to keep re-examining his own ideas
and attitudes.

Admittedly, self-doubt is a luxury for men who have to
make or confirm hundreds of decisions daily. The reality
they process into words and images is chaotic, and there are
times when it requires a monumental display of will and
confidence to direct a large organization in imposing order
on such disordered material. The line between confidence
and arrogance is hard to draw. Fred Friendly, when he was
in charge of CBS News, used to quote, not without pride, a
remark made by one of his subordinates: "Fred Friendly will
never have a heart attack, but he's a carrier." One of the most
commercially successful magazine editors of our time would
regularly replace managing editors like used cars; one of
them once called me to apply for a job from a hospital bed
while undergoing treatment for an incipient ulcer. Henry
Luce is reported to have resolved a major controversy among
his editors by calling a meeting and announcing: "My name
is Luce. I'm your boss. I hired you and I can fire you."

But this kind of self-assertion is becoming rarer as time
goes on. For the most part, major issues seldom lend themselves to clear-cut displays of authority. One reason is that
power in the media, as elsewhere in the society these days,
is usually given to those who can be trusted not to use it.
The large newspapers, magazines and television networks
are high-powered vehicles. Those who are chosen to operate
them are sober, skillful at steering and not likely to exceed
the speed limit.

The tradition of editorial independence, which has acquired a rich patina over the years, is almost tangible in the
offices of most editors. It sits in a place of honor, like a valuable antique — treasured, often discussed with visitors, but

seldom used. Like a cobbler's bench in an automated shoe factory, it is a source of pride but not of much practical use in a mass-production enterprise.

This is not to imply that most editors today are cynical or corrupt. Far from it. Many would threaten to quit — and mean it — if their managements tried to force them to publish something against their will or to stop them from publishing something they felt strongly about. But this only creates an illusion of independence that protects them from the more difficult questions: To what extent do their judgments and values automatically operate within the framework that their publications' commercial interests require? What forms of blindness to important subjects do they voluntarily acquire and unconsciously perpetuate? How often do they compromise their readers by good-naturedly going along with a request from their business offices when they might have resisted a directive? In short, to what extent do they absorb into their own standards the very pressures they pride themselves on resisting when they come from the outside? A veteran producer of outstanding public affairs programs for NBC, Fred Freed, summed up the prevailing principle in *Television Quarterly* some time ago: "I have never been turned down for a program I wanted to do for censorship reasons. On the other hand I'm not sure I have ever asked to do one I knew management would not approve for these reasons."

It is difficult to document the results of a state of mind that is largely unconscious, but the treatment of one important subject — cigarette smoking and health — over the past two decades reflects some of the problems involved. In 1963, the *Columbia Journalism Review* examined the subject up to that point. After noting that "the news and information media of the United States have treated the smoking-and-health issue in ways ranging from courageous and outspoken to indifferent or timid," the editors concluded: "Only a few individual organizations have come close to giving the issue the kind of in-depth accounting that would seem to be owed to the public. Here journalism has failed to assume the kind of initiative that it has shown in many other issues of public health."

The report brought out very few examples of editors who attempted to distort or hide the facts in response to pressures by advertisers. But it is the indirect influence that is crucial: The coincidence of their own self-interest with that of an industry built on massive advertising expenditures reduced the press and television generally to the role of cautious bystander in dealing with an issue on which they normally could have been expected to take the lead in educating the public.

Item: Since the *Columbia Journalism Review* article in 1963, the campaign to protect the public from smoking hazards continues to be waged by agencies other than the media. A young lawyer named John Banzhaf 3d organized a legal fight that resulted in compelling radio and television stations to broadcast "anti-commercials" pointing out the dangers of smoking, and it was the FCC that took the initiative that finally resulted in the removal of cigarette commercials from the airwaves at the end of 1970.

Item: In recent years, the lively reporting on marijuana has provided a sharp contrast to the muted concern over tobacco. Disinterested scientists who have questioned the medical case against marijuana have been treated with much less respect by editors than their well-paid colleagues employed by the tobacco industry to issue ritual rebuttals to every new study connecting cigarettes with lung cancer and heart disease.

Item: In a widely publicized editorial in the mid-1960s, Norman Cousins, then editor of *Saturday Review,* banished cigarette advertising from his publication. Early in 1971, after being removed from radio and television, cigarette advertising reappeared in *Saturday Review.* This time, there was no explanatory editorial.

Item: The women's magazines have traditionally taken the lead on public health issues — for example, breaking the barrier against open discussion of venereal disease. But they have been strangely silent about cigarette smoking. What makes their silence particularly suggestive is that women's magazines, until the recent ban on broadcast commercials, carried very little cigarette advertising over the years. Rather than resulting from direct self-interest, the reticence of women's magazines seems to reflect a general discomfort about prosecuting the case against a powerful American industry. My own experience may be instructive. In 1960, when I was editor of *Redbook,* we published a report under the title, "Cigarettes: Are the Facts Being Filtered?" The article, which one of our editors had prodded me to assign him, reviewed the medical evidence against smoking, pointed out the massive efforts of the tobacco industry to discredit it and criticized the mass media for their failure in public education. Then, for the next seven years, as editor of *Redbook* and later *McCall's,* I did nothing on the subject. At first I could tell myself that we had done a full report in the past year or the past two years or the past three years. Then, when the subject was proposed by a writer or editor, there always seemed to be other pressing public-health issues to pursue. And I could point out that, despite the publicity about smoking hazards, people were smoking more than ever before; would they be impressed by still another article on the subject? But the answer, in retrospect, seems to be that I was exercising my editorial independence in more comfortable areas. It may have been more urgent to deal with the dangers of nuclear fallout and air pollution, but it was also a good deal safer in terms of not ruffling advertising agencies and the larger commercial world they represent.

Not long before he died, Henry R. Luce proposed a definition to a group of younger editors around a luncheon table. "Good editing," he suggested, "is figuring out what's going to happen and advocating it before it does." It would be comforting to report that the remark was accompanied by a mischievous twinkle in Luce's eye. It was not.

By this definition, the editor is a courtier to the public — impressing readers with his sophistication and inside information, seeking favor by identifying himself with the prevailing wisdom, trying to stay one step ahead of a public dialogue in which he assumes no risks by taking a substantive part. Luce himself, on such issues as recognizing the existence of Communist China, was not a consistent adherent to his own definition, but it does fit a good many editors today, particularly of the largest publications. The need to appear knowledgeable and even prescient exerts a powerful influence.

For some executives, the fear of appearing to be naïve is much stronger than the fear of seeming unscrupulous. A few years ago, *McCall's* published an article about the bestseller lists in book publishing. One publisher, who received fairly rough treatment for his tasteless and rather questionable business practices, called me cheerfully and asked for several dozen reprints of the article. Another publisher, who was cited for failing to recognize the potential popularity of

one of his books until the public started buying it spontane-
ously, wrote a furious letter and threatened to consult his
lawyer. The two responses suggest the prevailing values of
many media executives: To accuse a man of not always being
shrewd in his judgments is far worse than calling him un-
principled in pursuit of commercial success.

In a far more significant case, the Presidential campaign of
Eugene McCarthy, particularly in its early stages, reflects
this vulnerability on the part of editors. When McCarthy
declared his candidacy in November 1967, it was clear that
a strong current was running in the country against the
Johnson Administration's conduct of the war in Vietnam and
its policies in a broader sense. But since no incumbent President had ever been successfully challenged for renomina-
tion, journalists refused to see any connection between Mc-
Carthy's chances and Johnson's unpopularity. As a result,
the hard-headed news judgment was that McCarthy merited
only minor coverage. The attitude of the *New York Times*
was especially striking. Until the last two weeks of the New
Hampshire primary campaign, the *Times* concentrated its
attention on the sight of George Romney lurching toward
political obscurity and virtually ignored McCarthy. One
day, shortly before the Michigan governor's abrupt withdrawal, the *Times* devoted space to his every movement as
well as a long story about Mrs. Romney's activities, while dismissing McCarthy's speeches in a few paragraphs. In private
discussions, I found some misgivings about the *Times'* approach among its own editors. Displaying great institutional
courage, the newspaper had been editorially criticizing the
conduct of the war in Vietnam for some time, yet it refused
to take seriously the only political challenge being made to
that policy. In effect, the *Times* was willing to risk being

unpopular in its editorial position but not to risk appearing naïve in its news judgment.

During this period, Michael Janeway was pointing out in *The Atlantic* that some members of the Washington press corps regarded running against the war "as a fool's errand and doubt that McCarthy can affect the war any more through a sizable primary vote than through Senate resolutions." Covering the New Hampshire campaign in the same magazine, Ward Just reported that McCarthy's "press was bad. The press likes professionals." In a conversation several weeks before that first primary, Senator McCarthy's wife told me: "When I'm up in New Hampshire, it looks encouraging. Then I come back to Washington and read the newspapers, and it looks hopeless." In *Harper's*, David Halberstam's notation for January 1968 was that "the McCarthy campaign is getting minimal attention in most of the press."

Why? Just as journalists can lend significance to people and phenomena that attract their concentrated attention, so can they deny the existence of important political currents by letting them go unreported. In late 1967 and early 1968, the conventional political wisdom denied the possibility that Lyndon Johnson might not be renominated. To have taken that possibility seriously before the New Hampshire vote confirmed it would have exposed political reporters and their editors to the risk of appearing unrealistic. On the evening of March 12, when the tallies showed McCarthy within several hundred votes of Johnson out of a total of 56,000 cast for the two men, the result came as a surprise to most journalists. Naturally, the surprise itself was converted without hesitation into a new kind of conventional wisdom; for the remainder of the primary season, the complex constituency that had rallied to McCarthy's support was reduced to a simple stereotype of doorbell-ringing students. No turn of events, regardless of how unexpected it may be, serves to wipe the knowing expression off the media's face.

"Freedom of the press," A. J. Liebling wrote in 1960, "is guaranteed only to those who own one."

Around the turn of the century, the legendary publisher E. W. Scripps, who founded and revitalized newspapers in a number of communities, boasted that none of his successful papers had required an investment of more than $30,000. "All two young men need to start a newspaper," he remarked, "is a basement, a second-hand press, four linotype machines, and a message." Two thirds of a century later, conditions had changed somewhat. In 1966, Scripps-Howard (E.W.'s corporate descendant) undertook a $16 million modernization and expansion program for *one* newspaper: the Cincinnati *Post & Times-Star*. In 1835, James Gordon Bennett started the New York *Herald* on $500; in 1841, Horace Greeley launched the New York *Tribune* with $3000. In 1967, after the death of the *World Journal-Tribune*, the owners of the *New York Times* estimated that it would take at least $25 million and probably twice that much to start a new afternoon paper in New York.

Competition in what publishers and broadcasters expansively describe, in commencement addresses, as "the free marketplace of ideas" is becoming more and more the province of corporations with high price-earnings ratios than young men with a message. Newspapers and broadcast outlets are increasingly being swallowed up into larger and larger concentrations. Owners have monopolies in 96 per cent of the 1500 American cities that are served by daily newspapers; in many of these cities, the same owners also control a television and/or radio station. In an article entitled "The Media Barons and the Public Interest" in *The Atlantic* in 1968, Nicholas Johnson of the FCC warned:

"I fear that we have already reached the point in this country where the media, our greatest check on other accumulations of power, may themselves be beyond the reach of any other institution: the Congress, the President, or the Federal Communications Commission, not to mention governors, mayors, state legislators, and city councilmen. Congressional hearings are begun and then quietly dropped. Whenever the FCC stirs fitfully as if in wakefulness, the broadcasting industry scurries up the Hill for a congressional bludgeon. And the fact that roughly 80 per cent of all campaign expenses go to radio and television gives but a glimmer of the power of broadcasting in the lives of senators and congressmen."

Commissioner Johnson's concern is framed in the context of his experience in politics; at one point he asks his readers to "imagine, for example, what the structure of political power in this country might look like if two or three companies owned substantially all of the broadcast media in our major cities." It is prudent to worry over the exercise of political power by those who control large segments of American journalism, but that danger is rather remote. The media are concerned primarily with profit rather than political power. No matter how large a segment of the media they acquire, it defies the imagination to picture as ideological dictators such managers as Frank Stanton of CBS or the faceless committee that succeeded Henry Luce at Time Inc. or Samuel I. Newhouse, who keeps adding newspapers to his chain the way others add laundermats and who operates them on similar philosophical principles. Because the networks and publishing corporations are after our money rather than our minds, the main danger that Media Power poses is not tyranny but inanity and irrelevance.

The historian Oscar Handlin has observed: "The way in which the contents of the mass media are communicated deprives the audience of any degree of selectivity, for these contents are marketed as any other commodities are. In our society it seems possible through the use of the proper marketing device to sell anybody anything, so that what is sold has very little relevance to character of either the buyers or of the article sold. This is as true of culture as of refrigerators or fur coats. The contents of the magazine or the TV schedule or the newspaper have as little to do with their sales potential as the engine specifications with the marketability of an automobile."

It is a measure of the media's difficulties that they can be accused, on the one hand, of exercising a dangerous degree of power in our society and, on the other, of functioning without conviction or purpose — and, in both cases, with some justice.

And yet . . .

All of these shortcomings do exist: Corporate managers *are* preoccupied with commercial rather than social values; editors and executives *are* obsessed with their own appearance of infallibility, and many do practice editorial freedom in the narrowest rather than the broadest sense; middle-level supervisors *are* self-protecting and resistant to change; reporters and writers *are* susceptible to their own preconceptions and the seductions of those who hold power. And yet . . .

Journalistic organizations can and should be criticized. But the wonder is how often they pierce the clamor and confusion of a disordered society and, somehow almost in spite of themselves, focus attention on the underlying issues of our time and place in history. One towering example is the change in public opinion toward the war in Vietnam.

If the growing disaster in Indochina escaped public attention in the early 1960s, part of the blame belongs to the news judgment of American editors. As late as 1963, the only full-time staff correspondent of an American newspaper in Vietnam was David Halberstam of the *New York Times*. Yet Halberstam and a few reporters for the wire services and newsmagazines, despite great pressure from politicians in Washington and Saigon, told the story of the Diem regime's corruption and the self-deception involved in official optimism over the course of the war. Halberstam was rewarded by President Kennedy's suggestion to the publisher of the *Times* that he be replaced in Saigon and by the invective of Madame Nhu, President Diem's sister-in-law ("Halberstam should be barbecued, and I would be glad to supply the fluid and the match"). *Newsweek*'s correspondent was expelled on the flimsiest grounds by the Vietnamese government after seventeen years of residence in the country. Two correspondents for *Time* resigned after their editors, from the perspective of New York, published an attack on the American press corps in Saigon.

Despite censorship and intimidation on the scene and pressure on their editors back home, a handful of stubbornly honest reporters managed to tell the truth to that minority of the American people that was then willing to inform itself about a distant and dirty little war. A year later, in 1964, Halberstam received a Pulitzer Prize, which he shared with Malcolm Browne, then of the Associated Press. Two years

later, the American Embassy press officer of that period in
Saigon acknowledged: "Our feud with the newsmen was an
angry symptom of bureaucratic sickness."

During the Johnson years, in which a military and diplomatic morass was being converted into a national disaster,
it was the media that brought some measure of reality to the
American people about Vietnam. The performance was a
mixed one: The *New York Times* tenaciously kept pointing
out the folly of our policy, while most other large newspapers accepted the government's optimism and obfuscation
uncritically; *Newsweek* told its readers that the war was
going badly, while *Time* refused to lose its composure; young
writers like Jonathan Schell in *The New Yorker* and John
Sack in *Esquire* brought the war home in long, disciplined
and dramatic narratives, yet some magazine editors, with
access to millions of readers on a weekly or monthly basis,
did less to enlighten the country than the presumably slower
moving book publishers, such as Random House, which
put out illuminating volumes by Jean Lacouture, Richard
Goodwin, Senator J. William Fulbright and Halberstam,
among others.

Above all, it was television, with pictures rather than
words, that brought the war into the minds of millions. "The
war in Vietnam," Richard H. Rovere wrote in *The New
Yorker* in the fall of 1967, "is close to the center of national
consciousness because of the ease with which we can 'follow'
it — 'live,' or almost. Because of television, it is impossible
to be unaware of, and hence indifferent to, the war, as the
people of the European colonial powers in the eighteenth
and nineteenth centuries were largely unaware of the prolonged and costly campaigns — many of them much like
the war in Vietnam — being carried on by their armies and
navies in distant parts of the world." To read the word

"pacification" in newspapers was one thing; to see on television that it meant women and children, those whom we were presumably protecting, running in terror as we burned their villages was quite another.

The issue was comparatively simple in 1733 when John Peter Zenger began his journalistic attacks on the British governor of New York, only to be arrested for libel and finally freed on the basis of Andrew Hamilton's defense, which established the lasting precedent for freedom of the press in America. By contrast, the war in Vietnam has been complex, confusing and unsusceptible to simple conclusions. But the reporters who resisted the official versions of what was happening there were fighting for an important modern corollary to Zenger's accomplishment: freedom of the press from being coerced in the name of patriotism. Long before the Pentagon Papers brought the question to the Supreme Court, Dean Rusk posed the issue in its baldest form when a reporter, at an off-the-record meeting, questioned him about the failure of our intelligence to warn of the devastating Tet offensive early in 1968. Rusk's answer was an angry comment that he sometimes wondered which side reporters were on, followed by his announcement that "I'm the Secretary of State, and I'm on *our* side." (In an informal meeting about a year earlier, I got a similar reaction from Hubert Humphrey when I asked about his remark that a coalition government in South Vietnam would be inviting "the fox into the chicken coop." When I pointed out that even General Maxwell Taylor did not sound as intractable on that question, Humphrey glared at me and announced: "*I'm* the Vice President.")

Rusk's outburst might be attributed to the nervous exhaustion of a man nearing the end of a long period of difficult service if the substance of his attack had not been applied a year earlier to the reporting of Harrison Salisbury of the

New York Times from Hanoi. Shortly before Christmas of 1966, Salisbury was admitted to North Vietnam. In his first dispatch from Hanoi, he reported: "Contrary to the impression given by United States communiqués, on-the-spot inspection indicates that American bombing has been inflicting considerable civilian casualties in Hanoi and its environs." The Defense Department, which had denied civilian casualties up to that point, several days later conceded that "it is impossible to avoid all damage to civilian areas," prompting the conservative Chicago *Tribune* to conclude that "the Communists have been more truthful than the Washington news managers." In the following weeks, the Administration launched a bitter campaign against Salisbury, through friendly columnists and commentators, reflecting its outrage that a reputable journalist had chosen to report his own observations at the risk of contradicting his government. Before it was over, Salisbury had been accused of everything short of treason, including a rhetorical question by Joseph Alsop, who had come to consider himself the personal proprietor of the war in Vietnam, as to "whether a United States reporter ought to go to an enemy capital to give the authority of his by-line to enemy propaganda figures." When the carping was over, Salisbury's reporting had held up and the fact that American bombing was causing considerable civilian injury and damage in North Vietnam was generally accepted.

A comparable response, albeit in private rather than public, was made to the efforts of two Los Angeles *Times* correspondents, David Kraslow and Stuart H. Loory, who spent seven months traveling to diplomatic centers all over the world in order to unravel the official misrepresentations and outright lies about United States policy and practices. Their prize-winning articles, published in April 1968, included the revelation that our government had blocked an opportunity for negotiations with North Vietnam early in 1967 by hardening our position after groundwork for talks had been prepared in discussions between Soviet Premier Kosygin and British Prime Minister Wilson. While Kraslow and Loory were working on their series, Walt W. Rostow, one of President Johnson's closest advisers, reportedly told them: "I want you to know that we know just what you are doing and I think it is the most reprehensible thing any newspapermen have done since the Chicago *Tribune* published the fact that we had cracked the Japanese naval code."

Looking back at more than a decade of reporting about and from Vietnam, the war offers a reasonable yardstick by which to judge the performance of journalism in our time. At first, we were told too little of what was happening there and, as our commitment of men and money reached frightening proportions, we were told too much that was self-serving, wishful and ultimately deceptive on the part of our own government. Throughout it all, a minority of reporters was cutting through the confusion to show us the realities and the implications of what was to become the most unpopular war in American history. It is ironic that many young people, who were prompted to oppose the war by what they saw on television and read in newspapers and magazines, came to regard all of the media as part of an Establishment that requires destruction by revolutionary action. If they ever succeed in their objective, it will be instructive to see if what they perceive as their superior morality will entirely overcome human imperfection, incompetence and inconsistency in creating not only a more just society but a more just network of communications.

In 1969, Western journalists learned that a thirty-one-year-old Soviet radio reporter had been released after serving eighteen months in a prison camp. He had been convicted of "slandering the Soviet system" by reporting on the secret trials of fifteen Ukrainian intellectuals in 1965 and 1966. There are passionate critics who will see little difference between a system that exercises direct suppression of this kind and one that undermines the integrity of its editors and reporters by more subtle means. But the difference exists nonetheless. It exists because individual human beings with conviction and imagination can break through the oppressive self-deception and self-satisfaction of our corporate media; those qualities would be much harder to exercise from the inside of a jail cell.

4

Publicity Saints and
Disposable Celebrities

A FEW WEEKS after Lyndon Johnson left the White House, I had occasion to visit him in Texas. The former President, preparing to write his memoirs, was still brooding over the reporting of his Administration, particularly the war in Vietnam. "Why," he asked, "do the newspapers and magazines and television people keep on describing Rusk and Rostow as hawks, and McNamara and Bundy as doves? There were so many times when Rusk argued for de-escalation and McNamara wanted to step up the war."

I doubt that my answer afforded the former President any comfort, but it does reflect a basic fact about the media: In the continuing public drama (or soap opera, if you prefer) composed by editors and reporters out of the vast disorder of events, it is vital that each public figure be assigned his role. The pace and scale of the spectacle do not allow for inconsistencies or nuances of character. After Dean Rusk took on his public role as chief prosecutor of the war in Vietnam, the fact that one Tuesday in 1967 the actual person named Dean Rusk wanted to stop the bombing of North Vietnam could not be readily reconciled with the media character named Dean Rusk. The show must go on, and the actors cannot be allowed to confuse the audience.

Of all people, Lyndon Johnson should have been most painfully aware of this hard fact of political life. Most of his time in office was spent fighting his public shadow and the harder he fought the more deep-dyed it became. More openly than any President in recent history, he tried to stage-manage his own media scenes and was baffled when the headlines and television screen kept departing from his script. A small but suggestive example of his efforts and the frustrating results took place early in his term. As reported in the employee publication of United Press International, one of the wire service's editors received a phone call one night and found himself involved in a conversation about an item that the President had obviously just read on the UPI ticker in his office:

"Hello?"

"Hello, Pat, this is Lyndon Johnson."

"Yes, Mr. President."

"Say, I have here . . . (pause) . . . A101N from Johnson City, Texas, about the homestead, by Kyle Thompson. Let's see . . . (pause) . . . you say in there that there's going to be a fee for the tour. Well, that's not right at all. The idea is to give it to the people."

"Just a minute, Mr. President, and I'll get the story."

"You see what it says. It says 'the home was opened to the public for fee tours.' That isn't right. You see, it's for free. That's the idea. Do you see that?"

"Yes, Mr. President. It looks like they dropped the 'r' in the word 'free.' I guess they omitted it in transmission."

"Well, Pat, it sure does mean just the opposite of what we mean."

"It sure does, Mr. President. I'll fix it."

"Well, we want it to be free."

"Certainly, Mr. President. I'll straighten it out right away."

"I'd appreciate it if you would clean this up for me."

"I certainly will, Mr. President."

"We hope you will take the necessary steps to straighten this out."

"Yes, sir, Mr. President."

"Thank you, Pat."

"Thank you for letting us know, Mr. President."

The UPI's story of the conversation was widely disseminated among media people, and long after they had forgotten whether or not there was an admission charge to the Johnson homestead, editors and reporters across the country retained the picture of a President of the United States avidly monitoring the wire-service tickers and calling in a minor change of detail with the kind of alacrity that might have been embarrassing in a Broadway press agent.

Of the three billion people living in our time, only a relative handful at any given moment can be assigned speaking parts on the media stage — the others are seen only dimly in the crowd scenes as victims of war and natural disaster or in fleeting appearances as the man in the street. This overwhelming majority is separated from those who are awarded public identities as political or religious figures, star entertainers or athletes, best-selling authors or business leaders, master criminals or master detectives, "authorities" on something or other, or as members of the Beautiful People. The process by which these selections are made and the conditions that govern the chosen can tell us a good deal about the power and principles of the media as well as of the society they reflect.

To begin with, the main requirement is not an individual's worth or accomplishment but his ability to attract and hold interest. It is not the most talented actors, original thinkers or dedicated politicians who rise to the first rank of celebrity but rather those with a combination of determination, flair and willingness to risk appearing over-ambitious, foolish or even malign. This last quality is crucial. It defines those who can capture attention amid intense competition. Long before she became a symbol and finally a legend, Marilyn Monroe was a joke in editorial offices for her willingness to pose for the most obvious publicity pictures and to mouth the most blatant wisecracks her agents could devise. The Kennedys, in their pre-White House years, were unabashed in their pursuit of publicity: The first time I ever talked to Robert Kennedy was in 1959 when he phoned long-distance to see if I would publish some pictures of his family that a photographer had submitted. In the pre-convention days of 1960, John Kennedy at his own request came to my office to inspect and offer his advice on potential cover pictures of his wife and daughter. (During this same period, the future President displayed another related quality that is essential to anyone applying for media stardom: the ability to absorb criticism along with puffery. When we proposed an interview with Mrs. Kennedy, he pointed out to me that "Mrs. Kennedy" had been displeased with a previous story we had published about his senatorial career, which had included the observation that the author of *Profiles in Courage* in some of his Senate votes might have shown a little less profile and a little more courage. He relented quickly, however, when I suggested that "Mrs. Kennedy" might appreciate the usefulness of a story that would be appearing in the midst of the 1960 primaries.)

Attention is a precious commodity in our noisy and distracted society. The media themselves are in the business of mass-producing attention and selling it to advertisers. In order to get and hold power of almost any kind today — political, social, cultural or economic — individual men and women must get and hold the attention of large numbers of people. The media provide the means but, as in other human endeavors, the means have a way of profoundly influencing the ends. In a classic anecdote, a farmer, after proposing to reason with a reluctant mule, hits him over the head with a heavy plank: "I *am* going to reason with him," the farmer explains, "but first I have to get his attention." The choice between an inattentive audience and one that is dazed by attention-getting devices faces editors constantly, and the same choice confronts aspiring public figures as they solicit the attention of editors.

In the search for celebrity, many call but few are chosen. To some extent, attainment depends on whether or not the media have a vacancy. Jayne Mansfield, Kim Novak and countless others with comparable acting talent and statistical qualifications lost out because Marilyn Monroe had already been appointed National Sex Symbol. Literary merits aside, Carl Sandburg always labored in the shadow of Robert Frost as the media's Wise Old Poet; when both were gone, editors turned to Archibald MacLeish and Mark Van Doren. For years now, any attractive young politician has automatically been classified as a "Kennedy type," thereby placing him on the waiting list for a position already occupied; within months of the murder of his brother Robert, Senator Edward M. Kennedy, up to then a "Kennedy type" himself, suddenly appeared in third place in the annual Gallup Poll of men the American people most admire. As in all drama, media casting depends more on the needs of producers than on the ability of actors.

There is no precise way of measuring the moment at which a name attains critical mass and becomes a Big Name but, as in a nuclear chain reaction, the results are soon visible:

Television directors (as Eugene McCarthy observed after his primary victories) stop superimposing his name on his chest during interviews; gossip columnists begin printing any pointless anecdote in which he is involved; magazine editors start putting his name on their covers in the expectation of selling more copies; book publishers besiege him with offers to write or sign his name to a book; and headline writers are careful always to use his name rather than his designation (it is invariably "Kennedy Claims" or "Muskie Reveals" rather than "Senator Predicts" or "Lawmaker Says," as in the case of non-Big Names).

The process is not nearly as haphazard as it may appear to be. In editorial offices, there are many occasions that require lists of names be drawn up: Whom shall we ask for opinions on what makes a man (or woman) attractive? To write (or have ghost-written) heartwarming little pieces for the Christmas issue? For philosophical comments on man reaching the moon? The names that come to mind on such occasions are the ones that stand the test of celebrity, and their published responses to these requests only increase their stature. The television talk shows and interview programs are the electronic equivalent of this process. Draw up a list of the most sought-after guests for Johnny Carson, Merv Griffin, Dick Cavett and "Meet the Press," and you have a reading of the celebrity market as accurate as the stock listings in the morning newspaper. Each appearance adds a point to the name value.

Almost invariably, the Big Name and the media find themselves locked in a classic love-hate relationship — needing each other for survival yet resentful of the demands that derive from their mutual dependency. This condition explains why, in private conversations, editors and reporters are almost always scornful and suspicious of even those celebrities about whom they seldom publish or broadcast an unkind word. No public man is a hero to his media valet. As magazine writer Tom Morgan put it in introducing his book of profiles: "I want the whole Truth. They want to be Beautiful . . . I pretend that I think they are beautiful. They pretend they are telling the truth."

When the aspiring celebrity is courting publicity, the media may appear as desirable and unattainable as a harem of exotic beauties. Once he has caught their eye, however, he often begins to feel himself being pursued by a swarm of insatiable harridans. In the spring of 1968, a handsome forty-eight-year-old bachelor named Pierre Elliott Trudeau was elected Prime Minister of Canada after a campaign that hinged less on political issues than on his reputation as a "swinger" — enhanced by appearances in colorful sportswear, high dives into swimming pools and dancing with beautiful women. Less than a year later, attending a Commonwealth Prime Ministers' Conference in London, Trudeau angrily reproached journalists for photographing and reporting his social activities. "I do not think it is any of your damned business," he told them at a press conference, "what particular person I am with or how we behave together."

The ultimate station in the realm of celebrity, which is reached by very few, is active resistance to and flight from the media. The surest sign that Frank Sinatra had become a household word came when he began refusing interviews and scuffling with photographers. And those three most durable of celebrities, Greta Garbo, Howard Hughes and Charles Lindbergh, held the media's interest by retiring from sight completely for decades. In the early sixties, an enterprising reporter produced a full-length magazine article out of his efforts to catch a glimpse of Garbo in her Manhattan neighborhood. And somewhere, if a veteran interviewer can be believed, are several hours of tape recordings in which I invested a good deal of professional effort and company money — tapes on which Garbo recorded the story of her life and the mystery of all those years in seclusion and which, after having made, she characteristically refused to release for publication. Early in 1972, Howard Hughes dominated the headlines as a disembodied telephone voice denouncing the authenticity of his alleged "autobiography." Such are the clouds of reticence that veil the highest peaks of celebrity!

One measure of the gathering impact of the media on our lives in the past decade lies in the radical change that has taken place in the manufacture of Big Names. It used to take years to achieve true celebrity, years in which a name, a face and a stereotype of personality were slowly being impressed on the public consciousness. This process produced a category defined by my friend Herbert Rowland as "publicity saints" — those who reached the level of newsworthiness where editors responded unquestioningly to any story in which their names were invoked. In the late fifties and early sixties, the publicity-saint classification embraced Dwight Eisenhower, Billy Graham, Albert Schweitzer, J. Edgar Hoover and Marilyn Monroe, among others — each representing a relatively fixed star in media heaven.

By the mid-sixties it was clear that a change was taking place. Just as the whole society began to buckle under the weight of problems such as Vietnam, the ghettos and the Generation Gap, the overloaded media discovered that their plastic publicity saints were too fragile to bear the freight of all that was assailing the American consciousness. (John Kennedy was mortal, and suddenly we had Lyndon Johnson.) That consciousness itself was breaking into fragments

defined by age, color and economic condition. The only way
the celebrity-making process could attune itself to this new
pace was to fall back on an old American custom: planned
obsolescence. Instead of publicity saints designed to last,
the media began manufacturing "disposable celebrities" —
Big Names that could be created quickly and used up
quickly, like Kleenex. (To illustrate the change in personal
terms, I had always had reason to believe that the names a
magazine editor put on his cover to attract readers were those
that had mellowed over many years: the Kennedys, Eliza-
beth Taylor, etc. One day in 1967, I realized that I had put
on the cover of the second largest magazine in the world,
McCall's, two names that even I had not heard six months
earlier: Svetlana Alliluyeva, Stalin's daughter, and Twiggy,
the newest phenomenon of the fashion industry. The cover
was successful, but six months later the two names had sunk
into media quicksand.)

The difference between publicity saints and disposable
celebrities goes beyond the question of durability. Publicity
saints were chosen to represent qualities the public cherishes
in itself: Eisenhower, honor; Billy Graham, piety; Schweitzer, charity; J. Edgar Hoover, rectitude; Marilyn Monroe,
beauty. They endured until a replacement came along (Tom
Dooley, had he lived, would have taken over Schweitzer's
role without a ripple). Disposable celebrities, on the other
hand, are designed to break through the boredom of a public
satiated with words and images; to accomplish this break-
through, they depend, not on familiar qualities, but on
novelty. And under pressure for novelty, there has been a
growing tendency toward the odd, the extreme and even the
grotesque: Fashion, representing the avant-garde of the pop
world, moved quickly from Baby Jane Holzer, who had a dis-
tinctive mane but was attractive in a relatively conventional

way, to Twiggy and Penelope Tree, who were not at all conventional looking. Youth idols progressed from the Beatles and Bob Dylan, distinguished by talent and long hair, to Jimi Hendrix, who ended his act by destroying his electric guitar; the Who, who went him one better by destroying their amplifying equipment as well, and Jim Morrison of the Doors, who was arrested after introducing an element of sexual exposure into his act. Liberace disappeared and up popped Tiny Tim. Andrew Wyeth continued to be our most respected painter, but Andy Warhol and a succession of put-on artists dominated the headlines. Pop religion left Norman Vincent Peale to the elderly and went on to the Maharishi, who blossomed briefly on campuses and magazine covers and then retreated, financially if not spiritually enriched, back to the mysterious East. On the racial front, Whitney Young and Roy Wilkins continued to receive invitations to the White House, but Rap Brown and Eldridge Cleaver made the news. As campus unrest intensified, Mario Savio of Berkeley was succeeded symbolically by Mark Rudd of Columbia, who was absorbed into the celebrity world to the extent that the *New York Times*, in a story on Jewish mothers inspired by *Portnoy's Complaint*, included a picture of a smiling Rudd being kissed by his mother, who cheerfully told the interviewer that she had just made chicken soup for "Mark and the other revolutionaries."

The pace at which the media now consume such figures can best be seen in the case of the seventeen-year-old, ninety-one-pound British model named Twiggy (nee Lesley Hornsby), who arrived at Kennedy Airport in March 1967 on her first trip to the United States to be greeted by one of the largest crushes of reporters and photographers ever assembled there. During her six-week stay, she posed for the major magazines (at first for $120 an hour, soon raised to

$240), was seen regularly on network news programs and in newspapers, served as the subject of two television specials, was mobbed by teen-agers, solicited for endorsements of all kinds and described as "a magic child of the media" in a *Newsweek* cover story, a description that was quoted in a *New Yorker* article about her trip that spanned 98 pages. At one point, photographer Bert Stern explained a complex maneuver to the *New Yorker* writer: "Since Twiggy was going to have her hair cut, I thought I'd photograph the hair-cutting for *Vogue*. Then . . . I thought that instead of just photographing the haircut for *Vogue* we'd have the whole press in for the haircut, and that we could take advantage of that to announce the Twiggy specials on A.B.C. . . . So we've done three things. We've announced the specials. The press has its pictures of the haircut and of me photographing it. And I've shot pictures for *Vogue* showing the press photographing the haircut." Within months, lines of Twiggy dresses, cosmetics and dolls were in the stores, and the "autobiography" of her seventeen years had been published in hard covers.

A little more than a year later, Twiggy's subsequent arrival in the United States went practically unnoticed. It was covered in one paragraph on page 10 of *Women's Wear Daily*, which reported that the airline had lost her trunk. (Four years after that, Twiggy reappeared in a new incarnation — as a movie star.)

"If *Time, Life,* and the television shows are full of Tom Fool this month, he's no fool," the poet Randall Jarrell once wrote. "And when he has been gone from them a while, we do not think him a fool — we do not think of him at all. He no longer exists, in the fullest sense of the word 'exist': to be is to be perceived, to be a part of the Medium of our perception. Our celebrities are not kings, romantic in exile, but

Representatives who, defeated, are forgotten; they had always only the qualities we delegated to them."

Under the circumstances, it is not surprising that some alternative had to be found to hand-crafting public personalities one at a time. Thus emerged the Beautiful People industry, a method for mass-producing celebrities to be consumed by the handful, like peanuts at a cocktail party. Parts of the machinery for such an enterprise had long been available in the journalistic fringe areas of society, fashion and cultural gossip. But in the 1960s media necessity mothered the invention of the Beautiful People — an amalgam of the very rich and bored, some of them remnants of royalty (formerly known as Café Society, later as the Jet Set); purveyors of elegance: dress designers and manufacturers, interior decorators, hairdressers, cosmetic tycoons, fashion-magazine publishers and department-store owners; the marginally creative — writers and artists of modest talent who find it more congenial to express themselves in conversation than on paper or canvas; and a selected number of actors and actresses with high cheekbones and an aptitude for looking well in evening wear.

What has brought and held these groups together in continual social intercourse is less their interest in each other, which appears minimal, than the creation of a new journalistic framework for marketing their activities. Prompted in the early 1960s by Jacqueline Kennedy's popularization of a life style that emphasized high fashion and the social graces, the Beautiful People (so named by *Vogue*) began to break out of their confinement to the fashion magazines and the women's pages of metropolitan newspapers. As they did, they brought with them a newly emerging journalistic attitude that would make it possible for mass audiences to consume their activities — an attitude that incorporated the fashionable new modes of "put-on" and "put-down" into the traditional gush of society and fashion reporters.

Two pioneers of this kind of reporting were Aileen Mehle, who under the byline of "Suzy" wrote a column syndicated by the Hearst newspapers and later by the New York *Daily News,* and Charlotte Curtis of the *New York Times* and points west, courtesy of the *Times* News Service.

For both the lower and upper ends of the mass audience, Suzy brought an ostensibly wide-eyed, breathless attitude toward the relentless party-giving and party-going she reported. The key to her success has been the always present note of self-parody. Like Alfred Hitchcock, whose irony allowed the sophisticated to enjoy movie thrillers without embarrassment yet failed to deter the unsophisticated from enjoying them unself-consciously, Suzy appeals to people who ordinarily would disdain society reporting as well as those who consume it avidly. As if to confirm her two-level approach, when she agreed to write a book on her milieu, the working title was "Putting on the Rich."

While Suzy perfected her put-on of the Beautiful People, Charlotte Curtis of the *Times,* who regards herself as more of a social historian than a society reporter, was gaining attention for her put-down style of dealing with the same material. Where Suzy brought an ambiguous dazzled smile to the proceedings, Miss Curtis came armed with a wry, somewhat stricken smile. (Smiling is a popular activity of the Beautiful People as well as their chroniclers.) Her success in subtly deflating while carefully describing the antics of the rich and socially ambitious brought Miss Curtis a promotion from reporter to women's page editor and put her in charge of a small phalanx of social historians to assist her in her work. She has been on the scene constantly, reporting the celebrity aspect of every major event, including the 1968 Democratic convention and the launching of Apollo 11.

Fittingly enough, Charlotte Curtis and Suzy soon became minor celebrities in their own right to be written about by others and imitated widely. "I call it as I see it," Miss Curtis told a reporter observing her as she observed her subjects. "I may be a clown but so is everyone else and the people who pretend they aren't are the funniest of all."

This chilling observation by a gifted editor of America's most respected newspaper toward the end of the 1960s can be seen as the logical outcome of Daniel Boorstin's observation in *The Image* at the start of the decade:

> The celebrity in the distinctive modern sense could not have existed in any earlier age, or in America before the Graphic Revolution. *The celebrity is a person who is known for his well-knownness.*
>
> His qualities — or rather his lack of qualities — illustrate our peculiar problems. He is neither good nor bad, great nor petty. He is the human pseudo-event. He has been fabricated on purpose to satisfy our exaggerated expectations of human greatness. He is morally neutral. The product of no conspiracy, of no group promoting vice or emptiness, he is made by honest, industrious men of high professional ethics doing their job, "informing" and educating us. He is made by all of us who willingly read about him, who like to see him on television, who buy recordings of his voice, and talk about him to our friends. His relation to morality and even to reality is highly ambiguous. He is like the woman *in* an Elinor Glyn novel who describes another by saying, "She is like a figure in an Elinor Glyn novel."

More and more, the people in a Charlotte Curtis story or a Suzy column find themselves behaving like people in a Charlotte Curtis story or a Suzy column. As they do, they become less and less distinguishable one from another. From two-dimensional stereotypes they are reduced to one dimension: names. They exist, in their eternal round of dinners, lunches, parties, cruises and charity balls, only to provide us with the opportunity of sharing vicariously their glittering life and at the same time feeling superior to its underlying emptiness and boredom.

There has always been a journalistic place for both serious and light reporting — for news of people and events of significance as well as those that provide only passing diversion. What is new is not only the multiplication of those who populate our consciousness but the blurring of the line between people we are meant to take seriously and those who are only meant to amuse. Our clowns acquire political power and our politicians behave more and more like clowns. While the young express themselves politically in "guerrilla theater" and "street theater" for the benefit of television, our Establishment politics increasingly resembles a theater of the absurd:

Item: The late Senator Everett Dirksen, one of the half dozen most powerful politicians in the country, would come onto the evening television news regularly to discuss public issues with the looks and demeanor of a carnival snake-oil salesman and then, to confuse us further, produce several campy long-playing records of patriotic readings in what can only be taken as self-parody.

Item: On the other end of the ideological spectrum, Adam Clayton Powell, temporarily deprived of his Congressional seat amid great racial tension, calls a news conference at his Bimini retreat in the Caribbean to make what he describes as an important announcement. He tells the assembled reporters about *his* new record, "Keep the Faith, Baby."

Item: During the 1964 campaign, a journeyman actor named Ronald Reagan reads a canned television speech on behalf of Senator Goldwater. Goldwater loses, but Reagan spends the next two years delivering his canned speech all over California and is elected governor of the second largest state in the nation, joining another journeyman actor named George Murphy who had been elected Senator two years earlier. Those of us whose sensibilities were heavily influenced by the movies of the 1930s and 1940s remember the Governor and Senator as supporting actors who seldom achieved stardom. Errol Flynn and Clark Gable, who always got the girl in those pictures, are dead; Reagan and Murphy, who usually held the hero's coat and were killed off before the final reel, are national leaders.

Item: Shirley Temple, who melted hearts in the 1930s as a movie moppet singing "The Good Ship Lollipop," runs for Congress in 1967 as a hard-line hawk on Vietnam and is defeated in the Republican primary. But, in 1969, she is appointed to the United States delegation to the United Nations General Assembly by President Nixon, one of the few Republican officeholders from California who cannot be seen regularly in old movies on television.

Item: It is now standard procedure for Presidential candidates to visit the Johnny Carson show to exchange banter while occupying seats still warm from the bodies of nightclub comedians and bosomy actresses plugging their latest movie. NASA did not send Apollo 11 off to land the first men on the moon without the presence of Carson, along with former President Johnson and leading government officials, in the VIP section to view the launching.

Item: Richard Nixon, several weeks after his election campaign, which followed a guest appearance on "Laugh-In," schedules a television show to make a wholesale introduction of his cabinet with all the aplomb and artistry of Ed Sullivan. After the splashdown of Apollo 11, the President is on hand to beat out Walter Cronkite and Huntley and Brinkley by interviewing the astronauts for television through a glass shield.

Item: Billy Graham, President Nixon's favorite theologian and a relentless critic of smut, also performs on "Laugh-In," which specializes in sneaking double-entendres past the NBC network censor.

Item: Two distinguished authors and sometime political candidates, Gore Vidal and William F. Buckley, Jr., climax their running commentary on the 1968 political conventions over network television by calling one another a "pro crypto Nazi" and a "queer." Buckley, famous for his urbane exposition of conservative political positions, advises Vidal, the elegant novelist and playwright: "Stop calling me a crypto Nazi or I'll sock you in your goddamn face . . ."

Item: Two other writers, novelist Norman Mailer and columnist Jimmy Breslin, run for mayor and president of the City Council of New York in the 1969 Democratic Primary on such slogans as "The Other Guys Are the Joke," "Throw the Rascals In" and "No More Bullshit." Mailer draws more votes than Congressman James Scheuer, a professional politician supported by an expensive and well-organized campaign.

Item: Advised by William Safire, who helped stage the Moscow "kitchen conference" between Nixon and Khrushchev in 1959 (Safire was publicizing the kitchen, not Nixon), Governor Claude R. Kirk of Florida appears uninvited at a rally being addressed by black militant H. Rap Brown (author of that televised classic, "Violence is as American as cherry pie"), welcomes him heartily to Florida and cheerfully asks: "Are you here in good spirits, are you here in good spirits?" Brown, himself a frequent exponent of the public put-on, departs in some confusion.

Item: Former Governor Orval Faubus of Arkansas, President Eisenhower's antagonist at Little Rock and the George Wallace of the 1950s, turns up in the late 1960s as the employee of a tourist park called Dogpatch, U.S.A.

Item: A Georgia restaurant owner named Lester Maddox dramatizes his opposition to Federal civil-rights legislation by turning away Negro patrons while brandishing an ax handle. He closes the restaurant, runs successfully for Governor of Georgia and, in 1968, is seen on national television, solemnly declaring his candidacy for President of the United States. Suitably enough, his career is immortalized in a musical comedy, which opens in Atlanta and moves on to New York.

It is as if, under the growing clamor of the media, we had lost all sense of connection between fame and its sources. Perhaps Marguerite Oswald, the mother of Lee Harvey Oswald, touched on some basic truth of our condition when, after appearing before the Warren Commission in Washington, she complained to a reporter about not being invited to the White House by Mrs. Lyndon Johnson. After all, Mrs. Oswald pointed out, Mrs. Johnson's husband had become President in the same series of events in which Mrs. Oswald's son had lost his life.

A year later, at the end of a busy working day, it suddenly occurred to me with a mild shock that I had taken part in two long-distance telephone conversations that day: one with Mrs. Oswald and another with Mrs. Joseph P. Kennedy, the late President's mother. I had been negotiating with Mrs. Oswald to cooperate with the novelist Jean Stafford in a long interview, which was later expanded into the book, *A Mother in History*, and I had been making arrangements with Mrs. Kennedy to pose with her daughter, Mrs. Stephen Smith, for one of a series of photographs of famous mothers and daughters. My journalistic purposes were different, but the methods in both conversations were quite similar: I was dealing with two celebrities.

In politics, it has always been necessary to attract voters with personal charm as well as political positions. But, under the growing intensity of the media spotlight, the line between a politician's public and private life has been dissolved almost totally. In the 1960s the experience of the Kennedy family mirrors this fusion of public and private with painful clarity: The Kennedys used the media, the media used them and, by the end of the decade, their public and private selves had been almost totally consumed. ("Marshall McLuhan Says That TV Killed Bob Kennedy!" reads the headline of a full-page advertisement for McLuhan's expensive newsletter in mid-1969. "Kennedy misused television," explains the copy. "Although he was supremely aware of its strengths, he was fatally unaware of its dangers. Thus — by heating up this essentially cool medium at a critical point — he practically begged for a try on his life." McLuhan's thesis, as usual, is dubious, to say nothing of his taste, but his commercial sense, as always, is infallible: The life-and-death connection between the Kennedys and the media is a fact that surely must have intrigued his potential customers.)

In the 1950s John F. Kennedy became a national figure largely through the magazines and newspapers, which treated him more like a movie star than a politician and were rewarded with photographs and articles that reflected the most marketable pop values: wealth, privilege and personal beauty merged with ideals and intelligence in the

cause of public service. When I first met the young Senator
in the studio of the photographer Howell Conant, it seemed
perfectly natural that he should inquire with considerable
interest about Conant's recent visit to Grace Kelly, another
descendant of a wealthy Irish-American family, who had
become a movie star and married a prince. At that point,
their careers were quite similar.

It was television, however, that raised Kennedy above the
fan-magazine level and put him in the White House. The
Kennedy-Nixon debates helped to swing the election of
1960, and Kennedy rewarded the medium by becoming the
first President to hold regular live televised press conferences. His use of television did not discourage the magazines. Far from it. After his inaugural, editors discovered
that Kennedys, all of them, sell magazines; the *Ladies' Home
Journal*, at that time in the process of being overtaken by
McCall's, temporarily recovered with newsstand sellouts of
three consecutive issues featuring the life story and picture
albums of Jacqueline Kennedy. From then on, all of the
Kennedys were publicity saints and, in their usual worldly
way, the members of the family made the most of their ele-
vation. The energetic young President, a former reporter
himself, read almost everything written about his Administration, offered advice and criticism, helped editors in their
planning and was more accessible to and more admired by
media people than any Chief Executive before or since.
"What he knew about your own business was discouraging,"
Look writer Laura Bergquist recalled. "He knew, for example, exactly what *Look*'s 'lead' time (i.e., deadline) was
when I had forgotten it." Another editor once told me: "The
Kennedy people not only cultivate the top editors, but they
know just who is on the desk of the *New York Times* at, say,
eleven P.M. so they can call directly if something important

comes up." (And unlike Lyndon Johnson, they made their calls with such finesse that they were never exposed to the kind of scorn reflected in the UPI house-organ story about the "fee tour" of the Johnson homestead.)

Yet, in Kennedy's tenure as President, the first signs were becoming visible of the growing disconnection between political reality and media reality. In the world of the newspapers, magazines and television, John F. Kennedy was a glowing figure of monumental proportions; in the world of political power, both international and domestic, his ability to act was sharply circumscribed. After his death, the debate over the style versus the substance of Kennedy's Administration reflected the divergence of these two realities.

I was involved in one incident that confirmed the difficulties he must have had in translating his power as a celebrity into Presidential power. Between the Cuban missile crisis of October 1962 and the signing of the nuclear limited test-ban treaty in July 1963, I served on an informal committee to stimulate public support for Senate ratification of the treaty. For several years, we had been publishing articles in *Redbook* about the dangers of fallout, the need for a test ban and other disarmament measures, and the activities of groups and individuals to prevent nuclear war. Several other mass magazines had dealt with these issues on an occasional basis, but many had simply ignored the entire subject of our possible nuclear extinction. I persuaded the editors of six other large magazines for women, with a total circulation of more than 30 million, to put aside their competitive differences, ask the President for a joint interview to answer questions about peace and disarmament for American women, and publish the results simultaneously. Pierre Salinger, Kennedy's press secretary, who was charged with fending off the constant requests of these magazines for stories about the White House children and pets, responded with enthusiasm when I broached the idea. The President, he explained, was starved for public forums for his ideas; he could make direct appeals by television only so often and, in press conferences, could not pursue any complicated subject at any length. I was struck then by the gap between Kennedy's power to command personal publicity and his inability to focus attention on an issue as important as preventing the world from blowing up.

As if to confirm this disparity, the editor of a large women's magazine, who before and since has published dozens of articles about the personal lives of the Kennedys, called me before the interview was held to express his concern that the material about human survival might be "too dull" for his readers. Could he attend without promising to publish a report on the interview? When I conveyed his doubts to Salinger, the press secretary, a former magazine writer, had a persuasive answer. "Tell him," Salinger said, "that the President does not work on speculation."

The interview was held, the results published, and shortly before his death, Kennedy sent a message that he was pleased. In the days following the assassination, I was haunted by the total national preoccupation with the death of a man who had had so much difficulty converting attention to his person into support for his policies.

From The White House Family, the media turned smoothly to the chapter of The Widow. Jacqueline Kennedy, who moved through a state funeral with stunned grace, was elevated to *the* publicity saint of the mid-1960s. Her widowhood became the common coin of newspaper columnists, feature writers, the women's magazines and even their slatternly sisters, the movie-fan magazines, which discovered that "Jackie" and "Liz" (Taylor) were an unbeatable and apparently inexhaustible source of best-selling cover lines.* It was *Women's Wear Daily,* the fount of the Beautiful People business, that stalked Mrs. Kennedy most relentlessly with photographers and reporters at her apartment-building door, her favorite restaurants and the local shops to which she took her children for hamburgers and haircuts. As editor of the world's largest women's magazine during that period, I gave in at one point to one of the worst temptations of a mass-media manager: to moralize over a situation while giving the audience a delicious taste of what is being self-righteously deplored (somewhat like Fellini in *La Dolce Vita* showing the depravity of Romans in loving detail while offering a high-minded comment on it). I assigned an article on "Jacqueline Kennedy Watching," which frowned on the tactics of those disturbing her privacy while inescapably offering a blueprint of how to do it. After some belated qualms, I declined to publish the finished article, pointing out that, even if the names and addresses of her haunts were omitted, it would still be an abuse of her limited privacy. The writer took the article to *The Saturday Evening Post,* which published it complete with names and addresses and, for the convenience of those who wanted to observe and deplore those dreadful people pursuing Mrs. Kennedy, added a detailed street map.

Perhaps my reticence went back to a strange incident in January 1965, some fourteen months after the assassination. Shortly after becoming editor of *McCall's,* I was told that Mrs. Kennedy was seriously considering going to work and

---

* In rebuking the fan magazines for their vulgarity, the *Columbia Journalism Review* inadvertently preserved for history a journalistic parallel to the proposition that a group of monkeys tapping typewriter keys at random for an indefinite length of time would eventually produce a great novel. One of the cover lines that the *Review* dismissed as unfounded nonsense in 1965 was: "Exclusive: Jackie: Onassis The Friend She Turns To."

that she would be interested in a position as a magazine editor. Along with several other executives of my company, I visited her at her Fifth Avenue apartment and listened as she tried to sort out her feelings and decide on her future. First, she explained why she had been refusing interviews and trying to discourage publicity. "I don't intend to become another Princess Grace," she said firmly. She then went on to explain that her only interest in working would be to find some way of helping to preserve President Kennedy's ideas and ideals. It was not in her nature, she said, to do this directly by writing or speaking publicly, but perhaps if she worked with some man she trusted . . . "Robert Kennedy would be ideal," she mused, "but, of course, that's not possible." For an hour, as we held our coffee cups and listened, it became increasingly clear that Mrs. Kennedy had, more than a year later, still not come to terms emotionally with the death of her husband and was attempting to find some way of reconstructing her life as it had been before November 22, 1963. Nothing came of that meeting, of course, but after that it was difficult to reconcile the public picture of her strength and imperiousness with the uncertain woman we had seen that day.

Under each media stereotype lurks its potential antithesis. In the three years that Jacqueline Kennedy was being canonized for mass consumption as The Noble Widow, there was always an opposing image waiting in the wings. The Manchester Affair brought it out. When Mrs. Kennedy went to law to force William Manchester to delete certain sections of his book *The Death of a President*, late in 1966, the gates were opened, and the anti-heroine bearing her name and likeness began to emerge. "Jackie Kennedy Comes Off Her Pedestal" was the title of one magazine article, later syndicated by newspapers throughout the country. She won the battle with Manchester but lost the war: The disputed sections were taken out of the book but were cheerfully published as "news" by newspapers across the country, and she was saddled at the same time with her share of long-standing public resentment over "Kennedy arrogance."

During the Manchester furor, I was involved in a project with Mrs. Kennedy, the outcome of which illustrates some of the prices paid for celebrity, both by those who bear it and those who have to deal with it. For some months I had been working toward an article to be published on what would have been John F. Kennedy's fiftieth birthday in May 1967. The original idea had been prompted by a remark of Theodore Sorensen's to the effect that Kennedy was being remembered too much for how he died rather than what he had lived for. On the fiftieth anniversary of his birth, it seemed fitting to summarize both his accomplishments and his unfinished political work. After long negotiations, Jacqueline Kennedy agreed to take part in the project. She would join in a tape-recorded discussion with Sorensen and Arthur Schlesinger, Jr., both of whom had been close Kennedy advisers in the White House and had written books about his Administration. The edited tapes would be published in *McCall's*. Sorensen, Schlesinger and I worked out the details carefully and set a tentative date. Then the Manchester dispute became public, and Mrs. Kennedy sent word that she was too upset to go through with our project. Her decision was disappointing but understandable.

At just about this time, I was offered American rights to a long article that was about to appear in a British magazine, *The Queen*. Written by the late Robin Douglas-Home, it contained recollections of a series of very personal conversations with Mrs. Kennedy during her White House years. I had read the original Manchester manuscript, and even those sections over which Mrs. Kennedy was willing to go to court seemed mild to me compared to the Douglas-Home material. I declined to publish the article and, at the same time, in a self-serving gesture, sent word to Mrs. Kennedy of its impending appearance so that she might be prepared for it. I was duly thanked, the article appeared but, for some curious reason, the American newspapers made very little of it.

Several weeks later, a multi-part exclusive interview with Jacqueline Kennedy appeared in a publication that had been one of the worst exploiters of her distress during the Manchester dispute. When I complained, Mrs. Kennedy's staff acknowledged my right to be angry and professed bafflement at her actions. Some months later, I was given a perfectly plausible explanation by a disinterested editor: The other publication had bought American rights to the *Queen* article and had persuaded Mrs. Kennedy to grant an interview rather than see the article published. There is no need to use the obvious word that describes this procedure, but the underlying lesson is clear: The celebrity game is not played by Marquis of Queensberry rules.

The final turn of the screw in Mrs. Kennedy's public fortunes came after she married Aristotle Onassis, a gentleman of Greek origin almost thirty years her senior and a good provider. The media turned on her with a vengeance for stepping completely out of the character they had carefully constructed for her. In 1969, after five years of discreet silence, her former secretary surfaced with a widely publicized book-length account of their White House years. "Jackie Kennedy was like a sister to me," Mary Barelli Gallagher wrote, as she detailed Mrs. Kennedy's household expenses and the President's annoyance with the amounts of money she spent for clothes and hairdressers. These historic revelations were first published in the *Ladies' Home Journal*; the magazine that had started the decade with a gushing paean to Mrs. Kennedy finished it with a peevish and petty exposure of her household accounts.

Jacqueline Kennedy Onassis may have finally freed herself from the media's obsequiousness but not its attentions. Just after publication of the Gallagher book, Mrs. Onassis was accused of using judo to deposit a New York *Daily News* photographer on the sidewalk as she left a theater showing *I Am Curious (Yellow)*. Witnesses suggested that the photographer had tripped himself in his enthusiasm to record Mrs. Onassis' exit, but the evidence did not deter *Life* and *Women's Wear Daily* from staging re-enactments, with models, of how Mrs. Onassis may have accomplished her alleged feat of judo.

The 1960s, which had framed the Kennedys' rise and fall in the outlines of Shakespearean tragedy, also drew to a close with the last surviving brother contemplating his recently acquired standing as the third most-admired man in America as it disappeared below the waters off Chappaquiddick Island. Ted Kennedy's actions that July weekend were only barely eclipsed by the landing of the first men on the moon and, in the following days and weeks, the media worked hard to redress the balance. The *Ladies' Home Journal*, alert as ever, asked Agatha Christie to speculate on the mystery, but the venerable writer of fictional entertainments declined; others, including most of the nation's editorial writers, were not so reticent. Kennedy himself, responding to the new rules of media strategy first established by Richard Nixon's Checkers speech, went on national television to offer a tendentious account of the weekend's events and to "ask" the voters of his state for their verdict. Thus the ultimate humiliation of the Kennedys: The family that had

always prided itself on its mastery of the media was reduced
in 1969 to emulating the man it had taught a fundamental
lesson about the use of television in 1960.

Today, the eyes and ears of the media are everywhere,
and no one questions their right to be there. At the scene
of any accident, the newspaper photographer is there to
give us a breakfast-table view of the mangled bodies, and
the local radio and television reporters are on hand to shove
cameras and microphones into the faces of the dazed survivors. The average man invites such attention only at a
moment of disaster; for the celebrity it is a way of life.

It is also a way of life for those who tend the communications machinery as editors, reporters and broadcasters. They
are charged with filling huge amounts of time and space.
They are better equipped to deal with images than ideas,
and people are the best raw material for fabricating images.
In any event, their customers have much more curiosity
about people than about ideas. And so even those editors
who feel strongly their responsibility to deal with issues find
themselves devoting much of their time and energy to pursuing personalities. The result is that we all are moving
further and further from reality. In noting the growing
tendency of public figures toward "self-parody," Russell
Baker pointed out in the *New York Times*: "A politician
like Johnson or Nixon spends untold hours studying the
Johnson or Nixon who is constantly carrying on in newspapers and television film. It would be only natural if he
attempted to imitate in his own behavior the characteristics
he admires in this distorted image of himself, and to suppress those he dislikes . . . The communications miracle
tends to break a person in two — into real and the unreal
halves — and then to make the worst half flourish."

Worse still, the public figure soon loses sight of which part of him is real and which is not. And so do we all.

The Kennedys, the Johnsons, the Nixons were all more or less real to begin with. But their reality was slowly and inexorably transmuted into the reality of the magazine cover and the television news clip. If our national leaders must inevitably lose themselves to the fantasy-making machinery of the media, how long can the rest of us hold on to anything resembling reality?

A. J. Weberman may be the perfect symbol for our condition. Starting with an examination of the refuse outside Bob Dylan's home, Weberman has gone on to invent a new branch of investigative journalism, poring through the rubbish of the rich and famous to reconstruct their inner lives from the evidence of egg shells, coffee grounds and discarded scrap paper. For a time, his findings were published only by the underground press, but, late in 1971, he surfaced in *Esquire* with an analytical report, accompanied by color photographs, on the leavings of Dylan, Muhammad Ali, Neil Simon and Abbie Hoffman.

Once again, life imitates art. Some years earlier, Jules Feiffer tried to tell us something about urban society by making the hero of *Little Murders* a photographer of excrement. Now, Weberman has emerged to confirm the lengths to which we are driven to express our sense of alienation. It would be difficult to improve on rooting through other people's garbage as a metaphor for our mistrust of media reality and our frustration at being unable to discover what lies behind it. As we approach a post-celebrity world, we seem to be losing faith that there are real people behind the printed and electronic shadows of public men.

Weberman's search was no more likely to uncover the real

Bob Dylan than all the televised press conferences, commentaries, columns and cover stories have revealed the real Richard Nixon. In both cases, the enterprise itself was more significant than the results it produced. The medium is the message.

Richard Nixon is our first media President, but not, as those who misread Joe McGinniss' *The Selling of the President, 1968* might assume, as the master of television but as its creature. McGinniss' book presumably showed a corps of highly skilled manipulators successfully manufacturing and packaging a candidate, but the evidence shows that television elected Nixon on its own initiative, not as the instrument of his managers. When the home screen had finished projecting the chaos of the Democratic convention in Chicago, Nixon entered the campaign with a 15 per cent margin over Hubert Humphrey. Two months and more than $20 million later, he won the election by less than one per cent.

In the first two years of his presidency, Nixon and his critics continued to share the delusion that he was harnessing television to his own purposes. In press conferences and prime-time reports to the nation, he gave us a picture of Uriah Heep as President, surreptitiously blowing kisses to the camera while rattling off facts and figures from his lined-yellow-pad mind. During that period, Alan L. Otten in the *Wall Street Journal* described Nixon as "remarkably adroit and effective in using the mighty medium of television." Senator William Fulbright, on behalf of opponents of the war in Vietnam, complained in a statement to the Senate, that "the Executive has a near monopoly on effective access to public attention." Yet, during those two years, the public opinion polls showed opposition to the war in Vietnam growing and Nixon's popularity declining.

It was the President himself, rather than his critics, who first grasped the fact that television was doing more to him that he to it. His first impulse was to blame not the medium but the people who run it. Enter Agnew. The rise and fall of Spiro Agnew provides yet another awesome example of the media's ability to create self-destructing celebrities out of anyone, including its own critics. Like Abbie Hoffman, Agnew became an instant symbol. On the evening news, the talk shows and in ghost-written magazine articles, both were constantly paraded before us and, in a year or less, used up as objects of amusement and oversimplification. Nobody remembers much of what they said, but each remains in our memory with an invisible sign on his chest: Agnew, Repression; Hoffman, Anarchy. Agnew was sent off to distant parts of the world to make courtesy calls on dictators and despots, while Abbie was found guilty by a tribunal of his revolutionary peers of exploiting his fellow opponents of exploitation by failing to share the credit and the royalties for his opus, *Steal This Book*. Both had been consumed as media symbols. A. J. Weberman can sift their garbage till doomsday, but he is unlikely to find any human remains.

Among all the transitory media figures that pollute our consciousness, Richard Nixon has proved to be durable, not because he has consciously created a series of old Nixons and new Nixons for public consumption, but because he is compelled by some inner chemistry to sense and gratify our media needs. Eisenhower, Kennedy and Johnson, in diverse ways, held on to shreds of their true selves while responding to media pressure. (Johnson once refused to be photographed watching a space launch on television. "If I smile," he said, "I don't have concern for the safety of the astronauts. If I look grim, I've got cancer.")

Nixon is the complete media creation. There is no old

Nixon, new Nixon, private Nixon or public Nixon — there is only the media's Nixon. "When Presidents begin to worry about images," he remarked in a 1971 television interview, designed to prop up his sagging image, "when they begin to be concerned about polls, when they begin to read their press clippings, do you know what happens? They become like the athletes, the football teams and the rest, who become so concerned about what is written about them, and what is said about them, that they don't play the game well." The irony is that Nixon's game *is* media, just as Vince Lombardi's was football. "Winning," according to Lombardi's dictum, "isn't the main thing — it's the only thing."

In mid-1971, Nixon finally found his winning media game plan. While political analysts and commentators exhausted themselves in tracing the roots of the President's sudden reversals over relations with China, economic controls and Supreme Court nominations, the essential answer may have been staring them in the face as they watched each of Nixon's prime-time appearances: The President was giving the medium what it wanted — surprise. He had been, in line with another of Lombardi's principles, running for daylight. And, according to the public opinion polls, he was scoring.

The Supreme Court nominations may be particularly instructive. Without the concentrated attention of the media, Haynsworth and Carswell could not have been quickly enough converted into symbols of racism and mediocrity to build sufficient support for Senate defeat of their confirmation. The next time around, the process was speeded up. Before we had a chance to savor Herschel Friday and Margaret Lillie as symbols of the Administration's contempt for the Court, they went up in smoke, burned up by premature media glare. Nixon, running to the Right, had faked out the journalists. A quick cut back toward the Center, and we had

Lewis Powell and William Rehnquist on the scoreboard before anyone could lay a hand on the President.

James Reston, alone of the political observers, saw what Nixon was doing. In November, Reston wrote: "He hasn't been watching all those pro football games for nothing. He is a scrambling quarterback, in deep trouble and throwing the ball all over the field. It may not make sense, but it makes headlines, and in politics dominating the news is important."

We may already be living in a post-celebrity world. As our Presidents become media creatures, we are losing the reality of all public men. Approaching the 1972 election, Muskie, McGovern, McCloskey, Ashbrook, Jackson, Hartke, Lindsay, Mills, McCarthy, Kennedy, Yorty and Humphrey were a blur in our overpopulated consciousness. About the seventies, we may look back and, as Hemingway did a half-century earlier, say: "There were many words that you could not stand to hear and finally only the names of places had dignity." Mylai. Kent State. Attica. The places were real, but were the people?

5
The Truth as Private Property

GENERAL ROBERT E. LEE, who refused to give newspaper interviews throughout his career, also declined to write his memoirs. "I should be trading on the blood of my men," he is reported to have said. A century later, James Earl Ray, the convicted murderer of Martin Luther King, claimed that he had been pressured into pleading guilty in order to protect the publication and movie rights to his life story. In a court petition, Ray asserted that his attorney "never intended for him to have a fair trial and testify in his own behalf as this would then make the facts and testimony public property and no one would or could have exclusive rights in the matter."

The distance between Lee's refusal to trade on "the blood of my men" to Ray's assertion that he had been trading on his own measures one dimension of the current media landscape. There has always been interest in the reminiscences of great men. Today, there is also spirited bidding for the memoirs of criminals, pariahs, victims, servants and bystanders; we are anxious to enrich any witness to a great media event as long as he promises to tell us "the real truth" behind the outpouring of news that we have been consuming so avidly: James Earl Ray, Charles Manson, Lieutenant

Calley, Sirhan Sirhan, Jacqueline Kennedy's dressmaker,
the commander of a ship seized by the North Koreans, the
survivor of a heart transplant, the leader of a campus riot,
Judy Garland's last husband — we want to hear them all.

Soon after Charles Manson's arrest, the New York editor
of a German magazine spent an entire day tracking me down
by telephone on the mistaken notion that I was negotiating
with Sharon Tate's father to write a book. When I explained
that it was not true, she took the disappointment in stride.
"That's all right," she answered, with some excitement.
"We've signed up two of the girls who helped Manson with
the murders." Manson himself immediately got a contract
to record several of the songs that he had been so unsuccess-
ful in selling before the murders.

After the incredible bidding for what turned out to be
80,000 turgid words of memoirs by Stalin's daughter, I asked
the representative of a distinguished European publisher
who had endured various forms of humiliation in his efforts
to buy the book if he would have acted differently had the
memoirs been those of Hitler's daughter. "No," he answered without hesitation, "it would have been the same."

Such questions do not remain hypothetical for long. Less
than two years later, the Macmillan Company paid $250,000
for English-language rights to the memoirs of Albert Speer,
Hitler's Minister of Arms and Munitions, who had served
twenty years in prison as a convicted Nazi war criminal. "It
was not an easy decision to bid for the memoirs of a former
Nazi war criminal," Macmillan's editor-in-chief told a reporter, but he was persuaded that "Speer not only offered
brand new historical material but . . . was the only prisoner at Spandau who was willing to accept his guilt." The
justification of history is by now a familiar one, but there is
something inventive in a moral principle that sanctions en-

riching a repentant Nazi war criminal as opposed to one who refuses to accept his guilt. The test will doubtless come when an unrepentant war criminal offers new historical material for sale.

But perhaps it is self-righteous to invoke moral considerations when what is at stake is "the public's right to know." That all-purpose phrase has become a cliché during a period in which the idea of privacy has been almost thoroughly dissolved under the media's hot eye. It is used to justify every invasion of privacy, every piece of self-exploitation, every bit of slavering over the misfortune of others that can be packaged and promoted in the current seller's market for inside stories.

The public certainly has a right to know the essential facts about public business, and it is one of the time-honored tasks of journalism to uncover what officeholders may be concealing for their own selfish purposes. But even in this area, there has been a rapid erosion of the line between legitimate information and gossip. Less than a decade ago, Emmet Hughes was severely criticized for describing in his book, *The Ordeal of Power*, some of what he saw and heard as a member of President Eisenhower's staff, including Eisenhower's offhand remarks about public figures and some of the personal sidelights of policy deliberations. In his own book, Theodore Sorensen tells us that President Kennedy thought Hughes "had betrayed the trust of Republican officials by quoting their private conversations against them" and adds Kennedy's remark: "I hope that no one around here is writing that kind of book." Sorensen himself did not write that kind of book and was scolded by some reviewers for his reticence. But others, notably Arthur Schlesinger, Jr., and former Assistant Secretary of State Roger Hilsman, made headlines with their blow-by-blow accounts of the internal workings of the Kennedy Administration; Schlesinger was particularly uncomplimentary to Dean Rusk and Hilsman to Robert McNamara, who at the time of publication were still serving as cabinet members, positions that precluded any rebuttal on their part.

There is no simple answer to the question of whether or not such material serves the public as well as it does the private interests of those who reveal it. At the very least, it deserves the same kind of critical scrutiny that greeted *The Saturday Evening Post*'s account of Adlai Stevenson's recommendations during the Cuban missile crisis. Yet some of the columnists and editorial writers who were outraged by the one-sided revelations about Stevenson were not noticeably disturbed by the similar treatment of Rusk and McNamara.

Fairness aside, there may be compelling arguments for making public material that bears directly on national policy. But what can be said about our right to know about the Kennedys' sleeping arrangements the night before the assassination (*Death of a President* by William Manchester), how the Kennedy children learned of their father's death (*White House Nannie* by Maude Shaw) and how much Jacqueline Kennedy spent each year for clothes (*My Life with Jacqueline Kennedy* by Mary Barelli Gallagher)? There has always been a journalistic sub-genre of "backstairs gossip" but it is only in recent years that its authors have come to justify (or rationalize) it as historical necessity.

The Kennedys themselves clearly invited abuses of their privacy. They used their personal charm to acquire power and then had their staff members sign agreements that they would not turn the resulting interest to their own profit. Jacqueline Kennedy asked William Manchester to write his account for the historical record and then insisted on the right to censor it. As editor Arnold Gingrich later pointed out, this was an attempt to establish the principle of "the truth as private property." Wherever they could, the family sought to control reminiscences of Camelot. Perhaps the least offensive and certainly the most innocently intended of all the "Kennedy books" was one entitled *The Pleasure of His Company* by Paul Fay, a wartime friend whom John Kennedy had installed as Under Secretary of the Navy. Fay's book was a lighthearted account of their friendship, published by Harper and Row and serialized in *McCall's*. In advance of publication, Evan Thomas, the book's editor, and I were subjected to a series of excisions dictated to Fay by Mrs. Kennedy and Robert Kennedy. One or two excesses might have been embarrassing, but the one deletion that sticks in my mind is of a charming anecdote in which the President's son, then aged two and a half, splashed his father at poolside while calling him "pooh-pooh head." After the wave of changes, many in this vein, had been made, Robert Kennedy thanked me, solemnly explaining that the family's concern was solely for what the children would soon be reading that might wound them. But Fay's cheerful compliance with having his book gutted apparently did not appease Jacqueline Kennedy, who later publicly insulted him by rejecting a contribution of $3000 from his royalties to the Kennedy Memorial Library.

There is little doubt that the Kennedys tried to have it both ways, parceling themselves out to the media when it suited their purposes and then self-righteously trying to control what others did along the same lines. But what is more significant is the uncritical eagerness with which both the media and the public have become accomplices in eliminating the idea of privacy without the slightest apparent regret. "Everybody belongs to everybody else" was the slogan of the dehumanized society of the future envisioned by Aldous Huxley in *Brave New World*, and, in the media at least, we are well on our way to accepting it as our own.

Why? Competition is a large part of the answer. Every book publisher, every magazine editor, every television producer is under pressure to go further than his competitors, to give his customers exclusively what they have not read or seen or heard before. In an earlier and less hectic time, the usual response to this kind of pressure was investigative reporting: the exposure of corruption that often served the public by leading to reform at the same time it served the selfish interests of editors by attracting readers. Even the legendary "muckrakers" of the early twentieth century were accused of self-serving excesses, notably by Theodore Roosevelt, who gave them their generic name in scorn rather than admiration. But history has largely vindicated the muckrakers; their own profit was incidental to the public service they performed. In today's corporate media, this kind of reporting is the exception rather than the rule; it is often practiced only when all else fails, as in the declining years of *The Saturday Evening Post*, which pursued "sophisticated muckraking" with a kind of recklessness that resulted in more law suits than public enlightenment. The far easier and more prevalent response to the pressure for exclusivity is the checkbook — to buy someone's own version of events in the increasingly frequent auctions conducted by literary agents and lawyers.

The auction itself offers an interesting sidelight to prevailing values. A decade or so ago, when someone became involved in a headline-making event, he would be signed up by an enterprising editor or publisher, usually the first to reach him with a substantial offer. Today, such public figures — whether heroes, victims, indicted criminals or former employees of the famous — are often sophisticated enough to place themselves in the hands of agents and/or ghost writers, who can convert their experience into the maximum dollar value. Within days after the release of the *Pueblo* crew by North Korea, an agent was soliciting offers for the ghost-written first-person stories of both Commander Lloyd Bucher and Mrs. Bucher. Shortly after the funeral of Judy Garland, the memoirs of her last husband, to whom she had been married for three months, were placed on the block. Within a year of the campus disorders at Columbia, an agent was inviting five-figure offers for a manuscript by Mark Rudd, one of the student leaders. The prevailing tone of these negotiations with editors and publishers, those trustees of our right to know under the First Amendment, can be inferred from a memorandum that came to light on publication of Mary Barelli Gallagher's book. Mrs. Gallagher's collaborator, Frances Spatz Leighton, informed her agent of the book's existence this way: "I am sitting on the hottest property currently in the U.S.A. and possibly the world. I am almost in a state of shock . . . you needn't waste your time with any publisher who doesn't see this as earning several million dollars when all the rights are sold — for the authors, that is. He'll make more, naturally. I mean the publisher. He's got a winner."

The winning bids in media auctions are seldom revealed and, in view of complicated clauses and contingencies, cannot always be added up with certainty, but the market has been booming. In 1966, William Manchester's advance payments for *Death of a President* totaled about $1,000,000. The following year, in a frenzy of blind faith and greed, publishers all over the world paid — sight unseen — a total of more than $2,000,000 for Svetlana Alliluyeva's *Twenty Letters to a Friend*. Robert Kennedy's posthumous 21,000-word account of the Cuban missile crisis was worth $1,000,-000 in 1968 and, in 1969, Lyndon Johnson's unwritten memoirs went off the block for $1,500,000, while Mrs. Johnson's diaries brought over $1,000,000.

Matters of taste aside, what are publishers buying at these auctions? All memoirs suffer from what I think of as the Sam Goldwyn syndrome. According to a famous Hollywood story, once verified for me by an eyewitness, Goldwyn had asked an experienced writer to produce a screenplay based on a certain classic novel. After several weeks of work, the writer reported that he had failed and that he was certain that the novel could not be made into a successful movie. Goldwyn nevertheless gave the assignment to another writer and made the movie — with disastrous results. Several years later, in a story conference, someone suggested an assignment for the first writer. "Oh, no," Goldwyn answered without hesitation, "not him — he was associated with one of my worst failures."

We expect memoirs to be self-justifying and, in varying degrees, dishonest. But more and more, the premium is on disparagement. There have been many insiders' books on the Kennedys, but what made Mrs. Gallagher's "the hottest property" was its unattractive revelations. It is as though, while consuming the false images that public figures are constantly manufacturing through the media, the public is developing an appetite for the anti-image, the dark side that is being withheld. When it finally becomes available, what do we have? An ugly unreality to cancel out the beautiful unreality, a soap opera of household bickering to neutralize Camelot. This image-making bookkeeping is balanced, but

are we closer to any human truth about the people to whom
we give power, about ourselves or about the kind of world
we are making together?

As if to remind us that the first men on the moon were,
after all, only the first lunar celebrities, *Life* magazine immediately ran an advertisement pointing out that it was the
exclusive proprietor of the astronauts' "innermost thoughts."
As taxpayers, we were entitled to know what Neil Armstrong
and Edwin Aldrin did on the moon; as media customers, we
had to buy *Life* to learn how they felt and what they thought.

Life purchased the astronauts' personal stories at the beginning of the space program. At first, there was considerable
grumbling by other publications about the propriety of re-
serving such rights as property of government employees,
whose work is financed by tax revenues. But who, after all,
will persist in arguing against the enrichment of men who
take such personal risks every time they are rocketed into
space? The more subtle effects of such proprietorship never
came into question. If *Life*, in effect, had a substantial investment in the success of the space program, could its readers
have looked to that magazine for any objective reporting on
the shortcomings and disabilities of our space efforts or any
questioning of their value? The magazine was relentless in
its investigation of the impropriety of Supreme Court Justice
Abe Fortas' relationship with Louis Wolfson, and its published reports led directly to Fortas' resignation; what were
the chances of *Life*'s displaying similar doggedness in investigating or criticizing NASA, when its own financial stake
in that agency dwarfed Fortas' dealings with Wolfson?

In 1963, when *Life* bought into the space program, the
New York Times complained editorially: "The sale of the

astronauts' 'personal stories' represents a stain of commercialism on the record of the space program. The astronauts are not movie stars or baseball heroes whose achievements in some private field of endeavor have made them objects of public interest." In 1971, after *Life* terminated its arrangement, the *New York Times* Syndicate bought exclusive rights to the personal stories of the Apollo 15 astronauts to appear on its own front pages and to be resold to other newspapers.

As men were heading toward the moon to expand the limits of our external world, other men were opening new medical frontiers by transplanting hearts from one human body to another. And the agents of the media were also busy converting this accomplishment into private property. The first transplant by Dr. Christiaan Barnard in Cape Town, South Africa, in late 1967, caught reporters by surprise. But they soon flocked to Groote Schuur Hospital in huge numbers and, according to the London *Express*, "delighted by the friendly cooperation of the doctors, clubbed together to buy them a Christmas present." The patient, Louis Washkansky, died. For the second heart-transplant operation, according to one news report, Philip Blaiberg's room was put under twenty-four-hour police guard, "apparently to keep reporters away and to enforce strict sterilization. Reporters had complete access to Washkansky, who became infected and died of pneumonia."

Several days later, the news of Blaiberg's condition was overshadowed by an argument over who owned the television rights to his operation. "Transplant Patient Fine; Dispute Flares Over Sale of TV Rights to N.B.C.," read the headline in the *New York Times*. After the Washkansky operation, NBC had solicited Dr. Barnard's cooperation for a documentary program to be called "Dr. Barnard's Heart Transplant Operations," but CBS had moved in with an offer to pay the surgeon's fare to the United States to appear on an interview program, "Face the Nation." Lucy Jarvis, an NBC producer, later said she had advised Dr. Barnard that he should "not go as a TV star," but he made the trip, which included a visit to President Johnson's Texas ranch, reportedly arranged by NBC's White House correspondent. "Then we could hardly get near him," Mrs. Jarvis said. "Something happened along the line, and when he returned home we found ourselves completely shut out, and we were not able to do our coverage. We went to the Blaibergs to protect ourselves and they agreed."

What the Blaibergs agreed to, in a contract signed four days before a dying heart donor was found, was $50,000 in return for exclusive television rights to the operation. But the network's enterprise was nullified when the hospital superintendent refused to allow the camera crew into the gallery of the operating room because of the danger of infection to the patient. Afterward, reporters found themselves squabbling over interviews with the Blaiberg family after being told by correspondents inside their apartment that "the Blaiberg story is ours."

Some twenty years ago, Billy Wilder made a hard-edged, bitter movie called *Ace in the Hole,* in which a cynical reporter takes control of the efforts to rescue a man trapped in a mine shaft and uses them for his own profit to build up the suspense and prolong the publicity. The trapped man, of course, dies. (The movie can still be seen on television under a different title, *The Big Carnival.*) In real life, reporters and editors are still struggling to lock up stories exclusively; while they seldom endanger human life in the process, they can do considerable damage to human understanding. As the big media voices — the television networks and publishers — were fighting over property rights in the first heart transplants, they had surrendered the possibility of putting the operations in any perspective. While CBS and NBC were pursuing Dr. Barnard as "a TV star" and competing for his cooperation, they were not reporting the widespread doubts and criticisms of medical authorities about the transplant operations. It remained for John Lear, science editor of the *Saturday Review*, to point out that coverage of the first operation constituted "some of the most irresponsible reporting that has ever been done in medicine." Lear cited medical research that stressed the difficulties involved in transplantation and the relatively minor role that such operations can ever play in the treatment of heart disease. But Lear was writing for hundreds of thousands of thoughtful readers; the networks were staging a spectacle for many millions. In the wave of well-publicized transplant operations that followed, few patients survived for more than a few days. Blaiberg himself, after several relapses and return trips to the hospital, lived for nineteen months — a gratifying addition to his life span, but not long enough to see the worldwide magazine and book publication of Dr. Barnard's autobiography, *One Life*, and the television and movie adaptations of it that were sure to follow.

Traditionally, reporters and editors are at their best when they approach a story as complete outsiders without a vested interest of any kind. As soon as they acquire property rights, they lose some of their freedom to see people and events with an impartial eye. Of all our journalistic organizations, the *New York Times* prides itself most on its objectivity and incorruptibility. Yet, in the past few years, I have been involved in several incidents in which the *Times* lost some of its fabled composure as a result of proprietary questions. When *McCall's* paid $1,000,000 for Robert Kennedy's account of the Cuban missile crisis in late 1968, the *Times* reported the purchase on a back page, along with the shipping news. Early in the story, it was pointed out that the late Senator had originally undertaken to write the narrative a year earlier in response to a request from the *Times* magazine (presumably for the usual $750 fee). The tone and placement of the story made it clear that the *Times* was annoyed, although James Reston, then executive editor, denied the implication. To placate the *Times*, *McCall's* offered Reston exclusive New York newspaper rights to the book at any price he would name, for use ten days after the magazine's publication, along with other newspapers across the country. Reston considered the proposal and finally answered that the *Times* would accept only if it could publish its condensation a week earlier than other newspapers, a condition that could not be met. When the account was published in *McCall's*, the *Times* covered it with a news story starting on the front page that repeated the details about the manuscript's origins, stressed that Kennedy's version "adds little to what has been published" and then went on for 54 paragraphs summarizing the presumably stale information it contained.

(The New York *Daily News*, when the sale of the Kennedy book was announced, published an editorial criticizing the impending publication of "security matters which normally require review and clearance by an official government agency." On the day the editorial appeared, the *News* syndicate was negotiating for rights to the book, and the *News* itself later serialized it amid the usual self-congratulatory promotional advertising.)

Perhaps the *Times'* pique over the Kennedy manuscript was understandable, although its expression was somewhat unseemly for an institution of such customary hauteur. But I could not help thinking at the time about the *Times'* own

performance in late 1966 during the dispute over William
Manchester's book about the assassination. After reporting
the various moves and countermoves in the Kennedys' attempts to excise parts of the manuscript, the *Times* one day
began publishing substantial summaries of material from
Manchester's book in a front-page story and continued to do
so over a period of several days. The stories, always credit-
ing anonymous figures who had read the book, were clearly
drawn from illegal copies that had been made in one or more
of the offices of magazines that had bid for serial rights and
lost. The parts quoted were, of course, the most controversial
and most likely to be the object of the Kennedys' exertions.
On what basis the *Times* justified such appropriation of a
manuscript that belonged to *Look* and Harper and Row and
such unilateral nullification of the Kennedys' legal efforts, I
could never learn from the *Times'* editors.

But it is the case of Svetlana Alliluyeva, Stalin's daughter,
that shows most clearly what can happen to the *New York
Times,* among others, when a major news event also yields a
valuable journalistic property. When Mrs. Alliluyeva suddenly appeared at the United States embassy in New Delhi
in March 1967 and asked for asylum, she presented our
State Department with a delicate problem: how to accept
the diplomatic advantages of defection by Stalin's daughter
without complicating relations with the Soviet Union. The
solution was to process her gingerly through official admission to the country and place her affairs in private hands as
soon as possible. The private hands turned out to be those of
a former ambassador to the Soviet Union, George Kennan.
After reading the book she had brought with her to make sure
that it would not embarrass the State Department, Kennan
arranged to give custody of the manuscript to his neighbor

in Princeton, New Jersey, an elderly attorney named Edward S. Greenbaum. General Greenbaum (he earned the rank in the Pentagon during World War II) flew to Geneva to take charge of the Alliluyeva manuscript while its author was awaiting entry to the United States.

Then, in one of those cozy arrangements that lead outsiders to suspect that there may be an Establishment that involves government and private collusion on public business, scarcely more than an hour after stepping off the plane from Geneva, General Greenbaum turned the book over to his client, Harper and Row, whom he had recently represented in the Manchester dispute with the Kennedys. In the same clublike atmosphere, newspaper rights were sold to the *New York Times*, whose publisher happened to be a client of General Greenbaum's, and magazine rights to *Life*, whose parent company's chairman of the board happened to be the brother-in-law of the *Times'* publisher.

Before these familylike arrangements were made for Mrs. Alliluyeva, the *Times* observed editorially that "the intense world-wide interest aroused by her defection makes it unlikely that she can be kept away from newspapermen indefinitely," and that "to gag her for reasons of political expediency violates her rights as a human being." Urging that Mrs. Alliluyeva be free to express herself to American journalists, the *Times* proclaimed: "To continue on the present course is to follow the Soviet principle that the rights of the individual are subordinate to the needs of the state." After Mrs. Alliluyeva arrived here, with her manuscript safely the property of the *New York Times*, a subsequent editorial in the *Times* revealed that she required privacy even more than freedom of expression and urged that she "be permitted peace, quiet, freedom from curiosity and sensation seekers."

The Soviet principle may measure all rights by the needs of the state; the American counterpart seems to be the proprietary interests of the media.

From then on, it would be an understatement to describe the *Times'* treatment of Mrs. Alliluyeva as unctuous. Her arrival commanded half of the front page and more than a page inside. The transcript of her press conference several days later, carefully staged by a commercial public relations company, was printed in full — with somewhat more coverage than normally is given to a Presidential press conference (perhaps understandably, since the public relations company was recommended to General Greenbaum by the *Times*). The newspaper capped a long, solemn page-one story of its own acquisition of rights to her book with the observation that *"The New York Times* has previously serialized books by Sir Winston Churchill, President Harry S Truman, President Dwight D. Eisenhower, former Secretary of State Cordell Hull and Gen. Walter Bedell Smith." When an essay that Mrs. Alliluyeva had written was to be published in *The Atlantic,* an advance copy was given to James Reston, who wrote a glowing front-page review in the *Times* before the article appeared. "Her gift of analogy and the power of her lyrical prose," Reston wrote, "are exceptional. She has composed not only a political but a literary document." (Other reviewers, in publications without property rights, were considerably less enthusiastic.) And, of course, when the book itself finally appeared, the *Times'* reviewers were ecstatic. (By contrast, in *Book World,* a supplement of the Washington *Post* and Chicago *Tribune,* John Kenneth Galbraith wrote: "I do not think this is much of a book . . . Mrs. Alliluyeva has a near genius for the inconsequential." The American public must have agreed. Two months later, *Newsweek* reported the book to be "one of the major publishing disappointments of recent years." One bookseller explained it this way: "If the book was a good description of what Stalin was like, we would be selling it out. But all she says is that my heart belongs to daddy.") *

And so we end up with a picture of the *New York Times* and *Life,* two pillars of our Cold War policy during the Stalin era, solemnly sponsoring the smug and rather maudlin reminiscences of their former antagonist's daughter. It is not difficult to imagine the derision with which these memoirs might have been greeted had the rights to publish them been sold to *Good Housekeeping* or the *Ladies' Home Journal.* But sponsorship in the media makes a difference. When *Esquire* published a skeptical article about Mrs. Alliluyeva's defection and, with typical irreverence, drew a Stalin mustache on her cover picture, the magazine was so bitterly criticized that its publisher, Arnold Gingrich, later wrote a column marveling at the "instant sanctity" that had been achieved by the late dictator's daughter. In contrast, an *Esquire* cover during the same period showing Vice President Hubert Humphrey as a ventriloquist's dummy sitting on President Lyndon Johnson's lap, passed without a ripple of protest.

The American press accepts responsibility for acting as a jury in the vast, continuing trial of men and events in our society. It takes on the monumental job of sifting the daily evidence of our public lives and presenting it to us, if not with objectivity, since that is unattainable, at least as fairly and disinterestedly as possible. In a court trial, we would be disturbed to find a member of the jury in a business partner-

---

* The *Times'* exertions on Mrs. Alliluyeva's behalf were rewarded in her second book, published a year later, in which she criticized both the photographs ("I almost fainted") and headlines ("dreadful") that accompanied the newspaper's installments of her first book.

ship with one of the litigants. Yet editors, who are constantly alert to conflict of interest on the part of others, do not see themselves as compromised in similar situations.

This is not to argue that memoirs should not be purchased and published. But it should be understood that the purchase price usually involves more than money; almost invariably, it puts a publication or network in the position of lending its own reputation to the subject's point of view. In one of the rare exceptions that underscores the rule, *Esquire* put a mocking cover of Roy Cohn wearing an artificial halo on the issue that contained Cohn's self-justifying memoir of his work for the late Senator Joseph McCarthy. But how are readers to know that several leading magazines declined to bid on Mary Barelli Gallagher's vindictive exploitation of Jacqueline Kennedy Onassis until the *Ladies' Home Journal*, in deep financial difficulty, decided to lend the manuscript the weight of its 86 years of publishing respectability? And how is NBC serving the public's right to know in paying Sirhan Sirhan $15,000 for an exclusive interview the day after his death sentence was upheld to hear him tell us of his victim, Robert Kennedy, "Every morning when I get up, sir, I say I wish that son of a gun were alive so that I wouldn't have to be here now"?

Just beyond these questions of responsibility and judgment, there has been lurking another word that I have hesitated to use: taste. For, after all, what does taste have to do with our right to know? The word itself summons up all those elitist assumptions that democracy was supposed to leave behind, particularly the assumption that some people have the right to decide what the rest of us should see and hear. But the fact is that some people — editors, publishers and broadcasters — do decide what the rest of us should see and hear. And in the case of television, we can see the inevitable result when they apply only the test of democracy (how many people will watch?) without admitting responsibility for their own taste. We get hour after hour of dehumanized mayhem, mindless comedy and inane chatter. Democracy gives us the freedom to be degraded or turn away.

Is this to suggest that, in the light of our hard-won freedom of expression, there are some forms of expression that should be withheld or, to use the most brutal word, suppressed? The fact is that a good deal always has been and is still being, if you will, suppressed. Every day, editors and broadcasters make decisions about what is important, legitimate or worthy of being reported. It is only under the mounting competitive pressure for our attention that their standards have been changing. Because these changes have been unconscious, they are all the more dangerous.

While the newsmagazines publish their periodic reports on the disappearance of restraints on sexual expression in all the media, they have largely ignored a form of permissiveness that seems to me to be a far graver threat to the society. We have placed a premium on what Ray Bradbury has called "insane fame." Of course, we must know all we can about what Sirhan Sirhan and James Earl Ray have done. But does that require us to enrich them for strutting before us on the television screen and the printed page with self-serving versions of their crimes? Will their rewards go unnoticed by potential imitators? (On his way to jail after shooting George Wallace, Arthur Bremer asked FBI agents: "How much do you think I'll get for my autobiography?") Are we compelled to shower money and attention on the disgruntled former associates and employees of the rich and powerful — without making distinctions between their venom and the value of what they have to tell us? Must we make marketable properties out of our scientists and technicians, bought and paid for by the media, at the risk of obscuring critical questions about their accomplishments? We cannot answer with laws or explicit guidelines. But these questions are hardly being asked at all, either by the media or the public. If they continue to go unasked, we will get more and more seekers of insane fame and instant fame while watching more and more television debates and reading more and more commission reports about violence and corruption in our society.

The commissions themselves, those august bodies of social scientists and public-spirited elders who are appointed to correct media distortions of our assassinations and riots, are also showing signs of succumbing to the temptations of property. After Bantam Books sold more than a million and a half paperback copies of the Kerner Commission report on the 1967 summer riots and more than half a million copies of the Walker report on the violence at the Chicago Democratic Convention of 1968, there was considerable controversy about allowing a commercial publisher to profit from material prepared at the taxpayer's expense. A persuasive rebuttal was that the ultimate purpose of the commissions is public education and the Government Printing Office simply cannot match the mass distribution of a paperback publisher.

But mass distribution requires mass appeal, and before long the commissions found themselves using ghostwriters and acting as literary agents to shape their material for the market. A case in point is the report to the National Commission on the Causes and Prevention of Violence on the conflict between police and black militants in Cleveland during a six-day period in July 1968. Less than a year later, the report was published jointly by Bantam and the *New York Times* under the title, *Shoot-Out in Cleveland*. The story of how the report was written, rewritten and finally published was told by Geoffrey Cowan in the *Village Voice*:

A 400-page manuscript was submitted to the commission by two members of the Civil Violence Research Center at Case Western Reserve University, but the commission chairman, Dr. Milton Eisenhower, and its general counsel, James Campbell, turned it over to Anthony E. Neville, a free-lance writer living in Baltimore. "They felt it needed work," Neville told Cowan. "According to Campbell, Dr. Eisenhower believes the Commission's major task is to educate the public. Since he wants the documents which it publishes to be widely read, he feels that they must be well-written." Neville went to work preparing the report to market specifications. "From a literary standpoint," he explained, "you want to get the reader very quickly to the blood and guts."

When the manuscript reached the publisher, even the people at Bantam were "shocked" at the title, *Shoot-Out in Cleveland*. One of them told Cowan: "We expected it to be called *The Cleveland Report*." But in the process of transition from a long, scholarly account to a short, dramatic one, more than the title was sensationalized. One of the basic conclusions of the study was that the original gun battle between police and black militants was more a case of mutual provocation than a black ambush, as most news accounts suggested at the time. But, in Neville's version, there is a sentence that both original authors fought to have removed: "A small, well-equipped army of black extremists were [sic] responsible for the bloodshed (whether or not they fired the first shot)." This conclusion was stressed in most news accounts when the report was published, yet one of the original authors told Cowan: "It undermines the book. I would have tried to prohibit the government from publishing the report if I had known that would be in it."

The efforts of the National Commission on the Causes

and Prevention of Violence to achieve the widest possible market for its material bear more than a little resemblance to those of Mary Barelli Gallagher and James Earl Ray. The ultimate irony might have come when the Commission published its findings on the extent to which the mass media contribute to violence in our society. If a ghostwriter had been chosen for the assignment to get "the reader very quickly to the blood and guts," that report might have found not only a paperback publisher but a sponsor for a television special as well.

In "A Sad Heart at the Supermarket," Randall Jarrell asked: "Is the influence of what I have called the Medium likely to make us lead any good life? to make us love and try to attain any real excellence, beauty, magnanimity? or to make us understand these as obligatory but transparent rationalizations, behind which the realities of money and power are waiting?" But then Randall Jarrell was a poet and what, after all, can a poet tell us about the real world?

6

They Must Know What They're Doing or They Wouldn't Be Where They Are

Since World War II, the history of mass magazines has been one long deathwatch. At the end, the aged giants of American journalism did not die gracefully. They succumbed after brutalizing surgery, prolonged family squabbles and unseemly deathbed antics: *Collier's* expired soon after a sensationally tasteless World War III issue, while *The Saturday Evening Post* collapsed amid a welter of law suits, brought on by exposing such major menaces to American society as college football coaches.

The post-mortems were numerous and ugly. During the final years of the *Post*, so many people were keeping diaries of the office in-fighting that there could not have been much time left for getting out the magazine. The resulting articles, memoirs and novels have a tendency to blur into one large bloody corporate canvas, where we see editors, executives and board members in constant conflict.

Yet these accounts tell us little more about magazines in our time than a coroner's report tells us about the life of the corpse. Terminal illness can be dramatic, but it rarely brings out the best in either victim or survivors. And it hardly ever reflects the richness and complexity of the life that preceded it.

In my time as a magazine editor, which spans the period from the last years of *Collier's* to the last days of the *Post*, there was, without question, a good deal of corporate melodrama and even more farce. The undertaker for the Crowell-Collier magazines — *Collier's, American* and *Woman's Home Companion* — was a short, tough-talking former Marine combat officer named Paul C. Smith. He did not become president of the company to bury the magazines, of course, but to restore them to their former glory. One of his first acts was to accept a speaking invitation from the Society of Magazine Writers to inspire contributors to renewed interest in his publications. "I first came to this company a few months ago as one of fourteen vice-presidents," he explained. "Someone with a penchant for making organizational charts drew one up showing me all the way at the end of a line of vice-presidents with no one under me. Well, a few days after I became president, I called in that chart-maker and said, 'You know that dangling vice-president with no authority? He just fired you.'" The magazine writers were not visibly inspired.

Twelve years later, a short, fast-talking lawyer named Martin S. Ackerman became president of the Curtis Publishing Company to save *The Saturday Evening Post, Ladies' Home Journal, American Home, Holiday* and *Jack & Jill.* One of *his* first acts was to call together the editors and executives of the magazines to introduce himself. "I am Marty Ackerman," he told the assemblage. "I am thirty-six years old and I am very rich. I hope to make the Curtis Publishing Company rich again."

Less than a year after Smith's speech, all three Crowell-Collier magazines were dead. Less than a year after Ackerman's speech, the *Post* had been buried and the rest of the company dismembered.

Spectacular incompetence is far from unknown at the upper levels of American life. A book editor I know once proposed a volume to be titled "They Must Know What They're Doing or They Wouldn't be Where They Are," using as examples the captain of the Titanic, the designers of the Edsel, Lyndon Johnson directing the war in Vietnam, and so on. At any gathering of executives in cosmetics or computers or kitchen appliances, you can hear stories of self-appointed geniuses who consulted their "gut feelings" and came forward with revolutionary answers to business problems that resulted in corporate disaster. Because magazines have been in trouble, the opportunities for such suicidal brilliance have been particularly rich. In one company several years ago, the editor of a large magazine was told by the controlling stockholder: "I want you to spend a million dollars every month for something to appear in the magazine. *That* will make readers and advertisers realize how much better we are than the competition." When the editor demurred on the grounds that he had never seen *one* feature worth a million dollars, let alone twelve a year, he was replaced with another editor who made a heroic effort to spend the money. The magazine's troubles grew worse, the second editor was removed and the controlling stockholder went on to apply his genius to ailing companies in other industries.

I have known more than two dozen presidents of large publishing companies, either on a day-to-day basis or through working closely on industry matters. Although most were sane and intelligent, the group included:

A psychopathic liar (often, he knew you knew he was lying, even on small matters, but that served only to spur him on to more spectacular heights of untruth);

A hopeless drunk (he would consume four or five martinis before dinner meetings, lurch to his feet in mid-sentence over coffee and disappear into the night);

A textbook case of personal insecurity (he could not resist launching into a detailed recital of his net worth with perfect strangers, on one occasion including a Rockefeller);

And my favorite leader of men (when one of his executives was suffering a long period of severe pain in the jaw, he sent the company's personnel director to visit the man's dentist, not to inquire about the executive's prospects for relief, but to find out if he would be permanently afflicted with bad breath).

None of these men is still running a publishing company. Each was quietly removed by a board of directors that could never admit its own culpability in choosing him for the position. Unless there is a scandal involved, such deposed presidents usually leave with testimonials and stock option profits to be hired as chief executives or consultants by other companies in need of their experience and wisdom.

How do boards of directors happen to pick such misfits in the first place? In theory, a board represents the accumulated judgment of men wise in the ways of managing large enterprises. From my own experience, a board is no such thing. It is generally composed of two factions: one, insiders with a large personal stake as executives or representatives of large shareholders, and two, outsiders — presidents and chairmen of other companies, public figures who have been retired by the electorate and academic politicians — who sit on boards for the prestige and/or the large fees they receive for a few hours of their time every month. The insiders dominate meetings with tendentious answers to management questions, while the outsiders, very much like parents at the PTA, waste time asking pointless questions to show their interest and astuteness. If intelligent business decisions are made in such a climate, it is more often by default than as a result of the deliberative process. When editors and publishers are doing their job well, there is little that a board of directors can do to derail them. When they are not doing well, the directors' usual response is prolonged inertia followed by sudden panic. In their search for saviors, they turn to spectacular incompetents and megalomaniacs.

From this evidence, it would appear that the corporate process has been largely responsible for killing magazines that flourished in a time when companies were smaller and dominated by individual owners rather than boards of directors. This theory, assiduously promoted by editors and publishers of defunct magazines, has been warmly endorsed by social critics who see bigness as the main problem of American society. It is a comfortable conclusion that has some truth in it. The only trouble is that it misses the main point: Owners rarely make or break magazines. Editors do. By the time ownership, corporate or individual, becomes crucial to a magazine's existence, the magazine has almost always been suffering from prolonged editorial malfunction. The most obvious evidence to this effect is to be found in those companies in which one magazine remains healthy while another withers under the same corporate management. In addition, there are many magazines that have surmounted their difficulties after a change of editors; to my knowledge, few have been saved by a change of ownership.

Of course, the people who hire and fire editors play an important part in the success or failure of magazines. But I have seen enlightened management and foolish management in both large companies and small. The difference has been not in the size or structure of the organization but in the qualities of the men who run it.

A few years ago, at an industry luncheon, I had occasion to introduce Henry Steeger, the owner of *Argosy,* who had been my first magazine employer. In acknowledging the introduction, Steeger made a little joke about how he had been the first to recognize my ability by giving me a five-dollar raise. As the audience chuckled appreciatively, it occurred to me that I had left the magazine after a year and a half because Steeger had *refused* to give me a five-dollar raise.

But money isn't everything. What finally helped me decide to leave the magazine was a two-hour staff meeting one morning. *Argosy* had been doing well with talented editors and writers like Marion Hargrove, Merle Miller and W. C. Heinz (in fact, it never did as well before or after), but the owner had met a gentleman in the advertising business who had spent an airplane trip telling him in some detail what was wrong with the magazine. We were treated to a full reprise of his criticisms (all of them inane) and exhorted to find ways of doing better. My way was to start looking for another job while vowing to myself that I would never again work for a publication that was subject to the whims and insecurities of an individual owner.

In the years that followed, I learned that corporations can be just as capricious as individuals, but I could never subscribe to the comfortable theory that large companies are bad while small ones are good. "There is nobody more frightened than a man with his first million dollars," is a favorite maxim of Norton Simon, who was relieved of that particular fear at an early age. Working in a corporate empire controlled by Simon has provided me with some bizarre and frustrating experiences, but it also gave me the best years of my working life under one of the most unlikely men ever to head a major publishing company.

Late in 1956, Simon decided that the McCall Corporation needed a new president. One of his associates suggested that several experienced executives would soon be out of work: incumbent governors who would be defeated on Election Day. Since he regarded himself as a moderate Republican, Simon turned to a retiring governor of that persuasion (a man he had never met): Arthur B. Langlie of Washington, who had been the Republican Convention's keynote speaker that year before running unsuccessfully for the United States Senate. Langlie, a former lawyer and mayor of Seattle who had never been in private business, accepted.

At the time, I was managing editor of *Redbook*. Most of our editors, who were liberal Democrats, were dismayed at the new choice of president. We heard that, in addition to being a Republican, Langlie was a devoutly religious man, a pillar of the Salvation Army, who did not smoke, swear or drink. In the magazine, we had just published a devastating critique of Norman Vincent Peale's religiosity (in one of his books, Peale later wrote that the criticisms in the article by leading Protestant theologians had prompted him to compose his resignation from the clergy but that, at his father's deathbed, the elder Peale had dissuaded him from submitting it). We were constantly running articles in favor of Federal aid to education, nuclear disarmament and other political proposals that were bound to be distasteful to a conservative Republican such as Langlie.

At a welcoming party for the new president, I expressed my anxiety by mischievously telling Langlie a story about Henry Luce that might help him understand the composition of our staff. Luce had once been asked why, as a staunch

Republican, he employed so many liberal Democrats as
writers and editors. "Because," Luce is supposed to have replied, "those Republican bastards can't write." At the punch
line, Langlie smiled weakly.

In the following year and a half, I had occasion to see very
little of the new president. Then, in the fall of 1958, Wade
Nichols, the editor of *Redbook*, announced that he was leaving to become editor of *Good Housekeeping*. I was only in
third position on the staff hierarchy at that time, thirty-four
years old and philosophically uncongenial to Langlie; in
addition, in its 88 years of existence, the McCall Corporation
had never had a Jew as editor-in-chief of one of its magazines.
Although I was fully prepared to see the executive editor or
an outsider become the new editor, Langlie called me in and,
after an hour's conversation, gave me the job.

A few weeks later, the company was in turmoil. Otis Wiese,
who had been editor of *McCall's* for thirty-two years and
was now the publisher as well, walked angrily into Langlie's
office one morning, accused him of "interfering" with his
direction of the magazine and resigned on the spot. Several
other editors and business executives of the magazine walked
out with Wiese. The newspapers and newsmagazines, which
relish such corporate turmoil, reported the story in great
detail, almost invariably from Wiese's point of view.

Several days later, I attended my first meeting of the
company's management committee. The entire morning was
taken up by Langlie's recital of his difficulties with Wiese
(there had been many) and his attempts to solve the magazine's problems by having company staff members work with
the editor. Langlie was visibly shaken by the news reports
of the resignations, particularly a *Time* magazine reference
to him as "an amateur." When he asked for comments, I
volunteered to explain the designation: "If an editor is doing

his job well, it's the company president's responsibility to support him in every way possible. If he isn't doing his job well, it's the president's duty to replace him. In publishing, that's professional. Anything else is considered amateur."

"Are you saying," Langlie asked, "that I should have fired him?"

"I'm saying that you should have decided either to support him or fire him. When a team keeps losing games and the coach is removed from his job, nobody is surprised. But if you had someone sitting next to him on the bench during games, whispering suggestions into his ear, they would call you an amateur."

The following two years were the most productive I ever had as a magazine editor. Until he was forced to retire prematurely after a heart attack, Langlie gave me the kind of confidence and support that editors dream about but seldom get. When I asked for better schedules and more press capacity from our printing plant, Langlie spent two days backing my demands against the plant managers who wanted to reserve their best equipment for outside customers. When the magazine was given an award by the Family Service Association for supporting Federal welfare programs, about which I knew he had personal reservations, Langlie stood next to me during the ceremony and expressed his pride in the magazine. After we published an article criticizing frozen-food manufacturers for slipshod practices, Langlie greeted an industry delegation with the remark, "I suppose you've come here to thank us for trying to raise the standards of your business," and brushed aside suggestions that members might withdraw advertising from both of his company's magazines.

The magazine prospered during those years, and so did I. Afterward, I no longer subscribed to any sweeping theories

about corporations and individuals, liberals and conserva-
tives, or any other easy categories for describing what happens among people when money and power are at stake.

In the years following World War II, while their managements slept, most magazines were in the hands of editors who
recognized neither the threat of television nor the changes
taking place among their readers. The war had shaken the
comfortable insularity of American existence; high-school
and college education was expanding rapidly; small-town
life was giving way to urban growth. And the least sophisticated readers were being taken over by the most compelling medium of mass entertainment ever invented. But most
magazine editors continued to give their readers what Tom
Wolfe later described as "brain candy" — stories and articles
that stroked their prejudices and lulled them with reassur-
ance. As a magazine writer in the late 1940s, I was assigned
to do an article for *Coronet* on adolescent problems during
puberty. After reading the literature and interviewing psy-
chologists and teachers, I turned in a piece describing the
physical and psychological changes taking place in teen-
agers during that difficult period of their lives. It was rejected by the editor, who explained that he had simply wanted
an article giving parents "ten easy rules for handling the
little bastards." *Coronet* went to its reward a decade later,
still searching for those ten easy rules that would solve all
of life's problems.

Along with such contempt for their readers, some editors
of that time indulged themselves in unbelievable smugness.
One of them told a would-be contributor grandly: "If Shakespeare were alive today and writing sonnets, we would be
publishing them." At about this time, the gentleman who
fancied himself as Shakespeare's editor was nearing retire-

ment age. After a careful search of all the white Anglo-Saxon Protestants available, he selected his successor from the staff of a magazine in the Midwest. But the successor made the mistake of coming to dinner wearing two-toned shoes. The editor's wife was horrified at this lapse in taste, and the job offer was withdrawn. Upon hearing the story, the editor of a competing magazine, delighted with this proof of his rival's narrow-mindedness, immediately hired the rejected successor as a senior editor. It turned out that Mr. Two-Toned Shoes did not have much ability; he was eventually fired but went on to a number of impressive jobs on the basis of his high-level experience.

Until magazines ran into serious trouble in the 1950s, all but a very few were run along the lines of country clubs, with roughly the same values and standards for membership. In this closed circuit, it was possible for a personable nonentity to move from one top job to another until retirement. One, who had a black thumb as editor-in-chief, presided at the death of one magazine and left two others comatose before moving on to a well-paying position as an educational administrator suitable to the distinguished former editor of three national magazines.

Some of these molders of public opinion were almost psychopathically removed from reality. Toward the end of his career, one of the most publicized magazine editors of our time was sitting in his private dining room with several senior staff members and a number of advertising people assigned to a major automobile account. The purpose of the meeting was to have the editors offer their ideas on automobile advertising that would appeal to readers of their magazine. During the discussion someone came in and whispered to the editor-in-chief, who then excused himself. He returned a few minutes later to announce that President Kennedy had been shot. He then resumed the discussion about automobile advertising that would appeal to readers of his magazine.

If social historians of the future show any interest in what happened to magazines in the middle of this century, the record will consist largely of the memoirs of those who helped to kill them, supplemented by the easy generalization of business reporters: Television made the large general magazine obsolete for advertisers. The world of Norman Rockwell was replaced by the world of "Laugh-In," and nobody shed tears for high-button shoes when *they* went out of style, right?

Maybe. But before the final nails are hammered into the lid of the mass-magazine coffin, some mourner should say a few words about the virtues and legacies as well as the corruption and folly of the deceased. This testimony will suffer dramatically alongside the tales of intrigue and betrayal, but it may help explain, by contrast at least, what all the corporate melodrama was about.

Shortly after Paul Smith made his speech to the magazine writers, presumably designed to show that he was enough of a son of a bitch to save the Crowell-Collier magazines, I was offered a job there at a salary considerably higher than that I was getting as a junior editor at *Redbook*. At the time, *Redbook*'s future seemed even less secure than that of *Collier's*. The first issue to be distributed in the office after I came to work had fewer than half a dozen pages of advertising; one of the largest advertisers was Preparation H, a remedy for hemorrhoids. But I declined the *Collier's* job, simply because of the contrast between what I had seen of Smith and the two men I was then working for: Phillips Wyman, the publisher, and Wade Nichols, the editor of *Redbook*. Wyman had been put in charge of the magazine in 1949, when the company management had been inclined to kill it. Like other general magazines, *Redbook* seemed to have no future as television began to take over the job of entertaining large numbers of people. But Wyman was convinced that a magazine for a specific part of the mass audience, with an identifiable point of view, could survive the competition of television. To back his conviction, he gave up a secure position as circulation director of the McCall Corporation to become publisher of the failing magazine. His first step was to recruit Nichols, then thirty-four years old, as editor, and announce that *Redbook* would henceforth address itself to "young adults" between the ages of eighteen and thirty-five.

When I joined the staff in 1953, the magazine was still holding on by its unpolished fingernails. An inexpensive grade of paper kept down costs but also discouraged advertisers who prefer glossy paper for their four-color pages. The newsstand price had been raised, yet readers, who were getting something from the magazine that did not require slick paper, kept buying it in increasing numbers. What they were getting was an honest, if not distinguished, magazine. Amid the conventional fiction and the treacle about movie stars, there was a vein of reporting that reflected social and moral concern: about racial prejudice in the churches and elsewhere (before the Supreme Court desegregation decision of 1954 as well as after), about the damage that McCarthyism was doing to the country, about the dangers of nuclear weapons, about public-health problems such as air pollution and the indiscriminate use of pesticides and food additives, about all kinds of community meanness and dishonesty.

All of this hard reporting was presented without much self-congratulation or self-exploitation. Little of it made newspaper headlines, and even less resulted in law suits. Years later, after Jessica Mitford told me how advertiser pressure had resulted in the butchering of an article on funeral directors in *The Saturday Evening Post,* she seemed genuinely surprised to learn that *Redbook* had reported all of the criticisms of funeral directors several years before the *Post* article and before she herself wrote *The American Way of Death.* In those days, it was relatively easy to resist advertisers, since we had so little advertising to lose, but it was painful nontheless to hear that a large meat-packer was canceling a proposed schedule to show his displeasure with an article on inadequate meat inspection.

For years before the flamboyant efforts were made to revamp *Collier's* and the *Post,* Wyman and Nichols were working doggedly to give their readers, without fanfare, a magazine that had meaning for them. As advertising and circulation reached new records, other publishers looked everywhere for the "gimmick" but failed to find it. Wyman died in the spring of 1955 just as the magazine was turning profitable. Less than a month before his death, several of us went to Washington with him to receive the Benjamin Franklin Award for public service, won by *Redbook* over all other magazines for articles on the misuse of government security programs, dangers to academic freedom on the campus and the conflict over integration of a Northern suburb. Late in the night, after much drinking and reminiscing, Wyman, a reserved and rather shy man, allowed himself an observation he would undoubtedly have suppressed under normal conditions. "My greatest pleasure in life," he said quietly, "is making it possible for people to do more than they ever thought they could do."

In 1949, the year Wyman volunteered to save *Redbook,* the magazine had a circulation of 1,800,000 and advertising revenue of $1,467,128. In 1969, *Redbook's* circulation was over 4,500,000 with advertising revenue of $23,132,692. During that period, the magazine won numerous awards for public service and attracted as regular contributors two Americans who symbolized the values to which it was dedicated, Margaret Mead and Benjamin Spock. But one incident in 1969 may be more revealing than all the statistics and prizes. In February of that year, in a brief editorial prompted by its editor, Sey Chassler, the magazine expressed concern about starvation in Biafra and suggested that readers might want to help. In the following weeks, in coins and dollar bills, almost $50,000 came into the editorial offices.

There were other exceptions to the prevailing smugness and timidity. From the mid-1950s to the mid-1960s, a tough-minded editor named Dan Mich transformed *Look,* which up to then had been a rather poor imitation of *Life,* into a magazine of hard-edged reporting about civil rights and civil liberties, education, mental health and all the other social and political issues of the time. Under his direction, the magazine outdistanced the failing *Saturday Evening Post* and closed in on *Life.* During that period, *Look* was the only magazine of its size to consistently risk the wrath of McCarthy supporters and Southern racists. Mich was a stubborn and sometimes testy man who urged his reporters to "surround every assignment" until they had the answers to the hard questions involved. "Nothing we've done before will ever be good enough again" was his byword. Unlike some of his less-talented competitors, he shunned personal publicity. Not long before he died, I was asked to present an award to him on behalf of the Society of Magazine Writers. In doing so, I expressed my admiration in somewhat sentimental terms. He got up, grunted one sentence of embarrassed thanks and sat down. After the ceremony, his wife took me aside and whispered: "That was his way of showing he was touched."

If Mich had lived past 1965, it is doubtful that *Look* would have been suffering the prolonged identity crisis it was going through before expiring in 1971.

One of the pitfalls awaiting even the best of editors is the desire, conscious or not, to prove his own indispensability. More than one magazine has been ruined by an aging editor bent on leaving behind a monument to his own brilliance by sabotaging his successors. The most striking exception to the rule has been Arnold Gingrich, the first editor of *Esquire*. From 1933 to the mid-1950s, he built a publication based on literary distinction mixed with risqué cartoons and paintings of barely draped Petty girls ("the mind of Madame Curie in the body of Sally Rand," observed one contemporary critic). By the late 1950s, Hemingway and Fitzgerald were historical figures and the Petty girl was as dated as the mustache cup. Instead of grieving for past glories, Gingrich began hiring the brightest young men he could find—among others, Harold Hayes, his eventual successor; Clay Felker, who later became editor of *New York*; and Byron Dobell, who prompted Tom Wolfe's first essay into the New Journalism — in what Gingrich described as "a reforestation program."

Presiding over your own obsolescence is not easy, as Gingrich himself later admitted. At first, he fought some of his younger editors' innovations, vetoing publication of *On the Road* by Jack Kerouac, among other things. "It occurred to me along about that time," Gingrich has recalled, "that this was pretty ridiculous. If you get people in to influence a magazine by the contribution they can make, and then give them a dead hand that keeps them from making that contribution, you are defeating yourself. I finally decided to bar myself from editorial meetings. I used to run those meetings and get these kids in and start talking to them very earnestly about all I knew about this business, and I soon found, from the expressions on their faces, that all the people I was citing from my own experience might just as well have been my good friends Ben Franklin, Thomas Jefferson and George Washington."

Gingrich's loosening of the reins resulted in a sophistication for the magazine that eventually led to new circulation and advertising records. Yet his withdrawal was far from a negative act. His own judgment in selecting the new editors and his continuing presence as a sponsor of their freedom were crucial to the transition. The atmosphere Gingrich created had a liberating effect in a couple of unforeseen ways: One of the bright young men he brought in, Ralph Ginzburg, went on to make journalistic history in the courts. After *Esquire* rejected a rather turgid article he had written on erotica, Ginzburg, by far a better promoter than writer, published it himself as a small book and sold more than 100,000 copies through mail-order advertising. He then went on to publish *Eros*, which earned him a jail sentence, and *Fact*, which resulted in a successful libel suit by Barry Goldwater. During that same period a young *Esquire* promotion writer named Hugh Hefner decided to start a magazine called *Playboy*. Ginzburg earned adverse legal decisions while Hefner became a multimillionaire, but both began their careers under Gingrich's influence before setting out on their own in the attempt to outdo him.

The careers of Hefner and his female counterpart, Helen Gurley Brown, tell us something about the society which magazines have been serving in the past decades. Hefner and Mrs. Brown are easily the most famous magazine editors of our time (*Life*, for example, has published picture stories on each of them but on no others of their calling). Hefner launched the phenomenal financial success of *Playboy* and its related enterprises by publishing nude pictures of Marilyn

Monroe and Anita Ekberg; a decade later, Mrs. Brown initiated her editorship of *Cosmopolitan* with an article describing the duration of the late Aly Khan's erections, along with a report on "The Pill That Makes Women More Responsive to Men" (although the Hearst Corporation nervously ordered her to erase the last two words from the printing plates of the magazine's cover).

Hefner kept himself in the public consciousness with a series of pompous rationalizations under the title of "The Playboy Philosophy" (which were characterized by one psychiatrist as "the worst mélange of guilt and insecurity I've ever seen" but which served as the basis of countless sermons and articles by ministers attempting to stay afloat in the tides of The New Morality).

Mrs. Brown's press clippings were augmented by the publication of a memo she had circulated in her office asking women editors to contribute their thoughts to a proposed article on the proper erotic manipulation of breasts. For a brief time, television audiences were treated to a series in which she interviewed other celebrities. On one memorable occasion, Mrs. Brown asked a young woman who had written a popular novel for her opinion of the birth-control pill. When the author replied with a comment on the dangers of tampering with bodily chemistry, Mrs. Brown asked sweetly: "Then what kind of birth control do you use?" The author's response was to roll her eyes upward and exclaim, "My God, what kind of program is this?" Mrs. Brown persisted: "What I mean is, do you consider it the man's responsibility or the woman's?" Only after a strangled reply ("The woman's") did the interview proceed into more conventional channels. The series was canceled soon afterward, but Mrs. Brown continued to be a popular guest on the evening talk shows, during which such personalities as David Susskind invariably took the opportunity to lecture her on questions of taste.

In an era of vulgarity masquerading as enlightenment, the history of *The New Yorker* is instructive. If the phrase "editorial genius" has any meaning at all, it must be applied to Harold Ross, who edited *The New Yorker* from its first issue in 1925 until his death in 1951. Under his direction, the magazine attained a unique blend of urbanity, humor and impeccable reporting. The names of its contributors during that period comprise a roll call of pre–World War II sophistication: James Thurber, Robert Benchley, Wolcott Gibbs, S. J. Perelman, Dorothy Parker, Alexander Woollcott, Frank Sullivan, E. B. White, Ogden Nash, Peter Arno and Charles Addams, among many others. Ross himself was a brilliant, colorful and somewhat eccentric man who inspired an endless flow of anecdotes around the circuit of Manhattan literary bars from the Algonquin to Tim Costello's. Ross chose a successor of contrasting temperament: William Shawn, who had joined the magazine's staff in 1933. If the word "retiring" has any meaning, it must be applied to Shawn, who, to my knowledge, has not made a public speech, has not appeared on radio or television and has given only one extended interview in twenty years as editor of *The New Yorker*. He is the only editor of a major magazine during that period that I have not had the occasion to meet. He is also, by an enormous margin, the editor I most admire and respect.

It says something about the values of magazine editors and the society as a whole that this opinion is not universal. So-called sophisticated people have reserved most of their enthusiasm for the brash and the breathlessly chic. *The*

New Yorker, many of them say, "has not been the same since Ross." With that statement, I can agree. Shawn has transformed his magazine into the most socially and morally aware publication of our time; on every important question of the past two decades, it has contributed stunning reportage and analysis, often long before any other general periodical has even recognized the existence of the subject. A partial list:

Race: As early as 1962, the rage of black Americans that was to spawn the militants and the separatists was eloquently expressed in James Baldwin's "Letter from a Region of My Mind," which later formed the core of his book, *The Fire Next Time.* Later, young reporters like Renata Adler and Calvin Trillin gave us the texture of what was going on in the South as well as in Harlem.

Poverty: It was Dwight Macdonald's essay-review of a then-obscure book, *The Other America* by Michael Harrington, that first brought attention to the hidden poverty behind our affluence and prompted the Kennedy Administration to launch the "War on Poverty." This political war went almost as badly as the military war in Vietnam, but the poverty was no longer hidden.

Vietnam: Long before the country turned against the most disastrous war in American history, *The New Yorker* was reporting the reality behind the televised carnage: in Jonathan Schell's narratives of the destruction of villages our troops were presumably defending, in Susan Sheehan's profiles of South Vietnamese victims, in Robert Shaplen's reports from Saigon, in Richard Rovere's analysis from Washington, in Richard Goodwin's essays after his departure from the Johnson Administration and, later, in Daniel Lang's account of the rape and murder of a South Vietnamese girl by an American patrol.

Environment: Rachel Carson's series, "Silent Spring," in 1962 was the early-warning signal for the alarm over ecological disaster that was finally sounded in the early 1970s. For twenty years, *The New Yorker*, in a stream of articles and essays, had been quietly documenting the despoiling of our air, land and waters.

Government: Throughout the 1960s, a gifted reporter named Richard Harris was laying bare the workings and non-workings of our legislative and administrative systems, in recounting the struggles over drug safety, gun control and law-and-order — the last a brilliant series in late 1969 that put into perspective the critical shift of philosophy during the Justice Department's transition from the direction of Ramsey Clark to that of John Mitchell.

Religion: The most compelling exposure of the internal conflicts of the Roman Catholic Church was provided by the reports of the behind-the-scenes struggles during Vatican Council II by the pseudonymous Xavier Rynne. On the scholarly front, Edmund Wilson contributed the earliest and most striking reports on the discovery and meaning of the Dead Sea Scrolls.

Under Shawn, *The New Yorker* has displayed an immense range of moral and esthetic concern: from Hannah Arendt's account of the Eichmann trial in Jerusalem to Truman Capote's recreation of the Clutter murders in Kansas; from Lillian Ross' portrait of Hollywood movie-making in the 1950s to Jacob Brackman's essay on "The Put-On" in the 1960s; from Norman Lewis' narrative of the Mafia in Italy to Janet Flanner's reports on the student rebellions in France. In an age of corporate journalism, *The New Yorker* has found new depths in individual reporting: After Edward Jay Epstein presented, in 1968, the definitive picture of District Attorney Jim Garrison's confusing activities arising from

President Kennedy's assassination, I asked the managing
editor of *Time* if it would not have been more logical for his
platoons of reporters to accomplish what Epstein did alone;
he agreed that it would have been but had no explanation
of why they had failed to do so.

If there is any way of accounting for *The New Yorker's*
achievements, beyond the skill of its editors and contributors, it seems to lie in a refusal to compromise with shortening
attention spans or increasing popular taste for vulgarity,
combined with a continuing effort toward refining and expanding its own scope and values. In his only interview,
published in *Women's Wear Daily* in July 1968, Shawn
himself explained:

. . . We used to be enamored of facts but a little embarrassed in
the presence of ideas — as if all ideas, rather than just some, were
pretentious and rather suspect.

We no longer feel that way. We've come to respect and enjoy
ideas as well as facts. We love information no less than we did,
but we are more hospitable to ideas than we once were . . .

There is no question that the magazine has come to have a
greater social and political and moral awareness, and to feel a
greater responsibility.

. . . *The New Yorker's* reporting . . . has changed in many
ways over the years, but almost from the beginning it has had, I
believe, certain characteristics — as close an approximation of
objectivity as we could humanly manage, straightforwardness,
thoroughness, fairness, clarity, truthfulness, and accuracy. In
reporting, we have preferred to hold down on explicit interpretation and, whenever possible, to let the facts themselves implicitly
convey the writer's interpretations and point of view . . .

There has been something constant, as well, in the tone of the
magazine — an attempt, perhaps, to hang on to sanity and reason-
ableness, no matter how turbulent or fevered or lunatic the world
became. We've tried to maintain our own oasis, no matter what.

And through it all we've considered humor indispensable, and we've searched for it, clung to it, and nourished it as if our life depended on it — and I think it did.

While editors and publishers of other magazines have been scrambling to adjust themselves to changing tastes, the external form of *The New Yorker* has remained almost changeless. In his only concession, Shawn added a table of contents in 1969, but the names of writers still appear at the end of articles, stories and reviews, which have retained their leisurely length and freedom from four-letter words ("It's a matter of literal truth as against a deeper truth," Shawn explains. "If you want a surface accuracy, you have to use those words").

By "pursuing our own tastes and interests and disregarding what might be popular or fashionable or commercially successful," Shawn has edited one of the most commercially successful magazines of all time, despite some advertising losses in the past few years. "I've deliberately never made any readership surveys," Shawn has said. "I don't try to find out who is reading the magazine (I'm opposed to the inhuman word 'readership' by the way) or why. We're not thinking about our readers when we edit. I never give a thought to what people want. Even if I did, I wouldn't know what they want anyway. People can't want what they have never seen, and we try to publish fresh and original work—or the unexpected."

Definition of a magazine editor: someone who knows exactly what he wants but can't tell you what it is until he sees it.

—Author unknown (probably a free-lance magazine writer)

If magazines can shelter a range of personalities from Hugh Hefner to William Shawn, it is because they offer their makers the greatest freedom of any large media enterprise in our society. No matter how diverse their points of view, newspaper, television and radio journalists work within a common definition of the day's news. They are closely bound by the expectations of their audience. A magazine editor, on the other hand, starts with his own vision and invents his readers: The more than six million buyers of *Playboy* did not exist as such until Hefner began offering them his obsessions on the newsstand every month. Next year's successful magazine exists only in the mind of some future Hefner or Henry Luce. Its readers will not emerge until he starts translating it into words and pictures; no market research surveys will find them before he does.

It is this basic fact that causes so much difficulty between magazine editors and the businessmen who manage their enterprises. The latter cannot understand why "the product" cannot be standardized or at least stabilized. Once the formula for a popular brand of soft drink or tomato sauce has been established, the genius of mass production consists of making each bottle or can an exact replica of all the others that have been produced. But sameness kills magazines: One of the last editors of the *Woman's Home Companion* relied heavily on reader research. He tried to repeat his successes and avoid the failures, only to find that readers were bored by the second or third variation of what had excited them the first time around. The only formula that can sustain a magazine is the taste and judgment of its editors, which must be continually applied to new and risky material in new and risky ways. Unlike soft drinks and tomato sauce, magazines are bought, not in the expectation that they will always be the same, but that they will be different within an expected framework. A magazine's only promise, according to Harold Hayes, editor of *Esquire*, is "the delivery, on a fixed schedule, of its own version of the world, its special attitude toward the reader."

In theory, at least, a magazine editor faces each new issue with his attitude and a blank slate. Human nature being what it is, no editor can have the confidence and imagination to make full use of this freedom. All fall back, to some extent, on proven subjects, proven writers and proven approaches. What separates a good editor from a merely competent one is the degree to which he enlarges on his successes, learns from his failures and persists in venturing into unfamiliar territory. The magazine that provides no surprises for its editor is not likely to provide any for its readers.

But what are the professional qualifications for working under such constant tension between freedom and anxiety? When editors talk publicly or write about their work, they tend to abstract it from their daily reality. They tell us about their intentions, but they do not show us how good intentions are eroded and often swallowed up by routine. They describe a coherent philosophy of editing, but they fail to indicate how much of that philosophy is composed of compromise, hindsight and rationalization. They expound on social issues but do not acknowledge the petty pressures and the mountain of detail that consume most of their time and energy every day. The larger the magazine, the higher the mountain.

When I became editor of *McCall's*, it had the largest circulation in the world, next to the *Reader's Digest*. The editorial staff consisted of almost one hundred people, and the other departments — sales, promotion and research — employed over one hundred more. The magazine itself was a business enterprise with an income of more than 50 million dollars a year. I had started my working life as an editor who conceived article ideas, discussed them with writers, read manuscripts, edited and sometimes rewrote them, planned layouts with an art director, and wrote titles and captions — a daily routine in which every task was directed toward feeding words and images to the printing presses, or, if you will, transferring ideas and information from my head into the heads of several million readers. As editor-in-chief of a mass magazine, however, my days were largely filled with duties as an administrator, negotiator, company officer, budget maker, voucher signer, meeting holder, speechmaker, handshaker and office psychologist. I would initiate assignments and approve the results, but dozens of people stood between me and what finally appeared in the magazine. Under the circumstances, I often felt that I was not so much editing a magazine as orchestrating it.

On a typical day, I would arrive with a briefcase full of manuscripts, reports and memos to be redistributed to the editors who had sent them to me; except for material on deadline, all my reading had to be done at home weekends and evenings. Each morning, my "in" box would be filled with a new accumulation, and in the middle of the desk would be a pile of final layouts, titles, cover lines and proofs that had to be glanced at and moved into production within the hour. By the time coffee arrived, people would begin appearing in the doorway with problems, suggestions, complaints and gossip. (Some editors shield themselves from such incursions, but they pay a price for keeping their door closed. The best people on a staff need constant access to whoever makes the final decisions, and some of the best ideas come out of seemingly aimless give-and-take.)

Then, meetings. I disliked having more than three or four people in a room because, in a larger group, I would find myself and others inevitably putting on a performance instead of carrying on a discussion. Therefore, there would be manifold small meetings to approve ideas, make assignments, establish deadlines, schedule advance issues, determine final makeup, set newsstand print orders, plan publicity and settle dozens of other details.

Between meetings, phone calls: from writers, agents, book publishers, promoters and aspiring celebrities. A good secretary was able to fend off most of the time-wasters or pass them on to other staff members, but I can list several valuable properties that eluded the magazine because I did not gladly suffer the fools who controlled them. To avoid missing out too often, I would find myself listening to hustlers like the documentary film producer who wanted the magazine to put up $25,000 in advance for rights to an unwritten manuscript by an unspecified writer that would be a by-product of a movie he had yet to make about an aging and impoverished former world figure.

Lunches, and often breakfasts and dinners, would largely be given over to such chores as wooing best-selling authors, their agents and book publishers, a process requiring courtship techniques reminiscent of Victorian novels: fine food and wines, elegant surroundings, flattery and small attentions, all for the privilege of paying large amounts of money for an article or story that many readers would later remember as having read in a competing magazine; industry gatherings, with brave formal speeches about social change and nervous cocktail talk about advertising revenue and postal rates; off-the-record get-togethers in the company dining room with aspiring politicians, both Establishment and revolutionary, where you could pick up useful inside information, i.e., Eugene McCarthy, three months before the New Hampshire primary of 1968, telling you he had decided not to enter that one, or Stokely Carmichael earnestly explaining how he planned to use Black Power to make political deals for his people in Alabama and elsewhere; and interminable awards luncheons, at which one of your editors or writers would receive a plaque for making the world a little better for teachers' trade associations, art directors or dog food manufacturers.

To Parkinson's Law and the Peter Principle, which provoke bitter laughter among men managing enterprises whose products are made by machines, editors can add their own corollary, a kind of journalistic Catch-22: The larger a magazine is, the more critical it becomes for an editor to devote himself to a vision that will attract and hold readers, yet the larger a magazine is, the greater the accumulation of daily problems and pressures that keep him from devoting himself to that vision. A determined editor can ignore a good deal of office routine or depend on others to handle it for him, but the price for doing so is often high. For example, my intention in asking Jean Stafford to interview Lee Harvey Oswald's mother was to show, through a gifted writer's eyes, the ultimate source of the warped personality that was responsible for President Kennedy's death. I arranged for the interview, read the manuscript, made suggestions for editing it and approved the pictures, captions, layout and cover line that went with it. But, under the pressure of other deadlines, I allowed a press release to go out that took out of context Mrs. Oswald's contention that President Kennedy had been dying of an incurable disease before he was shot. Understandably, the resulting newspaper stories made it sound as though we had reported that statement without qualification. In the following days, the magazine was denounced, in newspaper editorials and speeches by politicians, for publishing a sensational and tasteless article. When the same interview appeared later in book form, it was properly praised as a superior piece of journalism, but my own carelessness had seriously compromised all the skill and effort that had been expended in producing it for the magazine.

Under the pressure of routine, it seemed harder to hear your conscience, let alone obey it, on small questions than on larger ones. Before I became editor of *McCall's*, the magazine had made a commitment to pay Allen Drury $100,000 for his third novel in the series that began with *Advise and Consent*. When the manuscript came in, I found it offensive. I told the president of the company that I would rather resign than publish it. We paid $100,000 to Drury, who was later cited as Vice President Agnew's favorite author, returned the manuscript and swallowed the loss. On the other hand, several years after the television quiz show scandals, I assigned an article on what had happened to one of the most popular winners of the rigged programs. While our reporter was at work, I received a letter from the man's wife pleading that the article would damage her husband's efforts to rebuild his life and suggesting that it would be "kind and gracious" not to publish it. Although the piece was already scheduled for an issue we were working on, it would have been possible, with some effort, to take it out of the magazine. But I did not make the effort and my failure to do so has troubled me ever since. It was easier to take a stand on a question involving editorial pride than to stop the machinery for an act of kindness.

The larger the magazine, the more intense the competition for readers and advertisers, the more the machinery takes on a life of its own. Mass-magazine editors, who are given to easy moralizing on their pages, find ethical conflicts less manageable in their own offices. It may be harmless enough to allow table-setting pictures to be planned around credits to silverware manufacturers, because the other women's magazines do so and, if you refused, your magazine would lose advertising. But the cancerous effects of competition do not stop there. In 1967, we wanted to report what birth-control pills were actually doing to American women. Since no government or private agency had then done enough research in depth, we persuaded the American College of Obstetricians and Gynecologists to work with us in preparing an extensive questionnaire that would tell us what 8500 doctors across the country were experiencing with several hundred thousand patients. Working with the medical organization, the magazine spent about $15,000 and almost a year's time in making sure that the questions were properly framed and the results properly tabulated and interpreted. During this period, another women's magazine, after seeing our questionnaire, mimeographed a few questions on a single sheet and sent them to several hundred doctors selected at random from a commercial mailing list. Before our work was done, the other magazine had taken out of context all the negative answers and published a scare piece. It was denounced as irresponsible by medical authorities, but our own results, published several months later with all the qualifications required by a complex subject, had been hopelessly compromised. Competition, according to the American ethic, results in better mousetraps. In this kind of competition, it is not always the mice who are trapped.

On external evidence, mass magazines began dying when television became a more efficient vehicle for advertisers. True enough, but, seen from the inside, the decline of mass magazines has been experienced by their editors as a progressive sense of being trapped by the machinery, being drained by administrative and competitive problems of the energy that might have gone into making a better magazine for readers. Even worse has been the growing awareness that an essential connection has been broken between the quality of a mass magazine and its commercial success, i.e., the response of readers and advertisers. *The Saturday Evening Post,* in the last years of its life, was a better magazine than it had been for decades, but it was too late to arrest falling newsstand sales and advertising revenues. The gears of the machinery had been stripped, and its editors' efforts resulted only in wildly spinning wheels.

By 1970, much the same process was overtaking *Life* and *Look.* Despite renewed editorial vigor, particularly in *Life,* the demise of both magazines was being openly discussed and freely predicted. In an interview for one of those speculative pieces, Ralph Graves, *Life*'s managing editor, told a reporter: "It used to be enough. All we had to do was run a nice picture of a rhinoceros with a caption that read: 'This is a rhinoceros. He is running from left to right.' And people would be thrilled to pieces. It isn't enough anymore."

In his ruefulness, Graves was oversimplifying the past, but not entirely. The golden age of magazines in the first half of the twentieth century was made possible by the Industrial Revolution that produced cheap paper and fast printing presses, a rail network for distribution and, most important, national advertisers to subsidize low prices for readers in huge numbers. For a quarter of a century, before radio and television, magazine editors had a monopoly on creating an illusion of national reality for millions of Americans. But it was a tendentious reality, an America seen with blinders. The legendary editor of *The Saturday Evening Post,* George Horace Lorimer, came to his calling after a failure in the wholesale grocery business. He built the most

successful mass magazine of the time by romanticizing business values for millions of Babbitts and would-be Babbitts.
The Depression ended his career, leaving him confused and
embittered, but the following wave of mass-magazine editors came no closer to reflecting a reality that went beyond
the fantasies of the American middle class. Henry Luce, in
his lifetime of publishing, found only one President, Eisenhower, with whom *Life* and *Time* could be comfortable. The
Reader's Digest, the largest magazine of all time, has always
served only the same slice of the population: From its early
days, it looked askance at Jews, blacks and other outsiders;
resisted every major piece of social legislation proposed over
four decades; and remained consistent in its world view,
from its opposition to the war against Nazi Germany to its
wholehearted approval of the war in Vietnam.

The crisis for mass magazines began in the 1950s. On the
surface, television began taking away advertising dollars,
but readers presumably still cared. It was fashionable to
point out that *Collier's* expired in 1956 at the height of its
circulation, over 4,000,000. But the loyalty of readers was
illusory: Newsstand sales at full price were being replaced
by cut-rate subscriptions, sold through costly mailings and
high-pressure door-to-door tactics. Magazines were losing
their hold on the comfortable middle-class American who
was finding a more congenial false reality in television entertainment.

In retrospect, the 1950s offered mass magazines a chance
to move beyond the most conservative values and test the
rising waters of social change. Whether out of necessity or
conviction, a few of them did. *Look* and, to some extent,
Life began to report, often sympathetically, on the poor, the
black, the mentally ill, the pacifists, the victims of McCarthyism, the critics of conventional religiosity and other minorities

that had been ignored by Lorimer, Luce and DeWitt Wallace. During this period, *Look* prospered, *Life* held its own and the *Post*, still clinging to Lorimer's vision, became fatally ill.

By the mid-1960s, it was clear that cultural changes were coming too fast, and mass magazines were not flexible enough to deal with them. The American consciousness, exposed by television to the realities of war, riot, assassination and campus upheaval, was breaking apart. The illusion of a homogeneous mass audience could no longer be sustained. Specialized magazines began to find fragments of the mass, defined by specific interests, immediate preoccupations or political and cultural points of view: *Sports Illustrated, Redbook, Playboy, Cosmopolitan, Esquire, New York, Psychology Today*. These magazines prospered, while *Life, Look* and the mass women's magazines, *McCall's* and *Ladies' Home Journal*, floundered.

By 1970, mass magazines were cutting their circulations, page sizes and staffs, but a basic editorial solution eluded them. *Life*, a magazine that could no longer thrive on a rhinoceros running from left to right, was engaged in aggressive reporting, naming names in exposing the Mafia and questioning the ethics of national political figures. Such articles contributed to the resignation of a Supreme Court Justice and the political downfall of several governors and Congressmen, and earned laudatory newspaper editorials and journalism prizes, but there was no longer a coherent mass audience to be "thrilled to pieces." Newsstand sales continued to fall, and so did advertising revenue. The impression was that *Life* and its competitor, *Look*, were undergoing deathbed conversions. It was the mayor of San Francisco, Joseph L. Alioto, who made the point most sharply. In a libel suit against *Look* for linking him to Mafia figures, Mayor Alioto observed that the parent company, Cowles Communications, had been losing money for years and charged that *Look* was pursuing "a reckless policy of sensationalism under financial pressure."

During the period in which other mass publications were reducing their circulations, the *Reader's Digest* ran promotional advertisements trumpeting the fact that *its* circulation was at an all-time high. The only fact that such self-congratulation overlooked was that, for a number of years, the *Digest* had been building its circulation more on human greed than on the merits of its magazine, obtaining subscriptions through massive "sweepstakes" mailings that promised huge prizes of cash and merchandise to potential subscribers. Even this enterprise by America's most self-righteous magazine was tainted: At the end of 1970, the *Digest* was under government pressure because only a fraction of the prizes promised had actually been awarded.

A few years ago, Leo Rosten told an audience of college presidents and deans: "There is a myth that the mass media corrupt the masses and debase their intelligence. I am prepared to defend the proposition that in intelligence and insight and taste, the mass media are superior to the masses. I think the thing that is wrong with the mass media is the masses. What kind of people support the junk that we call junk? What schools did they come from? What homes?" Rosten has a point, but his use of "support" is in error. Readers and viewers do not support the mass media, they *accept*. The passivity of television viewers, who are given a choice ranging from the bland to the inane, has been translated to mass-magazine readers, who, for the most part, no longer buy what they want when they want it but are badgered and bribed into subscribing by cut-rate offers and sweepstakes.

Even the hard circulation figures by which advertisers used to judge mass magazines have turned television soft. Today, the criterion for placing magazine advertising is not paid circulation but readership estimates based on the same arcane sampling methods that measure television audiences. Thus, the distance between an editor's success in attracting readers and the response of advertisers to that success has grown larger and the connection more tenuous.

In a large magazine, the obstacle to innovation has never been the volatility of readers but their inertia. In presenting new ideas, editors have always had to worry more about baffling or boring readers than stirring them to anger. But the price for not having to fear readers has been high: The passivity that prevented them from punishing an editor who challenged their attitudes also protected them from having those attitudes seriously affected by his exertions.

Yet, in the 1950s and early 1960s, it was still possible to break through such apathy. Conscientious editors like Dan Mich of *Look* accepted that condition as a challenge to their imagination and resolve, rather than as an invitation to cynical manipulation. Through skillful use of words and pictures, Mich dramatized the social and political dangers of that time: murderous racism, hysterical anti-Communism, blindness to potential nuclear disaster. Unlike the fabled Lorimer, Mich spoke to millions of readers in terms of their concern for human life rather than their lust for property and self-protection. And it did make some difference.

Mich died in 1965. Six years later, *Look* was also gone. What happened in the years between is perhaps reflected in a sequence of incidents that took place in the fall of 1967. At a luncheon with *Look*'s chairman, Gardner Cowles, I expressed the opinion that the country was turning against the war in Vietnam and that most mass magazines seemed to be remiss in not recognizing that change, let alone playing any part in bringing it about. Several weeks later, one of *Look*'s top editors told me that Cowles had referred to our conversation in approving for publication an article by a minister explaining why he would counsel young men to evade the draft. Not long afterward, *Look* ran an article by General Omar Bradley about his trip to Vietnam, expressing wholehearted approval of the political as well as military aspects of the war. When I questioned a *Look* editor about it, he admitted some embarrassment that no one at the magazine had foreseen, when making the assignment, that Bradley would wax so enthusiastic about the war and that no one would take the responsibility for declining to publish the piece after it was submitted. My guess is that Mich would have turned against the war long before the end of 1967, but it is absolutely certain that, if he were still editing the magazine then, it would have taken a clear position on the war, one way or the other.

Today the organizational machinery of mass magazines has closed in to the point that even aggressive reporting of political corruption can be seen more as a self-serving bid for attention than as an expression of an editorial vision. Some will survive but the best impulses of the future Dan Mich's are more likely to emerge in publications that do not have to bear the weight of millions of undifferentiated and impassive readers.

7

Who's Afraid of
Tom Wolfe?

EVEN HER MOST DEVOTED ADMIRERS would hesitate to describe Mrs. Richard Milhous Nixon as a charismatic figure. During the two decades in which her husband kept rearranging the furniture of his public life in an effort to set a Presidential scene, she remained an important, if somewhat colorless, part of the background. Even as far back as the celebrated Checkers speech, she and her good Republican cloth coat took second billing to the Nixon dog. Her immobility was what remained in our consciousness, so much so that her tears during Nixon's concession speech on the morning after the 1960 election evoked the kind of astonishment we feel on learning that drops of blood have suddenly appeared on the polished surface of a religious icon. During the 1968 campaign, this impression was translated into the kind of cruel image that reporters can conjure up in private conversation: an inflatable life-size Pat Nixon doll brought out to stand behind the President-to-be during each speech, but only half-inflated for whistle stops.

Yet, for one journalistic moment in 1968, Pat Nixon came to life. On a flight between Denver and St. Louis, she granted a brief interview to Gloria Steinem of *New York* magazine. The exchange began with the usual bland answers ("stand-

ard phrase upon standard phrase") even to those questions
that sought to evoke how Mrs. Nixon felt about herself and
what she identified with. "We eyed each other warily as I
searched around for some fresh subject," Miss Steinem reported. "Then the dam broke. Not out of control but low-
voiced and resentful, like a long accusation, the words
flowed out."

"I never had time," Mrs. Nixon told her interviewer, "to
think about things like that — who I wanted to be, or who I
admired, or to have ideas. I never had time to dream about
being anyone else. I had to work. My parents died when I
was a teen-ager, and I had to work my way through college.
I drove people all the way cross-country so I could get to
New York and take training as an X-ray technician so I could
work my way through college. I worked in a bank while
Dick was in the service. Oh, I could have sat for those
months doing nothing like everybody else, but I worked in
the bank and talked with people and learned about all
their funny little customs. Now, I have friends in all the
countries of the world. I haven't just sat back and thought
of myself or my ideas or what I wanted to do. Oh no, I've
stayed interested in people. I've kept working. Right here
in the plane I keep this case with me, and the minute I sit
down, I write my thank-you notes. Nobody gets by without
a personal note. I don't have time to worry about who I admire or who I identify with. I've never had it easy. I'm not
like all you . . . all those people who had it easy."

Then the interview was finished, the fixed smile returned
to place and even the verbal thank-you note handed over
("I've really enjoyed our talk. Take care!"). Gloria Steinem
wrote, "I could see Mrs. Nixon's connection with her husband: two people with great drive, and a deep suspicion
that 'other people had it easy,' in her phrase, 'glamour boys'

or 'buddy-buddy boys' in his, would somehow pull gracefully ahead of them in spite of all their work. Like gate-
crashers at a party, they supported each other in a critical
world. It must have been a very special hell for them, running against the Kennedys; as if all their deepest suspicions
had been proved true."

Such moments are the fruit of the New Journalism, an
approach that rejects the embalmed reality of traditional
reporting, the vacuum of feeling that tells us what people
say and do in public but leaves us wondering who and what
they are in private. The New Journalism, with all its imperfections and potential corruptions, abandons the safety of
objective reporting and tries to show us people and events
through a pair of human eyes. Our glimpse of Mrs. Richard
Nixon through Gloria Steinem's eyes is only a *possible* truth,
but at the very least it creates a ripple on the smooth surface of authorized truth that is constantly being dispensed
by press releases and staged interviews to be recorded by
the headlines and television cameras. The conventional reporter does not try to give such glimpses and is likely to consider them irrelevant as "news" when they occur spontane-
ously.

In one sense, the New Journalism appeared in the 1960s
as a response to the overgrowth of media technology. In an
earlier time, our defense against official truth rested on its
limited power to engulf us. But television, transistors and
the proliferation of print changed all that. As the loosely
woven web of the media was tightening around our consciousness, it became clear that some instrument was needed
to poke holes through its suffocating sameness. The instrument turned out to be the New Journalism, a form of participatory reporting that evolved in parallel with participatory
politics and for many of the same reasons — to bring indi-

vidual views into an increasingly corporate enterprise, to
offset the corruptions of institutionalized power and, above
all, to reclaim some space for human expression amid the
computerized rhetoric of the society. In politics, this impulse
brought about a good deal of social awakening as well as a
good deal of self-indulgence and even chaos. So it has in
reporting. Each calling has its anarchists, hustlers and "crazies"; but those at the fringes do not define the basic impulse, they only mark the limits of its usefulness.

The New Journalism had been hovering in the atmosphere
for some time before it was officially discovered by a young
man named Thomas K. Wolfe, Jr., on a now-legendary night
in 1963. With a Ph.D. in American studies from Yale and
and a latent literary talent, Tom Wolfe was at that point a
restless feature writer for the New York *Herald Tribune*.
Sent by *Esquire* on a free-lance assignment to cover the California custom-car scene, he came back and found that he
could not write the story. What happened then Wolfe described in the introduction to his first book:

I had a lot of trouble analyzing exactly what I had on my hands.
By this time *Esquire* practically had a gun at my head because
they had a two-page-wide color picture for the story locked into
the printing presses and no story. Finally, I told Byron Dobell,
the managing editor at *Esquire*, that I couldn't pull the thing
together. O.K., he tells me, just type out my notes and send them
over and he will get somebody else to write it. So about 8 o'clock
that night I started typing the notes out in the form of a memorandum that began, "Dear Byron." I started typing away, starting
right with the first time I saw any custom cars in California. I
just started recording it all, and inside of a couple of hours, typing along like a madman, I could tell something was beginning
to happen. By midnight this memorandum to Byron was twenty
pages long and I was still typing like a maniac. About 2 A.M.
or something like that I turned on WABC, a radio station that

plays rock and roll music all night long, and got a little more manic. I wrapped up the memorandum about 6:15 A.M., and by this time it was 49 pages long. I took it over to *Esquire* as soon as they opened up, about 9:30 A.M. About 4 P.M. I got a call from Byron Dobell. He told me they were striking out the "Dear Byron" at the top of the memorandum and running the rest of it in the magazine. That was the story, "The Kandy-Kolored Tangerine-Flake Streamline Baby."

Tom Wolfe's moment of revelation launched a career that prompted *Newsweek* to label him "some kind of great writer": "Among journalists, Wolfe is a genuine poet; what makes him so good is his ability to get inside, to not merely describe (although he is a superb reporter) but to get under the skin of a phenomenon and transmit its metabolic rhythm." Wolfe himself has credited Gay Talese and Jimmy Breslin as his sources of inspiration: they showed him that "there are no more limits to nonfiction; everything that anybody has ever accomplished in fiction, you can now accomplish in nonfiction — if you have the stamina and the courage to do the reporting and the skill to put it together."

If. The key to Wolfe's and Talese's method is not the fictionlike form but the "saturation reporting" that precedes it. They soak themselves in the situation they are observing and wait for the emergence of scenes that will tell the story. The writer may or may not appear in the finished text ("I remove myself along with a lot of the superstructure," Wolfe says) but his attitude is everywhere. The action is seen not by an impartial journalist but, as in a novel, through an omniscient and often quirky eye. Visible or not, the New Journalist is always as much a part of the story as its subject — his perceptions and style suffuse the material.

Under these circumstances, a reporter's senses and sensibilities become critical. There will be only marginal differences between newspaper reports of a peace demonstration, no matter who is covering it. But Norman Mailer's version of the march on the Pentagon has about as much in common with a newspaper report as *Moby Dick* does with a tract on whaling. In the New Journalism, the eye of the beholder is all — or almost all. This diversity leads to a problem of definition. The original New Journalists were young men who broke out of the strait jacket of conventional newspaper reporting: Talese came from the *New York Times*, Wolfe and Breslin from the New York *Herald Tribune*. As they were developing their own style in the early 1960s, novelists like Mailer and Terry Southern were approaching the same ground from another direction, mainly at the behest of *Esquire*. Yet another expression of the impulse was evolving at *The New Yorker*, where Truman Capote was at work on his "non-fiction novel" (*In Cold Blood*) and Hannah Arendt was bringing a philosopher's perspective to reporting the Eichmann trial. And just below the surface, there were the first rumblings of the underground press. By the end of the decade, the individual voices of subjective reporting could be heard everywhere, breaking through the uniform chorus of the newspapers, wire services and television networks.

Not surprisingly, one of the first targets of the New Journalism was the Old. In a number of articles, later expanded into a best-selling book, Talese obsessively scratched away at the institutional façade of the *Times* in an attempt to dramatize the personalities and the power struggles behind it. In probably his worst piece of writing, Wolfe raged against William Shawn and *The New Yorker*'s "mummified" atmosphere. It may be too easy to see such attacks in oedipal terms, but there is a clear line of paternity from the fictionlike recreation of reality by such *New Yorker* writers as

Lillian Ross and John Hersey to the later efforts of the New Journalists. Perhaps it was Shawn's insistence on erasing the writer's fingerprints from the journalistic landscape, his determination to "let the facts themselves implicitly convey the writer's interpretations and point of view," that proved so infuriating to a reporter whose own style is stamped so heavily on his work.

The history of the New Journalism suggests that political changes are preceded by cultural: In addition to the media, the subjects chosen by its early practitioners — Wolfe, Talese and Breslin — were almost exclusively pop celebrities and pop phenomena: actors, gangsters, athletes, put-on artists, status symbols, new life styles among the young, the dispossessed and the new rich. But as the 1960s wore on, culture and politics began to merge; a second generation of New Journalists turned away from custom cars and baton twirlers to Vietnam, racial conflict and campus rebellion.

At first, the outlets for their work were limited — mainly *Esquire* and, from 1963 to 1965, *New York*, then a Sunday supplement of the late *Herald Tribune*. Early in 1968, *New York* was brought back to life by its editor, Clay Felker, as an independent weekly totally dedicated to the New Journalism. At about the same time, two of America's most venerable monthly magazines — *Harper's* and *The Atlantic* — were being reoriented in the same direction by new editors. In early 1968, Robert Manning devoted almost an entire issue of *The Atlantic* to Dan Wakefield's impressionistic report on the national mood; the same month, Willie Morris turned over *Harper's* to Mailer's narrative of the march on the Pentagon. Under the young writer-editor from Texas, *Harper's* was revitalized by a corps of subjective reporters, including Marshall Frady and Larry King from the Southern wing of the New Journalism, and David Halberstam and John Corry, two more disaffected alumni of the *New York Times*.

The time was ripe: 1968, a vintage year for street theater and political murder, was made to order for reporters in search of scenes. The New Journalists were in Vietnam for the Tet offensive and in New Hampshire for the McCarthy campaign. They were in Robert Kennedy's entourage when he decided to run for President. They were in the streets of Memphis and Harlem within hours of Martin Luther King's murder. When Columbia University exploded that spring, the siege was reported for *New York* from inside President Grayson Kirk's office by one of the student occupiers, James Kunen. The New Journalists were in Los Angeles for Robert Kennedy's last hours, in New York for the public mourning and in Arlington for his burial. But all this was only prelude to Chicago in August.

Future historians may judge the 1968 Democratic Convention as the point at which the country began breaking open before its own eyes, with the political middle ground being swallowed up inside the amphitheater and on the streets of Chicago. Television transmitted the instant sensory news of the upheaval, while newspapers and newsmagazines recorded the seismographic details. But ultimately it was a bizarre swarm of New Journalists who captured the essential drama: Jean Genet, William Burroughs, Allen Ginsberg, Elia Kazan, Arthur Miller, William Styron and Jules Feiffer led a phalanx of novelist- , poet- and playwright-reporters in covering the event for various magazines; Breslin, Halberstam, John Sack, Jack Newfield and almost all the other reporter-novelists were there as well. The underground press was out in force. Among them, they managed to convey to

that part of the population that was willing to listen the real
news of Chicago.

The contrast between their work and the limits imposed
on even the best traditional journalists was symbolized for
me by one comment I heard while I was in Chicago that week.
Just before we were enveloped by tear gas on Wednesday
evening in Grant Park, I was talking to a reporter for the St.
Louis *Post-Dispatch,* one of the nation's best newspapers.
"I wonder," the reporter was musing aloud, "if my paper
would let me say 'motherfucker.' No, I guess not. In yes-
terday's paper, they changed 'stink bomb' to 'stench bomb.'"
Before Chicago, profanity did not appear in polite print.
By the following year, it was commonplace in publications
dedicated to the New Journalism. There was no way to
report American cultural and political reality without it.

If the New Journalism needed a bench mark to certify
its ascendancy, it came in the ultimate reporting of the 1968
Presidential campaign — in book form. Theodore H. White,
who had pre-empted the 1960 and 1964 campaigns with his
Making of the President books, produced his 1968 volume,
which was serialized, as usual, in *Life.* But it did not, as
usual, dominate the best-seller list. That was accomplished
by a breezy young New Journalist from Philadelphia named
Joe McGinniss with, in his own words, "six months of surface
reporting" on Richard Nixon's use of the media. His book,
The Selling of the President 1968, was serialized in *New
York* and *Harper's.* White's subject was politics; McGinniss'
was the media. In 1968, the media, not politics, provided
the main arena for the struggle over power.

Aside from the style and scope of their books, the critical
difference between White and McGinniss was in their re-

lationship to the people they were observing. White has always been careful (too careful, his critics have said) to preserve his access to politicians for future campaigns and future books. McGinniss, with his unbuttoned description of Nixon's managers, undoubtedly forfeited his access to them — or any other conventional politicians, for that matter. After the shambles of the Democratic convention in Chicago, Arthur Miller remarked: "Can you imagine the reaction the next time someone calls the Hilton and asks to reserve rooms for a political convention?" The same reaction can be expected the next time McGinniss calls a politician and asks to cover his campaign.

If the New Journalism does not provide a clublike atmosphere with the rich and the powerful, it offers other compensations. One of them is instant celebrity. McGinniss went on a nationwide tour, appearing on television to sell his book about Nixon's selling himself into the Presidency by appearing on television. Just before the Johnny Carson show, McGinniss reported: "I am taken into make-up and discover that the make-up man is Ray Vojey, who is Richard Nixon's make-up man. So he puts make-up on me so I can go on television to talk about how Richard Nixon wears make-up to go on television." This revelation was imparted by McGinniss in his *New York* article, "The Selling of *The Selling of the President*," which fell short of the New Journalism record for mirror reporting. That mark is held by Gay Talese's *Esquire* article reporting John Corry's tribulations in reporting for the *New York Times* William Manchester's difficulties over his book reporting the Kennedy assassination.

The I-witness approach of the New Journalism invited self-exploitation. The reporter-as-celebrity was a natural development of a period in which politicians, entertainers,

athletes and others increasingly attracted attention by outrageous behavior in public. If Lester Maddox, Tiny Tim
and Joe Namath can do it, why not those who write about or
interview them? The question was definitively answered by
a young man named Rex Reed, who simply inverted the conventions of fan-magazine reporting: Instead of fawning on
stars, he approached them in a spirit of programmed bitchi-
ness. He perfected his art in *Esquire, New York* and, of all
places, the *New York Times'* Sunday drama section. In his
first book, a collection of interviews entitled *Do You Sleep
in the Nude?*, there were pieces that began this way:

> If there is anything more excruciating than sitting through a
> Michelangelo Antonioni film, it's sitting through a Michelangelo
> Antonioni interview.
> One thing about Barbra Streisand: to know her is not neces-
> sarily to love her.
> Sandy Dennis came flapping into the room like a Volkswagen
> with both doors open.

"I have never *ever* set out deliberately to be bitchy to
anyone in print," Reed has insisted, "but the conditions
often dictate the results." The results of the results were
magazine articles about Rex Reed (including a *Look* fashion
spread in which he modeled pajamas under the title, "Does
Rex Reed Sleep in the Nude?)"; regular television talk show
appearances; an acting role in the film, *Myra Breckinridge*;
and finally, the ultimate prize of New Journalism stardom:
an interview with himself. In the Sunday *Times* drama section, under the name of Jane Boylan (even in sex reversal,
life imitates art), Reed wrote: "One magazine called him
'a cross between Jack the Ripper and the nicest boy in Wines-
burg, Ohio.' Now that he's a movie star, they call him difficult, distant, aloof; they call him darling. But out here,

where fame and talent are the only lines left in the measuring cup, *everybody* calls him."

In Rex Reed's world, failure is a telephone that does not ring. We are a long way from the tweedy gentleman journalists whose interchangeable bylines in America's largest newspapers and magazines failed to make them famous beyond the press-club bars. Under the circumstances, it is not surprising that the New Journalism has produced its quota of hustlers who share the ambitions of Tom Wolfe, Gay Talese and Gloria Steinem but not their talent. In their wake has come a profusion of New Journalism hacks who are constantly taking shortcuts to Instant Truth. Once they have carefully researched their own feelings on a subject, they are ready for a spontaneous assault on the typewriter. Their responses to events have proved to be as uninteresting as their reporting is unreliable. What they chiefly have to offer is a prefabricated nastiness that may pass for sophistication with the kind of careless reader who confuses attitude and insight. By blackwashing every subject, the New Journalism hacks pander to readers with the same mentality, albeit different prejudices, as those served by the *Reader's Digest*. Their response to the heartless optimism of the Establishment media is a mindless cynicism.

Even the best New Journalists face a similar pitfall. They are preoccupied with sniffing out phoniness in every aspect of modern life. If traditional reporters are too prone to embrace conventional attitudes, the New Journalists are often too quick to deny them. If traditional reporters fail to question their own motives, the New Journalists may indict themselves too easily in order to establish their own honesty: How can we suspect a man's judgment of others when he tells us the worst about himself?

*

It was inevitable that the New Journalists would cross the border between reporting events and creating them, from showing us the world in the light of their own fantasies to acting out those fantasies for us. Early in 1968, many of them signed advertisements that they would refuse to pay taxes to support the war in Vietnam; many went to work in the campaigns of Eugene McCarthy and Robert Kennedy. Some became delegates to the Democratic convention, combining their duties as reporters and politicians during that week in Chicago. But it was not until the following year that the New Journalists conceived, organized and ran a political campaign all their own — Norman Mailer for mayor and Jimmy Breslin for president of the City Council in the New York City Democratic primary of 1969.

The campaign took shape at a beery lunch attended by Breslin, Gloria Steinem, Jack Newfield, Peter Maas and *New York* publisher George Hirsch, followed by an evening of whiskey and profanity at Mailer's home. (Profanity, in the New Journalism's brief history, was quickly elevated from a reportorial imperative to a proof of good faith — how can you doubt the integrity of an observer who dutifully records every use of "fuck" and "shit" in a conversation?). The job of campaign manager fell to a gifted *Village Voice* reporter named Joe Flaherty who, upon his appointment, conceded that "I wondered about my intentions. Like the rest of my breed who record everything from their first piece of ass to their last breath of air, I immediately sensed the possibilities of recording such a campaign." Flaherty did not have to wonder long. Soon after the campaign was over, he completed the manuscript of a book, *Managing Mailer*, which was published less than a year later. Even so, he was late. Weeks after the election, Doubleday published *Running Against the Machine*, a compilation of articles by the candidates and their backers, along with their position papers, press clippings, television transcripts and the text of their campaign buttons — in short, every scrap of paper that accumulated during those weeks with the possible exception of Mailer's laundry lists. The advance payment on royalties provided some of the campaign's heaviest financial support.

When it was over, Mailer had received 41,000 votes and Breslin 75,000, each running next to last among the candidates for his office. "I am mortified," Breslin announced in his concession speech, "to have taken part in a process that required the bars to be closed."

The main purposes of the Mailer-Breslin campaign were to provide some contrast to the venality and fakery of conventional candidates as well as to attempt the novelty of introducing ideas into the elective process. On the latter score, Mailer did offer the provocative notion of making New York City the fifty-first state in order to keep it from being fiscally strangled by state politics. On the question of contrast, the verdict has to be mixed: No one could picture Mailer or Breslin with his hand in the till, but it became equally difficult to imagine either candidate submerging his own ego long enough to get on with the dreary work of administering the world's largest city.

Along the way, a journalistic parallel inevitably emerges: The New Journalists are adept at spearing with words some fleeting fragments of reality about people and events. Most are poorly equipped, by talent and temperament, for the donkey work of giving us the external facts and figures that make up so much of the reality of our lives. Jack Newfield, for example, while brilliant at showing us the heart of Robert Kennedy in the last years of his life, in his other work has soared so high above the level of simple fact that his articles almost invariably bring in their wake swarms of letters-to-the-editor from readers who have an old-fashioned obsession with the truth. In the July 1970 issue, the editors of *Harper's*, instead of dealing with such cavilings on a retail basis, simply decorated their contents page with this note: "We are advised that there were a number of factual inaccuracies in an article about the *New York Post* by Jack Newfield in our September issue. We regret any harm that may have been done as a result of its publication." Newfield seems to be so impatient to get on with our moral instruction that he cannot be bothered with details. In 1968, he attacked Eugene McCarthy on behalf of Robert Kennedy with a piece in the *Village Voice* that distorted McCarthy's voting record in the Senate. Even after the usual corrections on the *Voice's* letters page and Kennedy's own repudiation of similar attacks by his overzealous supporters, Newfield blithely repeated the performance in an article in *Life*.

In 1968, Eugene McCarthy observed that columnists and commentators were in the business of making rash judgments. Today, many New Journalists give us rash judgments in the guise of reporting. Some — Pete Hamill comes first to mind — seem to be conducting their moral education in public, at our expense. They come roaring onto the scene with their responses at full throttle, and neither their own reflection nor an editor's perspective is allowed to stand between their typewriters and our overburdened senses.

Such assaults may be a small price to pay for the opening of new perceptual territory by the most gifted practitioners of the New Journalism. It was Gloria Steinem, for example, who, in the spring of 1968, foreshadowed the later disillusionment of many of Senator McCarthy's supporters in an article entitled "Trying to Love Eugene" and who, some weeks later, gave us a chilling premonition of the new Administration ("When Nixon is alone in a room, is there anyone

there?"). It was Gay Talese, for all his lapses into gossip for
its own sake, who brought out the human conflicts behind
the *New York Times'* faceless façade. It was David Halberstam, Michael Herr and John Sack, among others, who dramatized what was behind the bloodless headlines about body
counts and the smoking television footage from Vietnam.
It was Marshall Frady who showed us a flesh-and-blood
George Wallace rather than the wind-up demagogue of the
news stories and the home screen. It was Tom Wolfe who
skewered the idiocies of "Radical Chic" in the 1970s with
his narrative of the cocktail party for the Black Panthers in
Leonard Bernstein's Park Avenue apartment ("The very idea
of them, these real revolutionaries, who actually put their
lives on the line, runs through Lenny's duplex like a rogue
hormone . . . *These are no civil-rights* Negroes *wearing
gray suits three sizes too big . . .*").

There is no simple way to catalogue the New Journalism's
triumphs. A reader's response is likely to be as subjective
as the writer's approach. Just as the New Journalist must rely
on his antennae to detect authenticity in the political and
cultural situations he observes, so must the reader use his own
antennae to make judgments about the New Journalists themselves. The mediation of good editors can help, but the
reader is largely on his own, much as he is in confronting the
literature and art of his time. If the New Journalists accomplish nothing else, they will have made a contribution to our
grasp of reality by forcing us to refine and increasingly bring
to bear our critical faculties in dealing, not only with their
own work, but with the outpourings of all media.

By 1971, critics from Norman Podhoretz to Richard Goldstein were announcing that the New Journalism is dead —
killed, depending on the prejudices of the critic, by narcis-

sism, political rigidity or failure of nerve. Willie Morris and his crew had left *Harper's* in the wake of an internal power struggle, and Jimmy Breslin had removed himself from the masthead of *New York* because, he told a reporter, "it caused me to become gagged by perfume and disheartened by character collapse." The two departures suggest that the New Journalism, confined to a narrow political-cultural spectrum, may be too frail to support a publication with several hundred thousand readers. Morris had disturbed his management by failing to broaden his approach and, hence, his circulation, while Clay Felker apparently had offended Breslin in taking *New York* to the brink of financial success by dealing with the practical as well as the political and social concerns of his upper-middle-class readers.

Personal as well as commercial considerations were at work. Just as we all appeared to be in danger of becoming figments of Norman Mailer's imagination, Mailer himself was turning his interest back to the novel. Breslin had written one and was contemplating running for Congress. Gloria Steinem was becoming increasingly active in the politics of Women's Liberation. Jack Newfield seemed to have undergone some kind of religious conversion to hard reporting and was writing investigative series for the *Village Voice* on such subjects as prison brutality and lead poisoning of slum children. The first generation of New Journalists was moving on to other forms of expression.

Yet, even as the New Journalism was ailing, its spirit was being absorbed into the bloodstream of American journalism, as any casual reading of the large magazines and newspapers will show. The label may fade and even disappear, but the spirit will survive.

8
Action-Painting
the News

A WRITER-EDITOR I know, who does most of his work for
magazines like the *Reader's Digest* and *Good Housekeeping*,
had a puzzling conversation some time ago with his twenty-
year-old son, who was then the editor of a Midwestern underground newspaper. The young man was excited about his
paper's front-page story of a rally at which Kim Agnew had
appeared to denounce the war in Vietnam and call for the
legalization of marijuana.

"It's odd," his father said, "that we didn't hear about it in
New York. You'd think that the networks and the wire serv-
ices would have picked up a story like that about the Vice
President's daughter."

"Oh, well," the young underground editor replied, with
some impatience, "of course, it wasn't *really* Kim Agnew.
It was just some girl who *said* she was Kim Agnew."

At about the same time, the Washington *Free Press*, another underground paper, published a splashy page in red
ink about Communist China, complete with a cablegram to
the paper from Chairman Mao. Did the message, a reporter
later asked, really come from China? "Well," one of the editors answered, "it materialized here, very shortly after we
got the idea to do the page."

Conventional journalism has always demanded that its practitioners revere facts and suppress their feelings. The New Journalism came along to demonstrate that a gifted observer could use his feelings to get below the misleading surface of mere facts. The underground press contends that facts have always been used by the powerful to construct official lies that enslave the weak; therefore, what *ought* to be is often more important than what *is*. In the age of McLuhan, the underground press is less interested in how the world looks than in how it feels.

If the traditional reporter is a painter of official portraits, carefully posed, and the New Journalist a Picasso searching for essential structures beneath the surface, the underground writer is engaged in a form of journalistic action-painting, using people and events as a point of departure for expressing his own energies and visions. Each kind of canvas may have its uses and its charms, but life imitates art in that the adherents of each new media school have devoted a good deal of their creative energy to denouncing those of the past. From its earliest days, the underground press has spent almost as much time attacking conventional journalism as presenting its alternative view of the world. One of the milder critiques was offered in 1968 by John Wilcock, a founder of several underground publications: "There is a credibility gap between the press and the people, because the newspaper owners are plain and simple liars." A year later, Tom Forcade, editor of the Underground Press Syndicate, expressed his opinion more directly. As he joined a panel discussion of Sigma Delta Chi, the national journalism fraternity, he picked up a water glass and threw it across the room at the press table.

Wilcock's rhetoric and Forcade's direct action are fair samples of the underground journalist's style. Both modes of ex-

pression abound in the several hundred newspapers across
the country that, early in the 1970s, were reaching several million readers. The history of the underground press
is almost as murky as its circulation figures, but there is general agreement that its origins go back to 1955 when a small
group, including Norman Mailer, started the *Village Voice*
in New York's Greenwich Village. In the muted journalistic
chorus of the Eisenhower days, the *Voice* provided a refresh-
ingly discordant note but, true to the subsequent history of
the underground, the note soon began to sound flat to those
who wanted to amplify and extend its range. Mailer himself
abandoned his role as a columnist, complaining about his
partners: "They wanted it to be successful; I wanted it to be
outrageous . . . I had the feeling of an underground revolution on its way, and I do not know that I was wrong."

Mailer was less wrong than premature. In 1958, Paul
Krassner started his magazine, *The Realist*, described by
one observer as "the *Village Voice* with its fly open." Krassner, who qualified for even Mailer's definition of "outrageous,"
was a former comedy writer who specialized more in putting-
on than reporting. One of his inventions was a straight-
faced description of a post-assassination scene aboard Air
Force One, with Lyndon Johnson performing an obscene act
on John Kennedy's body. "The truth is Silly Putty," Krassner
told a *Life* reporter in 1968 when his circulation had passed
100,000.

But the *Voice*, which turned relatively respectable, and
The Realist, which Krassner used as a ventriloquist's dummy,
were only precursors of the underground press. Because the
full spectrum began to emerge in 1964 and 1965, there is
a temptation to assign political reasons to its coming. Vietnam was turning ugly and unmanageable; civil rights sen-
timents were giving way to Black Power realities; Kennedy,

with his plausible face, had been replaced by Johnson, with his mask of fake humility. The college generation, the first to have grown up with television from infancy, recognized the new President immediately. They had been seeing him all their lives as a cartoon character on Captain Kangaroo: J. Skulking Bushwhack, the cowboy con man.

Politics aside, it can hardly be a coincidence that the underground press found its audience in the first television-reared generation of Americans, a generation whose attention span and social attitudes were shaped by absorbing some four thousand hours of electronic brainsoaking before entering kindergarten. By 1964, many high-school graduates had spent more hours of their lives in front of a television set than in a classroom. That year, McLuhan wrote: "The young people who have experienced a decade of TV have naturally imbibed an urge toward involvement in depth that makes all the remote visualized goals of usual culture seem not only unreal but irrelevant, and not only irrelevant but anemic. It is the total involvement in all-inclusive *now-ness* that occurs in young lives via TV's mosaic image . . . The TV child expects involvement and doesn't want a specialist *job* in the future. He wants a *role* and a deep commitment to his society."

It certainly is this basic distinction between role and job, rather than mere political differences, that separates underground journalists from their counterparts in the traditional media, and it is the intense involvement of underground publications with their readers that is the essential difference between this new form of communication and all that has preceded it. The underground papers that materialized in the middle of the 1960s reflected a generation gap not only in politics but perception. Where conventional newspapers have always given their readers a structured picture of the world beyond their own senses — a world under glass — the underground papers, with their uninhibited language and makeup, attempt to shatter the glass by drawing readers into experiencing a world they share in attitude and feeling.

The characteristic illustration in the *New York Times* is a frozen rectangular photograph of two world leaders shaking hands before they disappear behind closed doors; its counterpart in the Chicago *Seed* is a free-form collage that is meant as a subjective comment on the police, the courts, the schools or some other aspect of the conventional culture (a Thanksgiving front page showed Mayor Daley's head on a platter with turkeys seated around the table). Reality, to the traditional reporter, is a huge, unending game to be reported from the grandstand, with scores to be kept, trends detected, strategies analyzed. The underground journalist is down on the field, describing how the scrimmages feel, rallying the wounded and cursing the officials for condoning foul play. It should not be surprising that their accounts of the spectacle are so different.

The influence of television on the underground generation reflects a basic irony. Just as young people responded to the lessons of the medium itself (keep moving, overload your senses, be spontaneous) rather than its message (be a consumer, lead a plastic life), so have they turned to their own uses other aspects of technology: Electronics provided the acoustical power for rock music. Pharmacology gave them new drugs for psychedelic purposes as well as the Pill, which made sexual liberation safe and convenient. And new developments in printing technology — inexpensive offset presses and cold type composition — reduced the amount of money and degree of skill needed to start a publication. Anyone with a hundred dollars and access to an IBM typewriter was

ready to produce an underground paper. By the end of the
1960s, it seemed as if everyone under thirty was doing just
that. With many false starts and sudden stops, by 1970,
there were hundreds of underground papers—in large
cities and small, on college campuses and army posts, even
in the high schools.

The first wave from 1964 to 1967, represented a sudden
flowering of a new outlook, mingling cries of outrage against
the world portrayed by conventional media with celebration of the values inherent in drugs, rock music and bodily
freedom. Looking back at 1967, Jesse Kornbluth, one of the
chroniclers of the underground, wrote in *The Antioch Review*: "For the first time, a lot of young people had the same
sense of life. And the same message came to many: It's beautiful. You can do more to enjoy it. And free yourselves, because the Crazies control the planet . . . There was so
much to enjoy at one time — Sgt. Pepper, stoned sex, Country Joe and the Fish, the Love-Ins and the beautiful newspapers — that we were overstimulated, living in a stunned
and prolonged ecstasy."

Lumping newspapers with music and sex under the heading of emotional experiences is something new. For previous
generations, newspapers may have been mild stimulants, like
the morning coffee, or aids to relaxation, along with the
evening cocktail, but, in any case, only accessories to the
primary private realities of work and love — politics was
out there, *we* were in here. But the underground press was
created by the first full-time inhabitants of the media world,
where there are no walls between private and public reality.
The early explorers of this new social landscape experienced
the exhilaration and sense of freedom that overcome pioneers
in new territory. They discovered that type could be run
sideways, ink fountains could be split to create multicolored

psychedelic illustrations, news stories could be written in the first person singular and plural, rhetoric and poetry could be used to report inner responses.

Predictably, the results varied in quality. Some papers, like the Boston *Avatar* and the San Francisco *Oracle*, approached the level of art form, while others were a visual mess. Some writers were genuinely talented, most simply ranted. But everywhere the impulse was the same: to break out of the perceptual prison of the old media. During this period, it was the Beatles and Bob Dylan, the idols of the underground papers, who carried the message to the over-thirty world. In *Partisan Review*, Professor Richard Poirier analyzed the Beatles' themes, among them that of "A Day in the Life," the seeking of "relief from the multiple controls exerted over life and the imagination by the various and competing media." Magazines like *Time* kept referring their perplexity back to Dylan's lines: "But something is happening/ And you don't know what it is,/Do you, Mr. Jones?"

The "stunned and prolonged ecstasy" that surrounded the hippie ethic did not last long. In his 1969 article in *The Antioch Review*, Jesse Kornbluth wrote: "It's difficult to say what destroyed this spirit. It's fashionable to argue that too much acid, too many undisciplined kids, and too much publicity made the underground press so self-conscious that it began to devour itself. . . .

"What happened, I think, is that too many papers started taking themselves seriously . . . Underground editors became mini-celebrities. It meant something to put out a paper, and the informal symposia conducted in the *Look* and *Time* articles on the hippies elevated the papers to the position of spokesmen for a movement."

At first, underground editors and readers thought they could free themselves from the mass media simply by turning away and creating a new journalism based on their own values. But they did not fully understand themselves or the media they were trying to escape. As underground papers grew in circulation, symptoms of the conventional world began to crop up in their own offices: At the Los Angeles *Free Press*, the publisher installed a phone in his car and a time clock in the office; Berkeley *Barb* staff members went on strike for more pay and eventually started a rival paper; and smut peddlers, with their own stake in sexual freedom, began to flood the papers with advertising for their wares.

On their own front pages, publishers soon noticed that sex sells better than politics. In New York, some enterprising underground figures took the discovery as the occasion to re-invent pornography. When the New York *Free Press* failed, former staff members began putting out *Screw* and, later, the New York *Review of Sex*. The business manager of *The East Village Other* went off to create *Kiss*. And the advertising manager of *Rat*, an austere SDS-oriented paper, became publisher of *Pleasure*, which claimed greater genital authenticity than the others on the grounds that the organs shown on its pages were not "unloved" before being photographed.

As they discovered impulses toward self-aggrandizement and exploitation among themselves, some underground editors began to suspect that their mass media enemies were also more complicated than they had thought. They had to re-examine the simplistic notion that Establishment journalists were consciously in league with politicians and businessmen to extol the consumer society and suppress alternative ways of thinking and living. If that had been true, mass media editors would have either ignored or ridiculed the hippie movement. Instead, they embraced and promoted it.

The reasons are not hard to understand. In my experience,

the most conscientious editors attempt to keep in touch with as many sources of information as possible — universities, political organizations, research people, foundations, knowledgeable individuals in various fields. Nevertheless, most editors get most of their information from the same sources as their readers—newspapers, television and magazines. This sets up a closed circuit in which the same ideas and approaches are circulated and recirculated, gaining acceptance by repetition until they become so obviously stale that they are abruptly dropped in favor of fresh but equally tenuous replacements.

Only a small part of such uniformity can be blamed on press-agentry. Noncommercial phenomena require no help in engaging the concentrated attention of publishers and broadcasters, who use up human experience at a terrifying rate. In less than a year, from early 1967 to late fall, the media helped to inflate the hippie movement and wrote its epitaph. In reviewing two books about the hippies a year after they had been officially interred, novelist Robert Stone commented: "Inevitably, the media of the Age of Explanations found them out, packaged them, and sold them back to themselves at the customary markup."

In the early days of 1967, the newspapers and newsmagazines slavered over the Flower Children and the Love Generation. At one point, it seemed impossible to pick up the morning's *New York Times* without encountering a rapturous description of what was going on in Haight-Ashbury or Tompkins Square. (A few months later, a *Times* editor confided to me that some of his colleagues had been expressing concern that the paper might have "overplayed" the story.) As the editor of a mass magazine, I was bombarded with memos from my staff, with clippings attached, urging that we "do" this colorful new phenomenon. From the resulting stories, picture layouts and television panel discussions in the following months, it is clear that many editors and television producers were under the same pressure. A San Francisco newspaper predicted that pseudo-hippie *Life* reporters would soon be interviewing pseudo-hippie *Look* correspondents in overcrowded Haight-Ashbury.

The publicity transformed and helped destroy the object of its attentions. Hippie communities blossomed in every major American city. In San Francisco and New York, tourists descended on Haight-Ashbury and the East Village to see the flower-painted youngsters. They were greeted by panhandlers willing to pose for the pictures the media had planted in their minds and by street sellers, hawking underground papers as souvenirs. The communities were swelled by "plastic hippies" — youngsters from nearby suburbs who affected the dress and manner on weekends and school vacations. What had started out as a sincere, if perhaps naïve, effort on the part of a small group of young people to live like early Christians quickly turned into a Disneyland of exploitation.

The hippies might inevitably have been defeated by the real problems brought on by their experiment — disease, abuse of drugs, hostility from their neighbors in the slums. Their touching desire to escape the computerized society did not have a philosophical or practical base on which to build an alternate way of life. But under the eye of the media, they never had a chance.

By the fall of 1967, the press and television, which had fed on the birth of the hippies, had a final feast on their death. *Newsweek* did a cover story, "Trouble in Hippieland." The *New York Times* magazine, which five weeks earlier had pub-

lished "The Intelligent Square's Guide to Hippieland," drove
a final nail in the coffin under the heading of "Love Is Dead."
San Francisco novelist Earl Shorris summed it up: "Without
a viable, unifying philosophy, the hippies became prey to
disease, commercialism, publicity, teeny-boppers, boredom,
one another and the psychopathic criminals who found them
the easy underbelly of the white middle class." Nowhere in
this or other obituaries was there the slightest hint of guilt
or self-accusation on the part of reporters, editors and television news producers.

Because this kind of exploitation of people and ideas is almost entirely unconscious — in effect, automatic — it is particularly dangerous. In following the rise and fall of the
hippies, I was reminded of an observation by Erik Erikson:
"The actions of young people are always in part and by necessity reactions to the stereotypes held up to them by their
elders. To understand this becomes especially important in
our time when the so-called communications media, far
from merely mediating, interpose themselves between the
generations as manufacturers of stereotypes, often forcing
youth to live out the caricatures of the images that at first they
had only 'projected' in experimental fashion."

In October of 1967, a mock funeral service was held in
Haight-Ashbury for "Hippie, devoted son of Mass Media."
That month, Richard Goldstein wrote in the *Village Voice*:
"Flower power began and ended as a cruel joke. The last
laugh belongs to the media-men who chose to report a cha-
rade as a movement. In doing so, they created one." But
even as the mass media were being indicted, there was some
sense that the blame was not exclusively theirs. In the Los
Angeles *Free Press*, Liza Williams described "an underground
paper office where there is a big sign on the wall that says

'Don't make magic, be magic' and 'Love' and you ask about something and receive cold indifference, they are too busy manufacturing love to give away any samples."

When the hippie experiment failed, one generation of underground journalists withdrew, and another — tougher and more political — moved in. In New York, the *East Village Other*, considered to be too preoccupied with poetry and sex, was confronted by competition from the *Rat*, organized by a former officer of Students for a Democratic Society. *Rat* did not bother much with poetry but became progressively more fascinated by revolutionary violence to the point that several staff members were accused of planting bombs in public places. But it was the fate of Liberation News Service, the first central source of news for underground papers, that most clearly dramatized the difference between 1967 (flowers and drugs in Haight-Ashbury, peaceful protest at the Pentagon) and 1968 (blood in the streets at Columbia University and the Chicago convention).

LNS was started in 1967 by two former college editors, Marshall Bloom and Ray Mungo. In October, more than one hundred underground papers carried LNS coverage of the march on the Pentagon. By the end of the year, there were 300 subscribers, and LNS had an international Telex machine for receiving and transmitting news from all over the world. The underground suddenly seemed organized and ready to become a Force.

But the growing strength was illusory. Mungo later explained in his book, *Famous Long Ago*, that "our movement was one of peace, sanity, and full enjoyment of the senses . . . It is impossible for me to describe our 'ideology,' for we simply didn't have one . . . I guess we all agreed

on some basic issues — the war is wrong, the draft is an abom-
ination and a slavery, abortions are sometimes necessary and
should be legal, universities are an impossible bore, LSD is
Good and Good for You, etc., etc . . . marijuana, that precious weed, was our universal common denominator. And it
was the introduction of formal ideology into the group which
eventually destroyed it, or more properly split it into bitterly
warring camps . . ."

In the summer of 1968, Liberation News Service moved
from Washington to New York, and the proponents of "peace,
sanity, and full enjoyment of the senses" came into conflict
with hard-eyed SDS veterans of the Columbia University
rebellion of that spring. Those who had tried to levitate the
Pentagon by chanting *Om-m-m* found themselves at odds
with those who had attacked the Columbia administration
with "Up against the wall, motherfucker." In a maneuver
straight out of a bad episode of "Mission Impossible," Mungo,
Bloom and their adherents staged a daylight raid on the LNS
office and made off with a printing press, addressograph
plates, office furniture and $6000 in cash. They trucked
their loot to a Massachusetts farm, on which they had made
a down payment with proceeds from an LNS benefit showing
of a Beatles movie.

The SDS faction immediately staged a counter-raid on the
farm, appearing in the middle of the night to beat and tor-
ture Bloom in a scene out of an old Nazi war movie. Before
they left, they had managed to retrieve most of the LNS
equipment. "All that had happened in that house that night,"
Mungo later wrote, wonderingly, "was not between rulers
and subjects, police and people, but between allies in a struggle for justice and freedom."

For a time thereafter, both groups sent out material under
the LNS banner. But the original editors soon turned from

journalism to farming, leaving the syndicate to the SDS people. A year later, at a convention of underground editors, when a motion was made to "informationalize" LNS, the LNS representative refused, patiently explaining that the service disseminated propaganda, not news. At this, someone from the audience shouted approvingly: "What are we anyway? Fucking journalists?"

"Underground" has always been a romantic designation for papers that are sold openly on street corners and sent through the mails, and whose activities are assiduously reported by *Time* and the *New York Times*. The label persists because there has been no general agreement on any other — "alternative press" has been the closest contender — and probably because it suggests conflict with authority, a condition that underground editors seem to need so badly that they will occasionally goad the law when opposition is slow to develop. After a Maryland judge asked a grand jury to investigate the Washington *Free Press* for possible violation of the state's law against subversion, the newspaper responded with a series of five articles attacking the jurist personally, illustrated by a cartoon of a naked judge masturbating in the courtroom. When street venders of *Avatar* were arrested in Cambridge for selling obscene matter, the editors devoted the center spread of the following issue to four words in large, elegant lettering: fuck, shit, piss, cunt.

For the most part, local authorities have required no prodding to harass underground papers, through obscenity charges, marijuana arrests of staff members and prosecution of street sellers. In some communities, enraged local patriots have bombed and burned underground offices. To those underground editors committed to the inevitability of armed revolution, such attacks are proof that American suciety is repressive. Those who approve of the attacks find the unremitting bias, profanity and violent rhetoric of most underground papers to be proof that the society is too permissive. To those who are committed to neither point of view, the underground and its antagonists often seem united in a campaign to suppress all awareness of human complexity and reduce life to ideology and slogans.

This tendency is particularly distressing in a movement originally intoxicated with the idea of intellectual and spiritual freedom. "Put down prejudice — unless it's on our side," read a sign in the Berkeley *Barb* office. An issue of the *Barb* once carried a banner headline: PARANOIA. Taken together, the two texts spell out the inner difficulties that have developed in the underground press. The ideal of openness, as opposed to Establishment orthodoxy, which inspired the original papers, has often been replaced by an orthodoxy of its own. One of the underground's intellectual heroes, Professor Herbert Marcuse, has legislated certain kinds of free speech as undesirable (generally by those who disagree with him), and many underground editors and writers seem to concur. "To the consternation of many liberal professors and students," wrote Allen Young of Liberation News Service in December 1968, "radical activists have shown their unwillingness to adhere to the niceties of bourgeois civil libertarianism when it comes to persons associated with war crimes, U.S. Imperialism, and reactionary and racist policies." Under this mandate, Young went on to justify disruption on various campuses of speeches by James Reston of the *New York Times*, an official of the U.S. Agency for International Development and a University of Southern California professor, who was discussing urban development.

As the underground increasingly frowned on free speech for its enemies, it became more irrational about threats to its own freedom. At the 1969 Radical Media Conference near Ann Arbor, Michigan, underground editors were greeted by a Black Panther guard carrying a loaded shotgun. At the meeting itself, the delegates decided to bar reporters from Detroit newspapers and made it clear that a *Village Voice* columnist was unwelcome. He left. Dom DeMaio, editor of a Philadelphia underground paper, described what happened then: "A final bit of paranoia came next when the presence of UPS (Underground Press Service) cameras and tape-recorders was questioned. The absurdity of the inquisition was brought to a climax when UPS head Tom Forcade suggested those who didn't want to be in the film could position themselves out of camera range. All that was left was for John Wilcock, himself a UPS founder, to question: 'Aren't we overdoing the paranoia business? First, we bar the establishment press, and now we say we can't even cover the meeting ourselves.' "

Since then, paranoia has become a staple of underground journalism. A striking example is the story that the Nixon Administration had been planning to call off the 1972 elections. In the fall of 1969, Paul Krassner ("The truth is Silly Putty") began telling his college lecture audiences, "in confidence," that he had learned of a Rand Corporation study commissioned by the Nixon Administration to determine possible consequences of canceling the elections. He had apparently heard of this sinister development from the wife of a Rand executive while they were both on LSD at a party. (Later, Krassner said that *he* was "stoned," but she was not.) The story spread quickly through the underground papers and even surfaced briefly in the Washington *Post*. Months later, *Scanlan's,* a radical magazine, published one page of a purported memo on Vice President Agnew's stationery, referring to "holding no elections in '72" and "the Bill of Rights repeal." The memo was labeled a hoax, of course, by the Administration, but the rumor of canceled elections persisted in the underground press. Ron Rosenbaum, a reporter for the *Village Voice*, investigated the story and wrote a long piece, which seemed to alternate between his desire to believe that the rumor had some basis and his reportorial failure to find any reasons to believe that it had. "I believe," Rosenbaum wrote, "that the Rand rumor is metaphorically and cosmically true, even if proven mundanely false. It's a truth about the way the Nixon/Mitchell/Phillips/Dent White House mind works." Or as Krassner once told a reporter: "You don't have to tell the truth. Sometimes the best way to comment on what's happening is to twist what's happening and not present it as commentary but to present it as what's happening."

Reviewing the brief, turbulent history of underground journalism is like watching a speeded-up film of human history. McLuhan's television children, with "total involvement in all-inclusive *nowness*," have not bothered to examine and reject the past. They have simply ignored it. In half a dozen years, they have experimented with most of the social arrangements people have devised over the centuries — ranging from various forms of utopianism to anarchy, not omitting a New Left brand of Fascism — combined with elements from Huxley's Brave New World, such as mood control by drugs and dehumanized sex. In trying to achieve love and freedom, they have also rediscovered power, ambition, hate, fear and exploitation.

While the underground may have failed in its grandiose objective of revolutionizing American journalism and the society as a whole, it *has* made a difference, more by the questions it has raised than by the answers it has found.

In some critical cases of social and political change, underground coverage has shown the limitations of conventional reporting. During the Columbia University disturbances of 1968, for example, the *New York Times* reported very little violence on the night police finally came onto the campus. The *Times*, whose publisher was a Columbia trustee, was acting on advance notice of police intentions. It remained for underground papers, such as *Rat*, with lines to students and their leaders, to delineate the darker side of the night's events. Taken together, the *Times* and the *Rat* provided a reasonably fair picture of what had happened. Alone, each paper seemed to be impaired by its underlying sympathies. Since then, underground journalism has provoked continuing debate in conventional newspaper offices on handling such stories as police conflict with the Black Panthers, the Chicago Conspiracy Trial and the legalizing of marijuana.

The underground has been influential in other ways. Four-letter words have seeped upward to such venerable publications as *Harper's* and such academically oriented as the *New York Review of Books*. The latter shocked its middle-aged intellectual readers in August 1967 by taking another leaf from the underground and publishing a front-page diagram of a Molotov cocktail. In 1971, Charles Reich's *The Greening of America*, a book celebrating the cultural values and sharing the political views of the underground, reached the top of the best-seller lists, after stirring up readers of *The New Yorker* in an advance condensation. By then, the *New York Times* was publishing communications from such underground figures as Bernardine Dohrn, a Weatherman leader hiding from the law.

One of the underground's recurring fears is that of being taken over by the mass media. But *Fifth Estate*, a Detroit

underground paper, has pointed out: "Actually we co-opt
their media, not vice versa . . . when *Playboy* runs an interview with Eldridge Cleaver or an article on the future age
by Alan Watts — we're using their media to get our message across to their people who are our people all the time
but just aren't hip to it. We couldn't buy that space, we
couldn't steal it, we couldn't make them give it up, but we
did get it by making our thing attractive enough to them on
their terms that they would use it for their ends too."

Who co-opts whom may be an academic question. Far
from being antagonists, the underground and the conventional media often seem locked into the same process —
packaging reality. Both reduce human complexity to
catch phrases: individual suffering is flattened out to repression or law and order; people are pigs and racists or hippies
and radicals; values are stripped down to love and peace or
free enterprise and democracy; and symbols are debased
to flag-burning or flag decals. Both speak the language of
certitude — doubt and contingency play a small part in
their vocabularies. Both are caught up in the requirements
of media melodrama, with reversible heroes and villains:
Abbie Hoffman is Spiro Agnew on LSD, two critics of the
media who became famous by expressing their disdain for
television in front of its cameras.

Hoffman's Yippies are a prime example of how much the
underground and mass media have in common. In 1968,
the Youth International Party existed only in the overheated imaginations of Paul Krassner, and of Hoffman and
Jerry Rubin, two New Left dropouts. The Yippies gained
instant fame by staging low-comedy routines for reporters
— dropping dollar bills from the balcony of the New York
Stock Exchange, cavorting in Grand Central Station, appearing in costume before Congressional committees. They

took their mischief to the Democratic convention in Chicago and, after being indicted for conspiracy, pleaded that it was all a put-on for the media. Meanwhile, both Rubin and Hoffman had extruded best-selling non-books and were collecting large fees for performing before college audiences. Hoffman was published by Random House, a division of RCA, one of the nation's largest defense contractors. "We're ripping off the Establishment," he told a reporter, "using them to promote the revolutionary consciousness." Rubin, who once was a crew-cut, bow-tied reporter for the Cincinatti *Post & Times-Star*, was published by Simon and Schuster, a house built on the inspirational works of Dale Carnegie and Joshua Loth Liebman. "I lay awake nights," Rubin wrote, "asking myself whether I was serious."

Television spawned the underground mentality, and television has always been the true north for its longings. In the 1960s, access to the home screen was limited to cameo performances by the Yippies on the evening news, an occasional raucous turn on the talk shows and one brief moment of radical glory on educational television in 1968: During a panel discussion about the underground on New York's Channel 13, a group broke into the studio, shouting slogans ("The Establishment press lies," "The airwaves belong to the people") and filming their own performance while studio cameras recorded the scene for the home audience. "This is what the underground really is," shouted one member of the panel as seven of his colleagues were being arrested for breaking and entering.

But the goal of underground television is to record and show its reality rather than simply act it out. Such groups as Global Village, Videofreex, Raindance and People's Video Theater have been filming and taping their highly subjective versions of events for some time. Without access to conventional means of transmission, they have been forced to show their work in dormitories, churches, private homes, lofts and abandoned movie houses.

Just as offset printing and electric typewriters gave birth to underground newspapers, new electronic technology promises to make possible the transmission of underground television. Inexpensive portable taping equipment is in the hands of young people on campuses and in urban ghettos across the country. They are convinced that cable television and video cassettes will eventually carry their work to large audiences.

In 1970, a publication, *Radical Software*, appeared to collect and share information among the members of the growing video underground. Ignoring the irony of using old-fashioned print for communication, Michael Shamberg, a former *Time* reporter who is one of the publishers, explains: "We are working on how to survive in an information environment. We say people should process and make their own information. And it starts with turning people on to making video about their own experience. For kids to be raised on TV and not to make TV is like learning how to read but not write."

As the television generation learns to use its medium, its members have been inflicting the equivalent of a good deal of bad writing on each other. At present, much of underground video bears the mark of the kind of earnest incompetence that equates bad technical quality with honesty and considers passing up a cliché to be a creative act. But the learning process has begun. In media terms, the members of the underground have seen the future, and they are determined to make it work.

9

The Newsroom Revolt

ONE AFTERNOON *during the 1968 Democratic National Convention, I came out of the air-conditioned Tribune Tower in Chicago to find a long line of demonstrators marching past on the sun-blistered sidewalk of Michigan Avenue . . .*

Then someone in the orderly line shouted at me. "Hey, Mr. Wicker," he called, rather politely, "come and march with us!"

All is vanity, and I was pleased to be recognized. But others in the line took up the shout: "Come on, Mr. Wicker! March! March with us, Mr. Wicker!"

I just waved, and stood there. Traffic went past. The line moved on, the shouts weakened, and one last call came back to me above the sounds of tires and horns, and is with me still:

"March, Mr. Wicker! Put up or shut up!"

So I stood there a while longer, and the picketers went on past, until those who had called to me were far up the avenue; and in the wilting heat I felt sad and old and out of shape. I had believed always that I belonged with the young and the brave and the pure in heart; but in the end I got into my rented car and went on out to the Stockyards and up to the press gallery.

— Tom Wicker, Associate Editor, the *New York Times* in the *Times* magazine, August 24, 1969

Wicker's experience recalls a conversation I had with another *Times* editor less than a year before that Democratic convention of 1968. The editor had telephoned to enlist me in organizing what turned out to be an ill-fated protest against the war in Vietnam, in which several hundred writers and editors declared their intention of withholding all or part of their income tax payments. After I had pointed out a number of reservations I had, both in principle and tactics, he answered with some distress: "I know, I know, but all those kids are out there marching against the war, and I'm sitting here, getting more and more middle-aged."

In the waning years of the 1960s, as the underground press joyfully leaped the barriers between the reporter and the reported, conventional journalists found it increasingly difficult to observe events without being drawn into them. Young men and women of McLuhan's first television generation, seeking a role in society rather than a job, came onto the staffs of newspapers, magazines and networks, and began to ask sticky questions. Conscientious older reporters, living and working in the same atmosphere, found themselves feeling "old and sad and out of shape" and "more and more middle-aged." Then, one man came along to earn a place in the history of journalism by crystallizing their feelings: Richard J. Daley, the mayor of Chicago.

If the new generation had invented a symbol for their complaints, they could not have improved upon Daley.

His misunderstanding of media was total. The last of the pre-television big-city bosses, the sixty-six-year-old mayor prepared for the 1968 convention under the delusion that politicians could still control the reporting of large public events. He surrounded the convention hall, like a concentration camp, with barbed-wire fences, armed checkpoints and platoons of helmeted policemen. (As I rode through the gates for the first time on a delegates' bus, someone remarked: "If they ask you to take a shower, don't.") Taking advantage of a telephone workers' strike, Daley made an arrangement that would allow the networks live coverage of the convention, but not the demonstrations outside. Mobile units were refused permits to park on the streets near the major hotels, and nearby parking lot owners were oddly reluctant to rent space, even for several hundred dollars a day. Richard Salant, president of CBS News, commented: "They obviously don't want us to cover any of the demonstrations live."

As it turned out, delayed videotapes of the street violence, much of it directed against reporters and television cameramen, were even more damaging to Daley than live coverage would have been. Instead of being seen by a smaller audience during the dinner hour, the bloody scenes came on during prime time and as a brutal commentary on the nominating procedures inside the convention hall.

Daley was in the position of an old-line general, using the tactics of trench warfare against a generation of media guerrillas. As Norman Mailer later explained the Yippie strategy: "They understand that you don't attack the fortress any more. You just surround it and make faces at the people inside and let them have nervous breakdowns and destroy themselves." Daley never did get the message of the medium. He allowed millions to see his throat-slashing gesture to the podium to cut off debate at one point in the convention proceedings and, when Senator Abraham Ribicoff complained about police brutality, Daley could be seen angrily shouting at him. The words were not audible, but lip readers later attributed to Daley some of the same obscenities which, when directed by demonstrators to policemen, the mayor deemed sufficient provocation for clubbing those who mouthed them. At another point, Daley was seen in a live interview by Dan Rather of CBS, blandly denying undue violence by the police and dismissing the charges as "propaganda by you and your station and a lot of Eastern interests," while the home screen was showing tapes of the bloody encounters downtown as a counterpoint.

When the convention was over, Daley was still blaming the media for what happened. The leaders of the demonstrations agreed, albeit with different emotions. Abbie Hoffman jubilantly told a reporter: "I think Daley was right when he said it was the newsmen and TV that brought the demonstrators here. Many of us understand the use of mass media both as a weapon and a battleground. In this country, it's what's news that's going to determine the future, and what's news is violence."

While Daley and the Democratic Party eventually recovered from that week in Chicago (Hubert Humphrey, after all, lost the election by the thinnest of margins), the effect on mass-media journalists was more profound. For the first time, both physically and morally, they had not been safely behind police barricades at the scene of a disorder — 63 of them were attacked by police, according to the Walker Report, prepared for the President's Commission on the Causes and Prevention of Violence. A few weeks after the convention, a black reporter for the Chicago *Defender* told a group of white reporters: "I'm really glad you people got your asses busted. Now you know what happens in the ghetto every night."

Just as campuses have not been the same since Berkeley, the officers of newspapers, magazines and television news departments have not been the same since Chicago. The

bruises healed, but a new awareness persisted. Young reporters began to look more closely at the policies and practices of their papers and, within two months, the Chicago
Journalism Review was born. In the first issues, the reporters rehashed the concessions and compromises their
editors and publishers had made in the weeks following the
convention ("Daley's Side of the Story . . . was almost a
standing headline"). But they did not stop there. In the
pages of the *Review*, they began comparing notes on other
stories that had been suppressed, puffery that had been ordered by the front office and reporters who had lost their
jobs by digging too deeply. They began to delve into the
business and political involvements of their publishers and
editors, and raise questions about why certain stories of
official corruption had not been printed. On subjects such
as the Chicago Conspiracy Trial and the deaths of Black
Panthers Fred Hampton and Mark Clark in a police raid,
they reported what had been deleted or distorted in the
daily accounts.

Before long, the Chicago *Journalism Review* had more
than 6000 subscribers, including journalists and journalism
students across the country. Similar publications were
started by reporters in other large cities. By the end of
1969, the dissidents were not only publishing their complaints but pushing for reform. They were asking aggressive
questions in their own offices, meeting after hours to compare notes and grievances, and, in some cities, forming organizations with staff members of other newspapers, magazines, television stations and book publishers.

In a number of striking ways, the history of newsroom
revolts parallels that of campus rebellions. Like universities,
media organizations are essentially communities of intense
young people working under mental, moral and psychologi-

cal pressure. Each community is dedicated to a social purpose but takes money from potentially compromising sources: advertisers in the case of media, government and industry grants in the case of universities. As the communities have grown larger and more impersonal, their members have felt increasingly powerless to assert their own values in the face of what they perceive as hypocrisy on the part of those who manage the enterprises. Once this discontent boiled to the surface on campuses, it was only a matter of time before students-turned-reporters would express it in publishing and broadcasting. And like their faculty counterparts, many not-so-young editors would support the dissidents. Together, they would have no difficulty finding occasions for confrontation.

If Chicago was journalism's Berkeley, the Moratorium protests in the fall of 1969 may have been its Columbia. As the October 15 demonstrations approached, reporters began asking questions, not only about covering the day's events, but about taking part in them. By then, many were wearing buttons with the words MEDIA AGAINST THE WAR, illustrated by a blood-splashed American flag. In an unprecedented decision, Time Inc. responded to a petition of 462 employees by lending its auditorium to antiwar discussions, while disclaiming company support or sponsorship. When the *New York Times*, on the other hand, refused a similar request, about 150 of its employees held a vigil outside the building before moving to a rally a few blocks away. Most publishers, like the *Wall Street Journal*, allowed individuals to take time off while their companies remained officially aloof. In November, the Minneapolis *Tribune's* Moratorium coverage was criticized by a group of reporters who had been getting together informally to express dissatisfaction with the paper's policies. Within a few months, they had created a formal organization and were meeting with management to promote their views of "what the hell is happening in this society."

By 1970, the problem of staff unrest had clearly spread to small communities as well as large cities and to every part of the country. In May, the *Bulletin of the American Society of Newspaper Editors* carried a lead article by Norman A. Cherniss, associate editor of the Riverside (California) *Press-Enterprise* on "How to Handle the New Breed of Activist Reporters." In an even-tempered way, Cherniss suggested to his fellow editors that they stop concerning themselves with how young reporters dress or wear their hair, listen seriously to their complaints, many of which he deemed valid, and then draw the line between proper and improper involvement in a story: "If conscience tells the reporter he must be an active participant in the demonstration he is supposed to report, we must not love him the less for responding to conscience, but to hell with him as a reporter."

At the 1971 convention of the American Society of Newspaper Editors, Thomas Winship, editor of the Boston *Globe*, delivered a blunt message on the subject: "Objectivity is such a nice trip for an editor. Every morning he swallows his little objectivity pill. It turns him off from all the long-haired kids in the city room who whisper dirty talk over the water cooler, words like 'Nader,' 'Hanoi' and 'Panther.' Objectivity is a code word for playing it safe, covering up and superficiality. These young people still think the newspaper is one of the most effective instruments for social change. They are not in the business to become stenographers.

"Certainly activist reporters are hard to handle. But what counts in the credibility issue is what gets into the paper. That's what we pay editors for. And, by God, these socially concerned young men and women *are* susceptible to good editing. They can be taught to be responsible and fair, if only editors will stay out of the executive dining room and the country club long enough to teach them and keep them interested."

Spiro Agnew, that tireless critic of the media, touched a sore point when he charged that journalists spend a good deal of their time, on and off the job, talking to one another and thereby tend to overestimate the dissidence abroad in the country. The best corrective, I have always found, is to lift one's eyes from the cocktail parties and dining rooms of Manhattan to the hills of Westchester County, some forty miles away, where the *Reader's Digest* stands firmly rooted, spiritually if not geographically, in the soil of Middle America.

As reporters began appearing in metropolitan editorial offices with antiwar buttons on their lapels, the *Digest* was preoccupied with a different symbol: the American flag. After thoughtfully providing flag decals for readers in the February 1969 issue, the *Digest* management began inserting them in the pay envelopes of employees with the suggestion that they be displayed on car windows. Anyone who failed to comply had his license plate number noted by security guards in the company parking lot and, in his next pay envelope, found another decal and a reminder. The fact that several young editors resisted should have served as a warning of the dissension that would arise by the end of the year.

The *Digest,* whose editors and readers have always been closer to the nursing home than the campus, had recruited a handful of young journalists in the 1960s as the magazine passed its fortieth birthday. Those who enlisted found

themselves in an antique-filled Georgian mansion on a peaceful island of wide lawns and formal gardens. As the *Digest*'s
flag decals flooded the mailboxes of America, its employees
were in their chandeliered cafeteria, enjoying an Apollo
Day luncheon of NASA Roast Turkey, Moon Glow Spinach,
Sea of Fertility Tossed Salad and Homeward Bound Cole
Slaw. In these surroundings, racial conflict and the war in
Vietnam could be seen in the comfortable perspective of
transitory problems rather than national disasters. But the
new young editors were not discouraged from pursuing
their interest in such subjects. One of them had cheerfully been given permission to sound out LeRoi Jones as a
potential *Reader's Digest* author, but it turned out that
Jones' article ideas were "not quite right" for the magazine.

Trouble came to Pleasantville at Moratorium time. Hobart
Lewis, president and editor-in-chief of the *Digest*, had been
a long-time friend and supporter of Richard Nixon, president
of the *Digest*'s subscribers. After Nixon's inauguration, the
two presidents continued exchanging house visits, and, in the
weeks before the Moratorium, Lewis had been observed
spending even more time than usual in the White House. In
October, a dozen or so *Digest* editors signed a petition supporting the Moratorium. As they did so, they discovered that
an editorial entitled "No Surrender" was scheduled for the
December issue, which would reach readers late in November. Contrary to normal practice, advance proofs had not
been circulated to the editors for discussion. Spiro Agnew,
who soon afterward attacked the television networks for
"instant analysis and querulous criticism" of Nixon's November 3 speech on Vietnam, never expressed concern about
the *Digest*'s prior analysis or its prescience in having in type
an editorial that paralleled the main points of the speech
several weeks before it was delivered. But a number of

young *Digest* editors were troubled, and an ensuing round of debates and memos resulted in minor editing and a change in signature from "The Editors" to "An Editorial."

In December, advance proofs of the lead article for the February issue were also strangely unavailable. When the younger editors finally saw a proof, they understood why. Titled "From Hanoi — With Thanks," it was a compilation of speeches and broadcasts (prepared, it was later alleged, with the help of the State Department) showing that antiwar activities in the United States "give aid and comfort to the enemy in Vietnam." The same issue was to carry an article by Spiro T. Agnew, "Enough of Government by Street Carnival." After another, more bitter, round of discussions and memos, one young editor resigned. Hobart Lewis circulated a memo acknowledging that "a certain amount of steam had been generated in the office" over the two articles, but urging all concerned to "work together for the betterment of the *Digest* and of mankind." In the following weeks, two more young editors, apparently disagreeing with Lewis' priorities for betterment, resigned from the staff.

Meanwhile, back in Manhattan, at other national magazines, dissension was less muted. In the fall of 1968, *Newsweek* had been granted a glimpse of the future on the occasion of Hubert Humphrey's arrival for a luncheon with the editors. As the Vice President and Presidential candidate was handshaking his way toward the dining room, a young researcher rejected his grasp and blurted out: "Mr. Humphrey, you are a war criminal and a murderer!" (She was not fired but left later of her own accord with a goodbye party and a Gucci suitcase.)

A year and a half later, in March 1970, on publication of a cover story, "Women in Revolt," 46 women on *Newsweek*'s staff filed a complaint with the Federal government, charging discrimination on the basis of sex. Soon afterward, 147 women from *Time, Life, Fortune* and *Sports Illustrated* submitted a similar complaint against Time Inc. to the New York State Division of Human Rights. After some negotiation, both managements agreed to hire male researchers and promote more women to positions as writers and editors. Women's Liberation came to the *Ladies' Home Journal* more dramatically when a group of women representing various radical media organizations occupied the office of editor John Mack Carter for eleven hours, haranguing him on their favorite subject while several of them smoked his cigars and, at one point, tried to separate him bodily from his desk. At *Playboy,* a secretary who had joined feminist picketing of Hugh Hefner's mansion was fired soon afterward for Xeroxing and distributing to the press a Hefner memo ordering an article that would serve as a "demolition job" on Women's Lib. "These chicks," Hefner had noted, "are our natural enemy."

A young black man I know, who, as he approaches the age of thirty, is well on his way to a brilliant career as a writer and editor, recently told me: "Sometimes I get awfully tired of The Subject. There are so many other things in life that interest me, but all my work revolves around blackness." Soon afterward, he was pleased when a magazine editor gave him two assignments, neither of which dealt with race. His reaction took me back more than a dozen years to my first meeting with a young reporter from Minneapolis, Carl Rowan. In my resolute white-liberal way, I insisted on seeing Rowan as a Midwestern writer, rather than as a black man, and proposed a number of possible assignments in that part of the country, none of them racial or political.

Rowan listened politely, but nothing happened. Some months later, he came in again and talked to another editor, who asked him to take on a Southern school-integration story. Rowan responded instantly and went on to write an article that won a national award.

In 1971, I took part in a discussion with a dozen young black men and women who were about to be graduated from journalism schools. They expressed two concerns: one, that white editors would not sufficiently appreciate their black perspective on the world, and two, that they would be exploited by being limited to racial subjects. They seemed to be torn between the possibilities of being denied their racial identity and being restricted to it.

Looking back at almost a quarter of a century in editorial offices, I could not tell them that their worries were unfounded. In 1961, when Margaret Mead was considering an offer to become a regular columnist for *Redbook*, she asked if we had any Negro editors. To my shame, I answered: "One, but he doesn't count because he's so talented we would have hired him even if he were white." I could tell myself then that my defensive flippancy was due to frustration. After being named editor several years earlier, I had told the company's Personnel Department that the magazine would hire people without regard to race or religion. (Not long before that, they had tried to veto the hiring of a young woman who had a Jewish-sounding name and who had worked for a trade union.) When no "qualified" applicants appeared, I instructed Personnel to seek out young Negro women for secretarial jobs. Finally, we were able to hire two or three black secretaries. But since we had no starting jobs for editors and since there were few experienced black editors, the upper level of our staff remained practically all-white.

After the urban riots of 1967, it became clear that this kind of liberal passivity was no better than overt exclusion. Even so, the awakening was gradual. Early in 1968, the executive committee of the American Society of Magazine Editors considered a proposal for having magazines jointly recruit and train young black graduates for editorial jobs. To my amazement, several editors who had been consistently indicting the society for racism on their pages found all kinds of organizational reasons for rejecting even such a modest program. By the end of 1968, however, under pressure from various government agencies, all branches of the media were scurrying to find and train minority employees. They should not have been surprised — but they were — to find that, by then, many intelligent and sensitive black graduates were suspicious of their motives and were concerned about "selling out" if they joined organizations that had excluded them for so long.

Since then, self-interest has forced newspapers, magazines and networks to take on not only black reporters and editors but others who see the world from perspectives that are not middle class, middle-aged and middle of the road. Social upheaval has become big news, and it cannot be adequately reported from the outside. But journalists who could be trusted by campus rebels and Black Panthers were not satisfied simply to bring back raw material and see it packaged by the traditional media machinery into what they considered comforting distortions for the mass public. Inevitably, they began to question and provoke their own organizations in the same way that their news sources were questioning and provoking the society as a whole.

The publications which made the most strenuous efforts to reach beyond their traditional limits were the first to come under attack. At *Newsweek*, the young woman who confronted Hubert Humphrey had been recruited from the Berkeley Free Speech Movement several years earlier. She contributed her own experiences to a cover story on marijuana, reported from occupied buildings at Columbia University and became a prime source of direct news from the Yippies, whom she surreptitiously provided with *Newsweek* office supplies. After her departure, she wrote of her experiences for *Scanlan's,* criticizing *Newsweek* and its editors, but also wistfully noting that the magazine "is easily the most permissive and relaxed of the large and established national media."

The new reporters — young, black and committed — not only created internal conflict but brought on outside pressures. The main source was no less than the United States government. For some time, law-enforcement agencies had been relying on the media for information about antiwar activities and campus disruption. Much of the evidence against Dr. Benjamin Spock and his co-defendants in their conspiracy trial, for example, had consisted of statements from press conferences and newspaper clippings. At protest meetings, it had become routine for police to pose as reporters. By 1970, the government went one step further and began to issue subpoenas, asking for reporters' notes and tape-recordings and unused film taken by television camera crews. Some media organizations complied, others resisted.

The issue was joined in February 1970 when a grand jury ordered the *New York Times'* San Francisco correspondent, Earl Caldwell, to surrender all his notes and tape-recordings of interviews with Black Panther leaders. Caldwell, a young black reporter, refused. As his case passed through the courts over a period of ten months, the debate went on in editorial offices: How could a reporter interview any political activist if both of them knew that the reporter, however unwillingly, might be doubling as a government investigator? How far could a reporter go in withholding what might be legitimate evidence of a crime in order to protect his news sources?

The subpoena issue, along with mounting outside criticism and internal dissension, showed that social change was shrinking the safe middle ground for American journalism. In the case of subpoenas, temporarily, at least, the government backed off. Attorney General John Mitchell issued a set of guidelines restricting Federal attempts to fish for evidence at the expense of reporters. Several months later, a Federal court supported Caldwell in his refusal to turn over his notes and tapes, but the Supreme Court overturned this ruling in a 5-4 decision in June 1972. The *Times* had backed Caldwell all the way, as had many other publications and journalistic organizations. But the basic issue was far from settled. The Caldwell case was clearly an opening skirmish in what promised to be a long war over the questions being raised by journalists who could not and would not take a neutral position in the conflicts that were racking American society.

In recent years, the *New York Times* has become a mirror not only for the rest of the media but, in many ways, for the society as a whole. What happens *at* the *Times* can be as revealing of our condition as what happens *in* it. One aspect of that condition is the current tendency to ignore history. Yet the history of the *Times* is critical to understanding the issues of the newsroom revolt, not only at the nation's most influential publication, but everywhere in the media. When Adolph Ochs bought the *Times* in 1896, he promised to "give the news impartially, without fear or

favor, regardless of any party, sect or interest involved."
It was not an easy or idle promise in an era of yellow journalism, when newspapers routinely invented news to attract readers and distorted it to serve the political or personal interests of their owners.

Over the next half century, the *Times* grew in profit and
power by honoring Ochs' pledge. In hindsight, it can be seen
that "All the News That's Fit to Print" was a policy with severe limitations of its own, defining fitness more in terms of
respecting vested political and economic interests than
questioning what went on below the surface of society. But,
more than any other single institution, the *Times* helped
to purge downright lies from American journalism and to
invest reporting with elementary standards of decency or,
to use the *Times*' own word, objectivity.

By the 1950s, it was becoming clear that objectivity was not
enough. The career of Senator Joseph R. McCarthy under-
scored the point. At first, McCarthy was indistinguishable
from traditional politicians who have always manipulated
the press for their own purposes. But it soon became clear
that his methods were different in kind, not simply in degree.
Rather than disseminating or even distorting information,
he actually created news out of thin air — calling press
conferences to announce future press conferences, making
accusations based on nonexistent reports, waving blank
sheets of paper as evidence. Because McCarthy was a United
States Senator, all of these empty theatrical gestures were
uncritically recorded by objective reporters and took on the
substance of high political drama.

Trapped by what one observer called "indiscriminate
objectivity," the *Times* could only criticize McCarthy on its
editorial page while dutifully reporting what he said in its
news columns. Finally, it was not the *Times*' editorials or

even Edward R. Murrow's courageous television journalism but the new media machinery, the camera itself, that brought McCarthy down. In hour after televised hour of the Army-McCarthy hearings, the camera eye discovered a new kind of objectivity, exposing the man and his methods to millions of Americans in a way that the printed page could never match. When the hearings were over, McCarthy's power had vanished. From then on, the *Times* would have to live with — even if it would not openly acknowledge — a new truth about political power: The media giveth, and the media taketh away.

Objectivity continued to be the professed faith, but interpretative reporting became a compatible dogma. And even objectivity could be tempered by sophistication: One measure of what *Times* editors learned is the contrast between their uncritical page-one treatment of McCarthy's wildest statements and, over a decade later, their cautious approach to District Attorney Jim Garrison's equally official statements about the Kennedy assassination, which turned up on the inside pages, along with qualification and skeptical analysis.

In the mid-1960s, A. M. Rosenthal, a gifted reporter, became metropolitan editor and began to emphasize what he called "hard reporting" — "not taking things at their surface value. You try to find the genesis . . . the why." Conditions as well as editorial convictions dictated the change. Television was exposing readers to the raw material of the news — battlefield action, Presidential press conferences, campus disruption — putting pressure on the *Times* to explain rather than simply record what was happening. More and more, it was necessary to investigate the motives of those whose words and actions were seen on the evening news, and to report the conditions behind the conflicts that were erupting nightly in everyone's living room. The reader was no longer a blank slate on which the *Times* could confidently draw its picture of the world the next morning.

Whatever its defects, old-fashioned objectivity was a comfortable standard for editors, who simply decided which events to cover, and reporters, who brought back accounts of what people said and did. The only hard judgments were what to put in and what to leave out. Once motives and conditions became legitimate news, the judgments increased in number and nature. Editors who had been playing checkers with the news suddenly found themselves in a chess game, with infinitely more, and more complex, considerations involved in each decision. They could no longer depend on reporters who would serve as pawns for politicians, police and other traditional sources of news. Under Rosenthal, who is now managing editor, many older *Times* reporters failed to adjust to the new demands. They retired or resigned, and ambitious younger men were recruited. Ironically, it was this overhauling of the staff that, in part, led to Rosenthal's own difficulties several years later; some of the young reporters he had brought in became as impatient with what they conceived to be the limitations of Rosenthal's editing as he had been with earlier standards.

In a sense, their dissatisfaction was a tribute to the slippery task that Rosenthal had set for himself and his staff. The *Times* continued to be the paper of record, that is, treating the news as though readers had no other sources for apprehending the world, or, in its own more grandiose conception, providing a daily document to be consulted by future historians. At the same time, Rosenthal was taking on burdens and risks usually assumed by magazine editors in selecting subjects to be reported in depth and, at least implicitly, committing the *Times* to a specific attitude in reporting those subjects. It was not a formula for universal popularity. Some readers would applaud the paper's efforts on the subject of urban apathy, set off by the failure of thirty-eight witnesses to call the police as a young woman was being murdered below their windows. Others would be less than enchanted with its inquiry into black anti-Semitism during the city-wide teachers' strike, which they took as implied support for the Teachers Union against black communities, particularly since the subject disappeared from the pages of the *Times* soon after the strike was ended.

The vulnerability of the new approach became dramatically evident during the Columbia University disturbances in the spring of 1968. From the beginning, the *Times* decided (rightly, it turned out) that what was happening had more than local and transitory significance. But its extensive coverage was clearly, as one observer pointed out, "order-oriented" from the authorities' point of view rather than "justice-oriented" from the students', culminating in a sympathetic interview with President Grayson Kirk by Rosenthal himself, depicting the Columbia administrator as a "Lincolnesque figure."

From then on, the *Times* itself became the object of increasing criticism, both from the outside and inside. By 1970, *New York* magazine was reporting the existence of a dissident group of editors and reporters, half-seriously designated as "The Cabal." Complaints ranged from suppression of favorable stories about the Black Panthers to distortion in editing J. Anthony Lukas' coverage of the Chicago Conspiracy Trial. What is more significant than the varying merits of the grievances is the fact that such questioning had taken on visible proportions at the nation's most influential newspaper, whose own institutional order has always been one of its hallmarks.

As it did elsewhere, the dissatisfaction at the *Times* led to memos, meetings and office gossip. In a communication to the staff, Rosenthal observed that "we live in a time of commitment and advocacy when 'tell it like it is' really means 'tell it like I say it is' or 'tell it as I want it to be.' For precisely that reason, it is more important than ever that the *Times* keep objectivity in its news columns as its number one, bedrock principle." Contending that revolutions usually take place, not when things are at their worst, but when changes produce rising expectations, he told Edwin Diamond of *New York*: "The *Times* has changed perhaps more than any other paper in the last ten years. Our concept of the news has expanded. No subject is taboo. Internally, we've broken the seniority system and opened up opportunities for younger men . . . We've opened up the decision-making processes. Where two or three people used to make up the front page, ten may participate now."

There is evidence that the *Times* is loosening up, albeit not as much or as fast as some staff members would like. The changes are more visible at the periphery, in cultural coverage and the Sunday sections, than in the news columns. Lukas' daily reports of the Chicago Conspiracy Trial were undoubtedly hampered by *Times* emphasis on the stenographic record at the expense of courtroom atmosphere, in contrast, for example, to Nicholas von Hoffman's free-wheeling coverage in the Washington *Post*. But when the trial was over, Lukas had a chance to redress the balance with a long, impressionistic piece in the *Times* magazine. (When an expanded version of the article was published in book form, Lukas took the occasion to reflect his chafing at editorial restrictions. At one point in the trial, one of the defendants, David Dellinger, had exclaimed, "Oh, bullshit!" and had been reprimanded by Judge Julius Hoffman.

Since "bullshit" is not an acceptable *Times* word, an editor suggested substituting "an obscenity." Lukas demurred and settled for "barnyard epithet." He titled his book, *The Barnyard Epithet and Other Obscenities.*)

In 1970, John Leonard, then one of the two daily book reviewers, was under some fire internally for "expressing too many opinions" in his pieces. Translated, that meant Leonard, a brilliant young critic, was making the hierarchy nervous with his outspoken social and political judgments. Somehow, in the Byzantine workings of *Times* staff politics, Leonard emerged a year later as the new editor of the Sunday *Book Review.* One of his first moves was to assign a staff reporter, Neil Sheehan, to write an 8000-word essay, "Should We Have War Crime Trials?" Based on thirty-three books documenting U.S. misconduct of the war in Vietnam, Sheehan's piece made a persuasive case for an affirmative answer. Leonard was rebuffed when he sought to have a news story based on the piece, but its appearance in the *Book Review* marked a radical departure for the *Times* as an institution.

While the *Times* itself has hardly gone radical, Lukas' and Leonard's experiences, along with subtle shifts in coverage of such subjects as the Black Panthers, argue for considerable flexibility. But it is a flexibility that remains firmly under the control of the top editors. In Rosenthal's words: "Decision-making authority can't be transferred."

Elsewhere, the transfer of decision-making authority is clearly becoming the main issue. For almost two centuries, American journalists have griped about but never seriously questioned the editorial prerogatives of ownership. "The best way to run an editorial page," a newspaper publisher once observed, "is to be strong, courageous and fearless —

and to own 51 per cent of the stock in the paper." In the 1970s, European journalists were showing how that cynical aphorism could be turned inside out. At *Le Monde* in France, editorial employees, through stock ownership, gained veto power over hiring, firing and editorial policies. Other French publications were moving in the same direction. In Germany, editorial employees of *Der Stern* blocked a proposed sale of the magazine ("We do not intend to be sold like cows") and went on to win participation in employment decisions and an agreement that "no staff writer or contributor may be required to write against his own convictions." Journalists in Britain and Italy have organized for similar purposes.

Inevitably, this un-American notion of democratic ownership and control of the media has begun to crop up on this side of the ocean. In several cities, employees now own newspaper stock through trusts. *New York* magazine has made stock options available to contributors as well as editors. In contract negotiations, American Newspaper Guild units are beginning to ask for some sharing of management power, along with better salaries and benefits. The first concessions, such as those made by the Denver *Post*, create committees that can offer advice without having specific power to act. But the door has been opened.

For the time being, the main fruits of the newsroom revolt have been informal recognition of various kinds. At many publications, staff members are now a constituency that management has to recognize in making policy decisions. In editorial offices, as on campuses, life is not as simple and orderly as it used to be. But those who hold power do not yield it willingly, and those who want it are not always wise in how they go about acquiring it. In such struggles, personal and professional issues are hard to separate. Private ambitions, frustrations and grudges become hopelessly entangled with questions of policy. The real test for both sides is to distinguish legitimate challenges from neurotic self-assertions and to find ways of allowing dissident viewpoints to enrich American journalism.

As in every other human enterprise, the results will vary according to the qualities of the people involved. It is unrealistic to close off debate, as one Time Inc. executive has attempted to do, with the remark, "They want to turn *Life* into the *East Village Other*." By contrast, the editor of another large magazine has held long, candid sessions with junior staff members and listened carefully to their complaints. "They have more impulses than ideas," he told me. "They're very good at telling you what's wrong, but they don't have much patience for figuring out how to do it right, and they're not much interested in detail. My job is to help them make the transition from critics to creative editors. If I can, we'll all profit from the experience."

Reporters and editors have always worked within a tension created by the demands of their conscience and those of their craft. Traditionally, it has been more comfortable and rewarding to let craft prevail over conscience, without questioning too closely the values built into craft. Now, the questioning has begun.

10

Old Banality
in New Boxes

IN A PRIVATE DINING ROOM a few years ago, I was one of
several editors being given a preview of the future by
Marion Harper, Jr., who had built an advertising agency into
a $700 million marketing-communications empire in half a
dozen years by the increasing application of technology to
the handicraft methods of advertising. Harper was explaining his latest innovation, a scientific method for predict-
ing the success of television commercials by measuring the
eye dilations of people watching them — the more dilations,
the more effective the commercial. He suggested that editors might want to test the sales potential of magazine covers
the same way. "Mr. Harper," one of the editors responded,
"I wouldn't count too much on that system. For example, as
I listen to you describe it, my eyes are dilating, but only out
of sheer horror."

Harper's empire collapsed soon afterward, but he seemed
to have impressed at least one of his listeners at the luncheon,
Norman Cousins, then editor of *Saturday Review*, a magazine of modest circulation, noted for its vocal resistance to
the encroachments of technology on individual freedom.
When Cousins was put in charge of a mass magazine,
McCall's, a few months later, one of his first moves was to

order a costly computer study to determine what makes magazine covers sell. The computer must have misled him, for, a year later, Cousins was back at *Saturday Review,* writing editorials denouncing the effects of machines on the human spirit.

In 1971, the Cincinnati *Enquirer* spent $25,000 on a computer study to find out what mixture of headlines would attract the maximum number of readers. Among the findings was that the combination of a Kennedy scandal and a no-hit game by a local pitcher would help circulation. Overall, however, the computer decided that the *Enquirer* was close to an "ideal" newspaper. Upon learning the results, the paper's editor commented: "You don't know whether to feel good you spent the money to find out you're doing well, or whether it was a waste."

In a larger sense, editors and publishers have displayed a similar attitude — a combination of awe, unease and astonishing gullibility — toward the application of technology to their profession. By temperament, they are hostile to the idea that machines will ever replace their own judgment or even seriously alter the conditions under which it functions. At the same time, they are haunted by the occupational fear that they may be missing out on something new. As a result, they are more likely to buy the Brooklyn Bridge from a technological pitchman than invest in real estate on the outskirts of a growing city. Like the original country rube, they are victimized by a combination of innocence and misplaced guile.

Their vulnerability also arises from their conflicting tendencies as journalists and business executives. As journalists, they are firmly rooted in the belief that perception is an exclusively human enterprise — reporters observe and listen, editors organize and evaluate. As businessmen, they know that mass marketing is susceptible to some of the same techniques that helped NASA land a man on the moon. This split was described by Paul Weaver, who spent two years studying the *New York Times* for a doctoral thesis before becoming an assistant professor of government at Harvard in 1968:

> The time will come, perhaps in five or ten years, when the top management on the business side of the *Times* will be infinitely more sophisticated than their colleagues in the news department about the information business — the types and qualities of information, how to manage its collection and production, and — what really counts — how to improve in a really significant way the output of the *Times* (if that can be done at all without incurring costs larger than the benefits). The reason for this is that the reporters and editors on the news side, in an unconscious articulation of their identities as craftsmen, insist on regarding their work and their abilities as "creative" and therefore in some ultimate sense mysterious, incapable of close analysis. The top business side executives, on the other hand, are in the best Harvard Business School tradition. They do computer simulations. They are sophisticated practitioners — or are become increasingly sophisticated practitioners — of the techniques of rational planning and management.

It is possible to accept Professor Weaver's description of these differing attitudes without endorsing his definition of sophistication. In magazine publishing, for example, the Harvard Business School mentality discovered in the mid-1960s that additional revenue could be brought in by offering advertisers regional slices of circulation — at first by sections of the country, later by state and even city. Publishers of several mass magazines were delighted to discover that indeed more money came rolling in. But soon afterward they found that printing plants were in chaos trying to sort out as many as 150 variations of the same issue of a magazine. The application of computers to press scheduling relieved the confusion somewhat, but it then became clear that, in many instances, more money was going out for printing and binding than was coming in from advertising. By the 1970s, some magazines were cutting back on their offers of regional advertising, while others were trying to figure out how to keep the linage and make a profit from it. A little sophistication can be more expensive than total ignorance.

Miscalculation aside, there is an anachronistic quality to the response of most publishers to the march of technology. They often seem to be in the position of the local grocer busily rearranging his shelves and counters while ignoring the fact that a new supermarket is being built on the next block. But publishers are businessmen, and it is understandable that their vision may be foreshortened by their own capital investment in older machinery and the uncertainties surrounding the new. What is less comprehensible is the inability or unwillingness of editors to look ahead and try to understand the professional and social implications.

In the spring of 1971, I held an informal seminar with members of the American Society of Magazine Editors on future communications technology. To my amazement, most of the editors had only the vaguest notion of what video cassettes and cable television are, let alone what effects such developments might have on their magazines and their readers, coupled with the cheerful confidence that "people will always be interested in print." Their response reminded me of a talk with David Sarnoff as he reminisced about the early days of radio. He had asked the Victor Record Company to take over his enterprise, since record companies had the capital as well as the artists and technicians to provide immediate content for the new medium. The Victor people, seeing radio as a potential competitor, refused. A few years later, Sarnoff's company took over Victor. When television came along, the movie companies, which were in the best position to supply programming, decided to fight the new medium instead. The radio networks moved in and, within a few years, the movie studios, under new management, began to grind out television series as suppliers rather than owners. Sarnoff's point was that each new medium represents as much of an opportunity as a threat for the older media. Records and movies did not disappear, they simply changed under the impact of a newer technology. But the people who made records and movies, by failing to look ahead, had rendered themselves obsolete.

In 1949, a shopkeeper named Robert J. Tarlton was having trouble selling television sets to the people of Lansford, Pennsylvania, because a nearby mountain was blocking reception from stations in Philadelphia, 65 miles away. Tarlton's solution was to build a large antenna on top of the mountain and string cable from it into the homes in his community. As a result, the residents of Lansford were soon getting clearer pictures than the people who lived near or even in Philadelphia.

Twenty years later, the unintended results of Tarlton's ingenuity were assuming enormous proportions for American society. As other entrepreneurs, in urban as well as remote areas, followed the Lansford example, it became clear that CATV (Community Antenna Television) was a simple improvement of existing television only in the sense that the automobile was an advanced version of the oxcart. FCC member Nicholas Johnson described the potential of the cable this way: "While it isn't much bigger than a telephone wire, comparing its capacity with that of a telephone cable is like comparing a river with a garden hose. The same wire that today carries television signals can also carry the signals necessary to print a newspaper in a home, connect a home information center with a distant computer or teaching machines, or provide closed-circuit television signals for visiting with friends or window shopping at home." All that, of course, is in the future. What CATV can do today — and is actually beginning to do — is double and triple the choice of programs available on uncabled sets. From a technical standpoint, new CATV systems could now be offering subscribers up to 80 working channels.

More is not necessarily better. But CATV has the capacity to do better as well as more. Unlike commercial stations, which broadcast to large numbers of undifferentiated viewers, cable systems operate in small, well-defined areas. As a result, they are in a position to create, in the midst of what former FCC chairman Newton Minow described as the "vast wasteland" of mass television, a series of local oases with lush and varied programming growth. Because channels are plentiful and transmission costs low (as little as five dollars an hour to reach 100,000 homes), CATV could provide not only cultural and educational fare for small audiences but a whole new range of community services. Among these are the televising of town council and school board meetings as well as a new, inexpensive kind of political campaigning in which local candidates could address voters with enough time to develop their positions instead of using brief, costly commercials that are seen by large numbers of people outside their electoral districts.

If these possibilities sound utopian, they are at least technically and economically feasible. In Farmington, New Mexico, for example, a debate on whether certain books, considered obscene, should be kept out of the local library attracted a larger audience than a program on the network channel. In other communities, high-school basketball games and other local events have outdrawn the offerings of NBC, CBS and ABC. In the Watts section of Los Angeles, a community group is at work on a CATV project that would gather and broadcast information on child care, welfare, jobs, legal services and relations with the police. Among other possibilities, cable television could give urban ghettos like Watts, which found its identity through riots in 1965, a nonviolent means of creating and maintaining a sense of community.

When the real promise of CATV became apparent, the television industry began to fight it, arguing over copyright infringement when distant signals were imported to compete with local stations and attempting to prevent cable owners from originating programs on empty channels. In 1968, the National Association of Broadcasters, in a 256-page report to the President's Task Force on Communications Policy, displayed a touching concern for "the poor, the elderly, the handicapped and the rurally located" who might be deprived of free television if CATV were allowed to develop without restriction. But, in the true spirit of American enterprise, many companies with a vested interest in traditional television began hedging their investments by buying into CATV, while supporting the industry effort to suppress it.

Because the stakes are so high, the battle over CATV can tell us a good deal about what happens in American society when public and private interests collide. For at least five years, it had been clear to media executives and government communications experts that a major issue was developing, but, until 1971, the public heard very little about it from newspapers, magazines, radio and television. By then, such noncorporate publications as the *Nation, Ramparts* and the *Village Voice* had begun sounding the alarm, but others like *Time* and *Life* were still strangely unconcerned, even though, by then, their parent company, Time Inc., was selling its radio and television stations and had bought up more than a dozen CATV systems.

While the campaign to hobble cable television was being waged quietly in Washington, an electronic Gold Rush was under way in communities across the country. Early franchises had been given to small businessmen like Robert Tarlton, but the large corporations soon moved in, buying out local operators with common stock and capital gains, and acquiring unclaimed territories by the time-honored method of buttering up and, where necessary, bribing local politicians. In 1971, the New Jersey Assembly voted a one-year moratorium on cable franchises. By then, in the absence of state regulation, nearly 150 out of 567 municipalities had given away franchises. In several communities, local officials were facing indictment for extortion. In others, such crude measures were apparently unnecessary. Politicians, unaware of what CATV is or could be, were willing to settle for campaign contributions and/or a modest share of the profits for hard-pressed municipal treasuries.

Perhaps such official stupidity and corruption can be shrugged off as the classic social price for the benefits of free enterprise. But, as the true dimensions of CATV emerge, it is no overstatement to say that what was being bribed and bartered away is future control of the American public's consciousness, through, in Fred Friendly's phrase, "these conduits that will determine what kind of people we are." As the London *Economist* put it: "Before very long, information theory will have been brought to its logical conclusion in public communications; there will be a single unified network for all kinds of messages . . . Information will flow through the network as on-off digital signals and appear as pictures, sound or print, according to the choice of those sending and receiving it."

By 1971, even our most conservative national politicians were beginning to worry over the spectacle. The Justice Department, under Attorney General John Mitchell, raised a nervous objection over the proposed union of two large CATV corporations, citing concern for "diversity in ideas, viewpoints and entertainment," but then did nothing to stop the merger. From the White House, President Nixon's Director of the Office of Telecommunications Policy called the system of exclusive municipal CATV franchises "absurd." And Governor Nelson Rockefeller proposed that the New York State Public Service Commission take a hand in regulating local franchising in order to, as he delicately put it, "correct the limitations in that system."

But such high-level clucking appears to be too little and too late. While the FCC was accumulating acres of hearing transcripts, the corporate poker players had been accumulating all the chips in the continental game for control of our frontal lobes. Corporations owning cable systems have merged, not only with one another, but with producers of televised sports events, cartoons and such ornaments to the First Amendment as the "Lassie" and "Lone Ranger" series. What they have in mind for that eventual "single unified network for all kinds of messages" is becoming distressingly clear. It is far from the utopia of diversified information, culture and entertainment that is described in the official pronouncements of the National Cable Television Association.

If we end up with electronic boxes in our homes that offer a hundred brands of banality, the corporate statesmen will call it a triumph of democracy — giving the people what they want. But the people, of course, will have had no choice. While the issue was being settled in the commercial and political back rooms, a rational alternative has always been available: to treat the cable as a common carrier, like the telephone and the mails. In that case, cable owners would be licensed to operate a public utility but would not decide how it was to be used. Local and state authorities would regulate rates, as they do with telephones and electricity, and set up safeguards against violations of obscenity, sedition and slander laws. Instead of creating a golden goose for cable owners doubling as broadcasters, the system would then provide access to anyone with information, ideas and entertainment to offer. But what we face now is what we would have had if the Founding Fathers had franchised the postal system, community by community, to private promoters and then allowed only those promoters to send newspapers and magazines through the mails.

The other prong of the approaching electronic pincers is the video cassette. Instead of watching the trash scheduled by the three major networks, the public will soon have the privilege of buying and renting custom-made trash for their television sets. Half a dozen systems, each incompatible with the rest, are being rushed into production by such cultural agencies as CBS, RCA and Avco. With an attachment costing from $500 to $800, viewers will be able to buy individual cassettes, estimated at $10 to $20 each, and enjoy all the glories of Western civilization when and as they desire. The cassette makers have been scrambling to buy up thousands of old movies, tapes of football games, how-to films and ancient children's shows, and they are already planning to offer one form of culture currently unavailable on television: pornography. But how much further video cassettes will extend our range of information and entertainment is an open question. Unlike cable television, when the technological conflicts have been resolved, cassette production will be open to anyone who can identify a market, and it *is* possible that new ideas will find their way into the cartridges.

Possible, but, considering the pressures toward mass selling, not probable. Yet, in October 1970, *Life* published an eight-page article, illustrated with those familiar multiple-exposure pop-science color photographs, under the title "A Good Revolution Goes on Sale," and the optimistic blurb "Cassette TV lets the viewer pick his own show." The article concluded by raising the future prospect that every household will be "plugged into a network of cable TV data banks containing — and available on call — all material on cassettes, all books and materials in libraries and museums and much else besides." When that time comes, according to *Life*, "we will have gained the power of virtually limitless choice over subject matter for our entertainment and enlightenment."

It would be uncharitable to make a direct connection between *Life's* euphoria over cable cum cassettes and its own company's continuing acquisition of CATV systems, along with the formation, early in 1971, of Time-Life Video, to rent and sell cassettes containing old movies, children's shows, sports, recreation, home education, current affairs, history, the arts and family services — mainly, it would appear, by putting the Time-Life imprimatur on films, old and new, produced by others. But a juxtaposition of personal impressions is irresistible: In 1970, I was one of the judges for the National Magazine Awards, administered by the

Columbia Graduate School of Journalism. We gave *Life* a well-deserved award for public service for its aggressive reporting on the questionable private dealings of Supreme Court Justice Abe Fortas and other national political figures. In 1971, we gave the same award to *The Nation*, largely for its comprehensive report on the power struggle over CATV ("The Wired Nation" by Ralph Lee Smith). It is important to expose personal political corruption, of course, but I could not help wishing that a mass-circulation magazine had taken on the issue that will have much greater bearing on the future course of American society.

Although timetables vary, most observers of the media foresee the ultimate joining of an electronic trinity: cable, cassettes and computer. When that happens, the most significant innovation will not be the form in which information is delivered — projection on a giant television screen or print-out on paper from an electronic console — but the change in the relationship between those who gather information and those who receive it. To this point in human history, the receiver of information — reader, listener, viewer — has been in a passive position. Editors, publishers and broadcasters have decided or, rather, guessed what would be likely to interest him and at what length. (The average newspaper uses only 10 to 20 per cent of the news that comes into its offices every day; radio and television pluck an even smaller percentage of items from the daily flow.) But, with high-speed processes for transmitting information and immense storage units for holding it until wanted, the reader / listener / viewer will find himself taking a much more active role in creating the picture of the world he carries in his head.

This is not to say that editors will lose their power — far

from it — but that they will take on the additional duty,
as Ben Bagdikian pointed out in *The Information Machines,*
of librarians. Future newspapers are likely to consist
mainly of headlines and brief summaries, from which the
receiver can immediately call up detailed information on
those developments that interest him. Future magazines
may, in printed form, serve largely as brochures for the new
material on various subjects that the editors have fed into
the computer that week or that month — whetting readers'
interest with capsule condensations, such as those now
found on the contents pages of *Fortune* and *New York,* and
perhaps the opening paragraphs of each article as a further hook for their attention.

If the new technology works this way, it will relieve one
traditional media problem: waste. In the ecological sense,
millions of trees will be spared from destruction to produce
unread areas of newspapers and magazines (*pace* the Sunday real-estate sections), since readers, instead of skimming
pages, will have printed out only what they want when they
want it. In the editorial sense, such a process will allow
minority interests to be served without putting unwanted
material in the hands of the majority. In editing a mass
women's magazine, for example, it has always bothered
me that a useful article on, say, childbirth would have
immediate value for only a fraction of readers. In the computer, such an article could be called up by pregnant women,
while others were asking for the latest information on day-
care centers, menopause or nursing homes, depending on
their needs.

The price for efficiency may be high. One of the classic
benefits of good editing is surprise: the pleasure and satisfaction a reader experiences from an article or story he had
no way of knowing he wanted or needed. Such experiences

are possible because a reader has learned to trust the taste and judgment of the editors of a particular publication. No matter how much diversity is built into the circuits, it will be difficult to sustain this kind of relationship through a computer. Moreover, as the link between readers and editors is weakened, it may seem logical, in the interests of efficiency, to reduce and simplify the amount and kind of material available in the electronic storehouses. Discussing these prospects, a journalism student once told me: "I would hate to push a button for information on Vietnam and get only the official point of view."

There is no suitable tone for expressing such anxieties. It is easy enough to label as too shrill Nicholas Johnson's warning about future freedom of information: "If we are unwilling to discuss *this* issue fully today, we may find ourselves discussing none that matter very much tomorrow." But his frustration is understandable in the face of almost total public apathy, matched by the complacency of most editors, publishers and broadcasters. It is likely that we will never be *completely* ensnared by the web of cables, cassettes and computers; that conventional newspapers, magazines and books will survive in some form; and that underground publications and broadcasts will undoubtedly manage to filter through the web.

Yet we should know by now that the technological society is designed to lull us with the appearance of freedom and diversity while maintaining control where it counts: Let the underground papers rant, but keep the pressure on network television to make sure that it does not "abuse" its freedom, i.e., take it too literally. In fact, the pressure seldom has to be applied because the larger the system, the more it becomes self-regulating. Network television controls its own possible excesses through built-in anxiety, in the same way that the power grid responds to a heavy demand for electricity, not by apportioning the available supply on some humane basis, but simply by shutting itself off. The system is designed, above all, to protect itself. If we are to maintain any human priorities in the operation of the new media technology, the time to raise questions and make social and moral decisions is now, before all the machinery is in place. After that, it will be too late.

There are small hopeful signs. While new commissions and study groups continue to pore over the same crushingly obvious facts, some communities and some states are dampening the franchise fever to take stock of what they might be giving away. A few politicians are beginning to embrace the common carrier concept, at least for a number of channels in the vast cable repertoire. In New York City, where an excellent survey was conducted for Mayor John V. Lindsay in 1968, two channels have been set aside as common carriers and, in the areas already franchised, have gone into service. What goes out over them may not always be polished or even polite, but it *is* free expression.

Someday, direct satellite-to-home transmission or some other technical development may supersede the cable, but the social, political and cultural questions will remain the same. The answers we develop now are very likely the ones we, and our children, will have to live with for a long time.

11

Two Cheers for
Freedom of Expression

I HAVE WRITTEN, *and then thrown away, several endings
to this book. Over all of them there hung that fatality of last
chapters, in which every idea seems to find its place, and all
the mysteries, that the writer has not forgotten, are unraveled
. . . The last chapter is merely a place where the writer
imagines that the polite reader has begun to look furtively
at his watch.*
— Walter Lippmann, *Public Opinion* (1922)

About the thousands of journalists I have worked with, the
hundreds I have known reasonably well, the dozens who
have become close friends, I can make one generalization
with confidence: Very few came to their work for reasons
that are not essentially moral, however embarrassed many
of them would be to apply that word to what they do every
day. To examine the workings of the world and reveal
them to others is not a neutral enterprise. Invariably, it
is rooted in some vision, conscious or not, of how things
should be as well as how they are. In our time, the underlying impulse may not be as simple as that classic journalistic credo — "The duty of a newspaper is to comfort the
afflicted and afflict the comfortable" — but it exists in some

form beneath the professional disciplines of detachment and fairness. For the most part, journalists are men and women who derive more satisfaction from exploring and explaining the world than wresting power and profit from it.

Life has a way of eroding even the best intentions. But the present dilemmas of reporters and editors cannot be fully explained by the compromises that are normally exacted by age and ambition. If none of my contemporaries has attained the undisputed moral stature of a William Allen White, a Lincoln Steffens or a Ralph McGill, the explanation lies deeper than the nature of individual character and commitments. In fact, there is persuasive evidence that, on the whole, journalists today are more honest, more idealistic and intellectually better equipped than those of any previous generation. What is new and different are the dimensions of the pressures at work to confound their moral impulses in serving the vast machinery of information today.

Many of these pressures come from the size and complexity of the society. American journalism developed its principles and practices in a far different world, a world of small communities in which people could test the authenticity of the news by looking directly into the faces of those who made it as well as those who reported it. "The environment," Walter Lippmann has pointed out, "was so familiar that one could take it for granted that men were talking about substantially the same things. The only real disagreements, therefore, would be in judgment about the same facts. There was no need to guarantee the sources of information. They were obvious, and equally accessible to all men." Now that the environment is global and unfamiliar, we are all strangers to one another — and suspicious strangers, at that. We cannot take it for granted that men are talking about the same things.

Fifty years ago, in *Public Opinion*, Lippmann wrote that the difficulties of journalism, like those of government and industry, "go back to a common source: to the failure of self-governing people to transcend their casual experience and their prejudice, by inventing, creating, and organizing a machinery of knowledge." Lippmann proposed the remedy that social institutions employ reason and intelligence to "work by a steady light of their own," so that journalists could concentrate on amplifying and transmitting that light to the public.

Now, it is clear that, as they have grown, institutions such as government and industry have indeed developed a "machinery of knowledge," but one that is geared to produce not understanding but obfuscation, not to invite criticism and correction but to promote and protect their own power. Between reality and reportage, the machinery imposes not only self-serving secrecy but what the historian Daniel Boorstin has called "pseudo-events" — interviews, speeches, press conferences, briefings, releases, reports, leaks, guided tours, presentations, receptions and many other forms of manufactured news.

The problem goes far beyond the issue of "news management" (a euphemism for official lying) that periodically produces self-righteous debate between government and media. Several years ago, the Associated Press reported that the Federal government alone spends $425 million a year on "public information, news, views and self-pleadings" — more than twice the combined expenditure for newsgathering by the two major wire services, the three large television networks and the ten largest newspapers in the country. The survey estimated that there were 6858 Federal employees creating tendentious news, several times the number of journalists employed in Washington to evaluate what spews out of government mimeograph machines and to uncover what information officers are paid to obscure. Much of this money spent to make and/or hide news is not even controlled by government agencies but by private companies with defense and space contracts, which routinely bill the government for public relations just as they do for other management costs. In the world of what President Eisenhower called the military-industrial complex, taxpayers even contract for fabricated news at cost-plus.

Like most technological systems, the machinery of obfuscation is designed to protect itself when threatened. In 1971, when CBS had the temerity to scratch its surface, however gently, in "The Selling of the Pentagon," the television program led to attacks on the network by the Vice President as well as a Congressional investigation, not of the Pentagon but of CBS. A few months later, when the *New York Times* brought to light what became known as the Pentagon Papers, the entire legal weight of the Executive branch was applied in an attempt to stop publication. Although the government pleaded in the courts, and lost, on the basis of the danger to national security, the White House's real concern, as Director of Communications Herbert Klein made clear, was to avoid future disclosures. In an affidavit, Max Frankel of the *Times* called the government's action "monstrous and hypocritical," since officials, for their own purposes, are constantly feeding secrets to reporters.

Any joy over the press' victory in the case has to be tempered by the awareness that journalists are usually willing partners in their own manipulation by officials and that, had not the Pentagon itself employed 36 analysts to assemble 7000 pages of material and then conveniently neglected to safeguard it properly, much of the information contained in the Pentagon Papers would have remained buried in government archives for decades. (Even retired politicians of a rival party are considered better security risks than journalists. There was no Republican outcry when Lyndon Johnson took several truckloads of government files with him to Texas to begin his own reconstruction of recent history after receiving a publisher's advance of $1,500,000.)

As reporters and editors exhaust themselves in penetrating this bureaucratic swamp, most of them are inevitably caught in its premises. No matter how much venality and deception is uncovered, the rules of journalism require that each instance be treated as an aberration rather than part of a larger problem. Those who attempt to report in a broader context are accused of forfeiting their objectivity. They have the choice of becoming pariahs and losing their access to sources of information, or commentators and losing their credibility as reporters. In either case, the machinery grinds on, immeasurably strengthened by those journalists who convince themselves they are doing their jobs by following the accepted rules — i.e., it's all right occasionally to point out that a bit of paint has been chipped off the social machine but not to ask where the machine is taking us. As a result, much of the real questioning of society is given over to radical rhetoric, and media people are confronted with a choice between two kinds of manipulation. Both Eldridge Cleaver and Spiro Agnew are telling them, in effect: If you're not part of the solution, you're part of the problem.

In a more rational world, journalism would not be required to mediate between a social juggernaut and those who are trying to destroy it. It is too much to ask media people not only to report American reality but hold it together. Yet, more and more, as other institutions default and Media Power grows, that seems to be their assignment. Under the circumstances, the crucial questions they will have to answer — for themselves as well as their critics — are neither political nor professional but moral.

If I were allowed to put up one sign in every editorial office in America, large and small, it would bear these words by Cesar Chavez: "When we are really honest with ourselves, we must admit that our lives are all that really belong to us, so it is how we use our lives that determines what kind of men we are."

How media people use their lives is at the heart of all the questions about freedom and responsibility. As publishers, broadcasters, editors and reporters work under the constant demands of deadlines and competition, their private values tend to be pushed further and further into the background until, in some cases, particularly at the executive level, they disappear completely. For years I have been fascinated by what happens to individuals (including myself) when they gather around a corporate table. Institutional responsibility seems to act simultaneously as a narcotic that suppresses conscience and a stimulant that brings out every bit of low cunning that can be used to profit the organization. I have seen prominent educators, editors and publishers sanctimoniously propose solutions to company problems that would make a carnival pitchman blush. Under the circumstances, to raise a moral question that would endanger institutional objectives is considered as unseemly as swearing in church. To express doubt about corporate practices is made to appear, at best, irrelevant, and, somehow, *unmanly*.

The prevailing mode of discourse is group rationalization, which can take on the fervor of an Esalen encounter session. At a meeting of the board of directors of the Magazine Publishers Association in 1971, for example, the subject was the policing of false and misleading advertising. By this time, under pressure from government and consumer groups, advertisers and agencies themselves were trying to work out some method of eliminating the most blatant lies that are used to sell products. The question before the publishers was whether, under the most careful safeguards, they would consider refusing to accept advertising deemed by an impartial industry group to be beyond the pale. The publishers were as shocked as if someone had suggested making cut-rate subscriptions illegal. To a man, they refused to entertain the suggestion, which, considering the source, might have taken them the smallest distance toward honoring the rhetoric of social responsibility in their speeches and promotional advertising. "After all," a leading publisher said to murmurs of general approval, "we're only distributors of advertising — we can't be expected to police it."

After all, said Eichmann . . . After all, said Lieutenant Calley . . .

This is not to say that we all become Eichmanns or Calleys under the pressure of institutional objectives, but it is to say that the pressure exists. Most publishers and editors are decent men. But, consciously or not, as they assume their professional roles each day, they put on corporate blinders that make it difficult to see, let alone honor, their personal commitments to human life. The worst derelictions are not committed directly for profit — few media executives would knowingly endanger people as casually as drug manufacturers and automobile makers do — but indirectly, by adhering to unexamined assumptions about the distance between personal and professional responsibilities.

At the working level, sophistication joins self-righteous-

ness as the most common means of sublimating moral conflicts. In private moments, over a quarter of a century, I
have found myself wishing I were as sure of anything as
many editors appear to be of everything. Without doubt,
they are under pressure to behave this way: Readers,
viewers and listeners not only want to know what happened,
rather than what may have happened, but they expect to be
told what is likely to happen as well. Should one publication
refuse to accommodate them, others will cheerfully fill the
breach. But, external pressure aside, professional omniscience protects editors and reporters from their own qualms
and scruples. Unfortunately, the best protection is provided by the meanest kind of certitude. Taking too generous a view of human actions and motives exposes a journalist to the risk of appearing naïve. There is no comparable
penalty for nastiness — at worst, he earns grudging respect as a hard-nosed reporter or editor.

Since journalism is poorly equipped to deal with doubt
and ambiguity, journalists often tell us more than they know,
particularly when they have to depend on official sources
for news. Conversely, in the absence of what they consider
legitimate channels of news, journalists tell us less than
they know. On some occasions, the subject is literally life
and death, on a massive scale.

In 1963, when he was trying to rally public support for
the limited nuclear test-ban treaty, John F. Kennedy was
frustrated by the excessive attention the press was paying
to military men and their apologists who opposed the pact.
Pointing out that three hundred million deaths might result
from a nuclear exchange, President Kennedy told me in an
interview: "That means that everybody is involved in this
debate. You don't need a military background or access
to top-secret documents." Yet, all during this period,

editors chose to patronize Dr. Benjamin Spock, for example, as an overwrought pediatrician, while gravely respecting the expertise of every Neanderthal general or Congressman who offered an opinion on the subject.

Ironically, as Kennedy was complaining about journalists' excessive awe of military men and politicians on the subject of nuclear controls, he was fuming over the refusal of *New York Times* correspondent David Halberstam to take at face value the Kennedy Administration's political and military estimate of what was happening in Vietnam. For years after that, the overwhelming majority of editors continued to accept the official version. Few allowed their concern for human life, American or Vietnamese, to prompt a critical questioning of the war until students, professors and housewives forced the issue into the open. Yet, as far back as 1963, when American deaths in Vietnam were 100 rather than 55,000, a nonpolitical women's magazine like *Redbook* was expressing concern over the war in an article that ended with these questions:

"How much are we being told about what is going on? To what extent are American resources and manpower being committed to combat without the nation's understanding and support? Do we have the moral right or obligation to fight to save from Communism people who do not always seem to *want* to be saved from it? Should we continue to make sacrifices for governments that are 'anti-Communist' but are themselves dictatorial or even tyrannical? How can we prevent the spread of Communism in situations where right and wrong and good and evil are blurred?"

When the Pentagon Papers finally came along, editors had official confirmation of what they may have suspected years earlier. In the midst of self-congratulation for defying the government by publishing the Pentagon material, few

editors reproached themselves and their reporters for failing
to dig out some of those facts at the time they were current.

Over that period, deep divisions were developing in
American life, not only over the war, but over racism, poverty, education and the destruction of the environment,
among other issues. As journalists were frantically recording the symptoms of this division, they found themselves
being accused, on all sides, of carrying the disease. It
took a long time for even the best of them to realize that
what was being brought into question was not their skill or
even their integrity but their time-honored professional assumptions. In 1971, Tom Wicker of the *New York Times*
told a group of journalism students:

To the extent that you are reliant upon institutional sources for
news you are reliant upon a self-serving source which, in every
case, will attempt to put the best face on the news, to interpret
information for you in the light of its own interest . . . These
institutions have stood still while the world has moved out from
under them. Therefore you are going not only to a self-serving
source for news but to a source that simply may not know what
it's talking about . . . Anybody who has been roaming the country as a reporter in the last few years can cite examples of having
gone to a perfectly respectable institution, to a highly official
source, and taken a statement that seems to have absolute surface
validity, only to find that as events unfolded it meant nothing because it was out of touch with reality.

The best reporters, like Wicker, refuse to screen out those
aspects of the world that have not been sanctioned by
scientific, academic, corporate or political authority. But
Wicker is a member of a journalistic minority, a man who,
in David Halberstam's phrase, has "never lost his sense of
rage." The *Times* is clearly much more comfortable with
Wicker as a columnist, a role in which he is speaking for

himself, than as a reporter, using his perception in a way that stretches the traditional language of objectivity.

The heart of the difficulty is that this language has always been the language of power. That is why so much reporting revolves around institutions and the organized groups that oppose them. But it is becoming clear that, beyond the noisy power struggles that occupy so much of our attention, the important news about American society involves values — what kind of people we are and how we live. Editors and publishers understand the etiquette of power, but values make them nervous. Power has always been hard news, but values were "Yes, Virginia, there is a Santa Claus," and editorials about free speech. Today, even as reflective an organ as the *New York Times* is willing to talk about values *ad nauseam* on its editorial and Op-Ed pages, but the news columns are reserved almost exclusively for power. (On a day in June 1971, the *Times* itself came close to admitting this disparity. Its front pages reported New York City in near-chaos because municipal workers, angry at the State legislature's refusal to ratify their pension agreements, had opened drawbridges and abandoned city trucks on the highways. On the Op-Ed page, the union leader who had ordered this sabotage and was threatening more of it, asserted in an essay that organized labor was the true friend of those "who struggle for civil rights, social welfare, the needs of the poor and the defense of the environment." In an editorial, the *Times* noted that his actions as a labor leader had made "a mockery of his protestations" as an author.)

On every issue, the media isolate values from power as carefully as the Victorians separated love from sex. Black militants and their skirmishes with police are news, but the daily reality of life in the black ghettos is not. The seizure of campus buildings brings out the television cameras and headlines, but we hear little about the education going on in those buildings during normal times. On Vietnam, the Administration's rhetoric, the official body counts and the tactics of protesters are news, but the meaning of Vietnam is obscured until Mylai explodes in our faces. Then it becomes the Calley case, an issue in which we can all acquit ourselves metaphorically or find ourselves guilty. Either way, the questions are tied up in a neat little package of legal and political conflict, to be pushed to the back shelf of our consciousness after a few weeks and forgotten. The war goes on, and we can return to the safe surface of body counts and protest tactics. Life and death in the Vietnamese villages, and our responsibility for it, is not news, only the occasion for an inside-page feature or a one-minute film clip on a slow day.

Television unwittingly introduced values into the news, but through a back door. While well-groomed announcers were giving us newspaperlike abstractions, the little screen has been showing us death, suffering and human anger. The connection between power and values, which the journalists, in their best professional manner, avoid making, is nevertheless being made in our nervous systems. One immediate result is that the power genie has escaped the institutional bottle, and we are beset by media-elected spokesmen to counter the professional politicians: Weathermen, Yippies, hard hats, Black Panthers, police unionists, environmental apocalyptists, Mafia statesmen, Jewish commandos, American Indian occupation forces, Women's Lib guerrillas — all making their power plays on the evening news and the next day's front pages. As the conventional politicians have always done before them, the anti-politicians insist they are educating us to values, but the only way to get our attention is to keep buttonholing us with power until our media teeth rattle.

It is this failure to transcend the language of power that underlies many of the complaints against journalists today, from the New Left through the Silent Majority to the Radical Right. For differing reasons and purposes, they all resent (even while attempting to exploit) the picture of the world they have been getting, the definition of news that is conditioned by a preoccupation with power.

"A bill is coming in that I fear America is not prepared to pay." James Baldwin made the prediction almost a decade ago in *The Fire Next Time*. The bill seems to have arrived, and it is not for racism alone. It is being delivered, not only through the media, but *to* the media, and it itemizes all the expensive assumptions that have permitted us to accumulate comfort and power while considering ourselves free, responsible and decent.

Traditionally, editors and publishers, to put it mildly, have not invited critical analysis of their work. Typical of their attitude was the response in 1947 to a report entitled *A Free and Responsible Press*, by a group largely composed of scholars including Reinhold Niebuhr, William Ernest Hocking, Harold Lasswell, Archibald MacLeish and Zecheriah Chaffee, Jr. In careful language, the report advocated more vigorous pursuit of a number of democratic principles: maintaining competition in the press through antitrust laws, extending First Amendment protection to radio and movies (television was in its infancy), wider distribution of information about government policies, better training of reporters, more mutual criticism by journalists and "establishment of a new and independent agency to appraise and report annually upon the performance of the press."

As a news story, the report met with outraged silence. The president of the American Society of Newspaper Editors did remark that the report had damaged freedom of the press throughout the world. Arthur Hays Sulzberger, publisher of the *New York Times*, was quoted by his own paper as observing that people who did not like one newspaper could read another, stop reading altogether or start one of their own. The Chicago *Tribune*, never a journal to mince words, ran a critique under the headline: "A Free Press (Hitler Style) Sought for U.S. Totalitarians Tell How It Can Be Done."

The "totalitarians" had been financed in their work by a grant of $200,000 from Henry R. Luce, administered by Robert M. Hutchins, then chancellor of the University of Chicago, later to be head of the Fund for the Republic and the Center for the Study of Democratic Institutions.

Introspection has not been the hallmark of people who control the media. Now, the questions they have failed to ask themselves are being asked by others. The reasonable voices of 1947 have given way to the more strident voices of the 1970s: the Agnews, the underground, the newsroom activists. It is understandable that publishers and broadcasters would respond, not to Agnew's challenges to their prevailing values, but to his clumsy hints of intimidation. But, in a sense, they had invented Agnew themselves by failing to recognize the right of *anyone* to question their values. Academic critics had been dismissed as woolly-headed and impractical, the underground had been packaged into a crackpot phenomenon, and the newsroom activists, for the most part, were being treated as a management problem rather than a source for self-examination. If those without power are irrelevant and those with power are a menace, who has a legitimate right to raise questions?

Until recently, the answer was no one. That answer has come back to haunt the media managers. In failing to recognize any partner in the debate over their principles and practices, they have opened the door to everyone who nominates himself. The first to come rushing through have been, not those who want to help them define and use their power more responsibly, but those who want to control or destroy it.

Yet, there are signs that a useful debate is beginning. Serious self-criticism is rapidly being institutionalized, not only through staff-management forums at various publications and broadcast organizations, but in print. For years, professional journals were either business-oriented like *Editor and Publisher*, or platitudinous, like the *Nieman Reports*. In 1961, the *Columbia Journalism Review* was born. It immediately began to deal with the harder questions, albeit on a craft level that often stopped short of the deeper issues. In the past few years, keeping pace with the rising activism of young journalists, the *Review*, under Alfred Balk, has moved energetically into those critical areas. In a special issue on Vietnam (winter 1970-71), for example, working reporters and journalism teachers reviewed almost a decade of coverage and analyzed its shortcomings: overreliance on government information, treating a guerrilla war in the language of World War II, discounting the peace movement at home, the delay in investigating on reporters' own initiative such crucial events as the battle in Tonkin Gulf and the Mylai massacre, and emphasizing military developments at the expense of the long-range social, economic and political situation. In short, journalists were asking themselves what was really going on while they were chasing deadlines.

At the same time, local journalism reviews have begun

to examine with a hard eye reporting in Chicago, St. Louis, Denver, Cleveland, Albuquerque, Providence and other cities. In mid-1971, a New York review was launched under the title "(*more*)" — the newspaperman's indication at the bottom of a page that his copy is not finished.

A parallel development in self-criticism has been the invention of the editorial ombudsman — a critic on the payroll. In 1966, at the Louisville *Courier-Journal*, a former city editor began to investigate about 500 reader complaints a year. By his own testimony, this work was not received with total enthusiasm by staff reporters: "Going into the city room, I know how a policeman feels going into the ghetto." Several other newspapers have appointed ombudsmen, and it remains to be seen whether the results in better reporting will outweigh the bruised egos.

Hard-headed, knowledgeable criticism by working reporters and editors can produce immediate results, but, sooner or later, the public will have to be invited to join the debate. If media people fail to issue the invitation, political demagogues will.

There are good reasons for journalists to be wary of outsiders. A newspaper, a magazine, a television news unit is a fragile organism that survives on a complex, delicate balance of craft, judgment and ego. The introduction of an irritant is just as likely to cause an infection in an organism as stimulate it to produce a pearl. But the laws of nature give organisms a hard choice: adapt to a changing environment, or sicken and die. So far, the pace of media adaptation has been glacial.

For years, newspapers had been urged to set up local press councils, at which community representatives could air their dissatisfactions and desires, and journalists could explain the complexities of reporting. In 1967, using a $40,-

ooo bequest by a newspaper editor to "stimulate responsibility in the press while maintaining freedom," several press councils were set up in small towns across the country. After three years, the publisher of the Bend (Oregon) *Bulletin* told a group of editors that he was satisfied with the experiment. "They do not tell us how to run our newspaper," he explained. "They do tell us what they think of the way we run it. They accept, and seek, complaints from readers about our performance, and tell us whether they think the readers are right. We were surprised and pleased when members of the council, after hearing a full explanation from both sides, agreed, at least in part, with the newspaper in most cases."

So far, the idea has not spread beyond a handful of communities, although Minnesota had organized a state council. As for a National Press Council, similar to the one that has been operating successfully in Great Britain for almost a decade, the response of publishers and broadcasters has been almost unanimous lack of interest. The British Council, made up predominantly of working journalists with a few laymen, considers disputes only if the complainant waives his right to use the findings in subsequent legal action and if the accused editor agrees to publish the council's decision. After five years, the number of libel suits in Britain has been reduced, and, in a survey, 86 per cent of the newspapermen questioned approved of the council's work.

In the absence of any rational social process for marking the boundaries of media freedom and responsibility, disputes lead to noisy and unenlightening public quarrels between politicians and journalists, followed by unfortunate attempts to settle the questions in legislative and judicial arenas. A National Press Council might have focused the serious questions involved in CBS' "The Selling of the Pentagon" and the *New York Times'* publication of the Pentagon Papers. Instead, those questions ended up in a Congressional committee and a courtroom, where coercion became the main issue, rather than the propriety and value of those journalistic efforts. Once again, power makes the news and values are pushed into the background.

Between upheavals, the vacuum of responsible debate produces bizarre and dangerous proposals from all sides. Vice President Agnew, with his inimitable logic, suggests that television panels of politicians interrogate journalists about *their* beliefs. Other public figures have proposed that licenses be required to practice journalism. The American Civil Liberties Union reflects its gloomy view of media responsibility by considering lawsuits that would enforce a "right of access" to the press of unpopular opinions under an expanded definition of the First Amendment. When the ACLU joins Agnew in placing more faith in the fairness of officials than journalists, it is time for media people to give up any remaining illusions about holding a privileged and trusted position in American society.

Our form of government assumes that the truth will emerge, in Judge Learned Hand's phrase, from "a multitude of tongues." As technology has multiplied and amplified them, however, the products of those tongues have begun to resemble a Tower of Babel. Since no intervening authority, political or legal, can be trusted to sort out the media's messages, the burden is squarely on those who send them and those who receive them.

The process is beginning. In addition to newsroom debates and journalism reviews, editors and broadcasters are starting to evaluate and criticize their own work for the public. *Harper's, The Atlantic, Saturday Review, The New*

Yorker, Esquire and *New York,* as well as some television and radio stations, have devoted increasing attention to journalism in the past few years, and a number of gifted critics have begun to explore aspects of the subject on a more or less regular basis: Nat Hentoff, Michael Arlen, Edwin Diamond, Ben Bagdikian and Edward Jay Epstein, among others. In the coming years, journalism will undoubtedly become a major subject of journalism.

All of this is to the good, but something more than corrective journalism is needed for the long run. The place to start looking for it is among future generations of readers and viewers. To judge from the curricula of elementary and high schools, it would seem that children still form their picture of the world from what they see and hear in the classroom, the library and at their parents' knees. Yet, while teachers are droning on about reading, writing and arithmetic, most children are receiving their real education elsewhere — not only from television and the periodicals that flood the family mailbox but from their own publications: *Mad, Rolling Stone, National Lampoon,* the comics and the underground newspapers. In some of the more ambitious schools, social studies will introduce children to ancient cultures but will fail to give them any way of dealing with the raw material of their own. While conducting the Carnegie study of American schools that resulted in his book, *Crisis in the Classroom,* Charles E. Silberman remarked: "An example of mindlessness is the failure of public schools as well as universities to recognize the existence of mass media. Teachers at both grumble about the media, but fail to provide their students with the means to criticize those media."

It may seem unrealistic to ask American schools, in their current state of disrepair, to take on the added responsibility of teaching children a few fundamental skills for evaluating the words and images that surround them. Yet, some of the schools' own difficulties can surely be traced to their unwillingness to recognize that the media have been giving children a concurrent and conflicting education that is vastly more effective than what they have been getting in the classroom. If only in self-defense, the schools will eventually have to recognize that conflict and address themselves to it.

If elementary and high schools are deficient, their failure is more understandable than that of colleges and universities. In higher education, until recently, the media have been relegated to two minor academic pigeonholes: journalism, where retired newspapermen analyze news stories and spin anecdotes; and communications, where social scientists reduce living issues to jargon and statistics. On a few campuses, notably the Columbia Graduate School of Journalism, something new is emerging: an attempt to bring both practical experience and academic skills to bear on the real problems and possibilities presented by such developments as the New Journalism, the underground, changing technology and the conflict of government and media. (It may be significant that such efforts are being made at Columbia, where, in 1968, campus rebels proved to be so adroit in exploiting the presence of the national media.) As Professor William L. Rivers of Stanford has pointed out, such programs are vital not only to train future journalists, but because "students generally need to be fortified against the perils of living in a world that is enveloped, if not drowned, in mass communications."

The real long-range hope is in the simultaneous development of a generation of both journalists and educated citizens with increased awareness of the social issues surrounding Media Power and the alternatives available to deal with them. If journalism is to maintain any human scale in a mass society, we will need critical readers, viewers and listeners as well as talented editors and reporters.

Almost a century and a half ago, Alexis de Tocqueville looked at American journalism and gave two cheers for its freedom of expression. "I confess," Tocqueville wrote in *Democracy in America*, "that I do not entertain that firm and complete attachment to the liberty of the press which is wont to be excited by things that are supremely good in their very nature. I approve of it from a consideration more of the evils it prevents, than of the advantages it insures." The heart of Tocqueville's reservation was that, while competition among large numbers of American publications guaranteed independence from political control, it inevitably resulted in a low level of journalism — "vulgar" and "coarse" were the words he used.

In our own day, freedom and vulgarity still seem to be inseparable. Human nature being what it is, however, we are well-advised to struggle along in this imperfect condition. Only those who can visualize Spiro Agnew or John Mitchell as the font of an intellectual renaissance will be willing to give up any measure of freedom in the hope thereby of raising themselves to excellence. But, unless the fears of the underground papers about canceled elections turned out to be justified, the Spiro Agnews and John Mitchells will come and go in public life, and their attempts at political control will be largely offset by the aroused self-interest of swarms of publishers, broadcasters and opposing politicians. While it would be foolish to discount such threats, it would be paranoid to accept them as the central issue in American journalism today.

The important issues, as I have tried to show throughout this book, involve not what outsiders do to media people but what they do to themselves, consciously or not. While they resist political control, many submit to various forms of voluntary enslavement — to competition and deadlines, to their own ambitions and anxieties and, most of all, to narrow professional standards that obscure the human implications of their work. If freedom of the press ever disappears in America, it will not be with a bang but a whimper.

Yet the turmoil of recent years, the outside criticism and internal dissension, may do more to extend freedom than weaken it. Now that the crust of self-satisfaction is being chipped away and journalists are asking whether the First Amendment is more than a gentlemen's agreement between politicians and press not to disturb each other too much in the pursuit of power and profit, they are ready to face even harder questions. The most important involves the effects of Media Power — how their work affects people. Traditionally, reporters and editors have contended that they do not make the news, they simply report it. In a typical response to Vice President Agnew's polemics, Walter Cronkite told a gathering of journalists: "I don't think it is any of our business what the moral, political, social, or economic effect of our reporting is. I say let's get on with the job of reporting the news — and let the chips fall where they may. I suggest we concentrate on doing our job of telling it like it is . . ."

"It" — reality — is what happens to people all over the world twenty-four hours a day. News comes down to selecting a small fraction of the day's events. Those choices themselves have profound moral, political, social and economic effects. That they are made unconsciously by "professional" standards does not relieve those who make them of some responsibility for the effects.

One day in November 1968, for example, 55 reporters and photographers waited three hours in a cold rain to see Jacqueline Kennedy Onassis get off an airplane on her return to New York after marrying Aristotle Onassis. That evening, television showed us her arrival in detail, and the next morning, the *New York Times* devoted nineteen paragraphs and two three-column photographs to the story, starting on page one, and including the comments of the plane's stewardess: "She was just the most lovely, lovely person. She was very charming, very natural." At the time, 10,000 people a day were starving to death in Biafra. Of all the national media, only the *Times* covered a press conference that same day by a relief worker who predicted that two million Biafran children might die in the following two months. That news was reported by the *Times* the next morning in five paragraphs on page 20. Elsewhere there was only silence.

Such choices are made every day. The people who make them, willingly or not, shape our consciousness. No matter how impartially they report the facts, their choices both reflect and help determine the kind of people we are. Is it too much to ask them to face that responsibility?

To ask such a question is to confront the complexities arising from the competitive, and therefore repetitive, nature of American journalism. In a free society, every editor must evaluate news in his own best judgment and according to his own conscience. No one can be allowed to police his judgment or his conscience. But this puts a heavy burden on the editor. If, under the pressure of deadlines, he fails to ask himself what he is doing in a larger context, the questions will go unanswered.

In speeches and at seminars, editors, publishers and broadcasters give lip service to freedom and diversity. In practice, most of them most of the time act like part of a herd. They use their freedom to send reporters and cameramen swarming to the same places to record the same press conferences and staged events. In 1971, Fred Friendly, former president of CBS News, made a modest proposal to reduce journalistic waste by creating a "nationwide electronic news service," patterned after the News Election Service, which was established in 1964 to provide pooled returns to all news organizations instead of having them try to cover 25,000 precincts individually, as they had done in the past. Friendly pointed out:

> The spectacle of a half dozen camera crews and a dozen microphones, several from the same organization, standing tripod to tripod at Andrews Air Force Base to witness the Secretary of Defense's departure for a NATO meeting, or to cover S. I. Hayakawa's, Abbie Hoffman's, or George Wallace's latest news conference, often says more about the newsgatherers than it does about the news makers. Such events . . . illustrate the fact that the profession must repeatedly commit its best troops to the urgent rather than the important to avoid being scooped. The price for such overkill is often paid by missing truly significant stories.

Journalistic overkill is not limited to the waste of equipment and manpower. How much time and space are consumed in telling us what we already know, or will soon know, in more detail than we could reasonably require? Here, we are approaching the slippery area where editors feel constrained by time-honored professional conventions to ignore the fact that their readers and viewers have other sources of news. Each editor feels compelled to act as though he alone were bringing them the news of the world.

He has no accepted way of dealing with the momentous change that has been wrought by the media of which he is a part: Most people are no longer separated from the world outside their own experience.

In the past two decades, television has brought that world into every form of isolation: the black and the poor in rural backwaters and urban ghettos, the Indians on their reservations, housewives trapped in their domestic routines, children who used to grow up in a world limited to classroom and home, working men whose lives were bounded by factory, lodge, union hall and neighborhood tavern. As television made the world visible to those who used to be isolated, it made them more visible to the world and each other. It brought them into history. Journalism, like history, had always been largely the record of what was said and done by the rich and the powerful. Now, it is a much more complicated enterprise.

But old habits persist. Editors still abdicate to the politicians and, now, to the anti-politicians, who claim to represent various minorities, most of the daily decisions about what we will know of the world. Doing so, editors can hide from criticism by insisting that they are "telling it like it is." By that standard, political power alone still determines the news. But, as in other fields such as medicine, law and education, a new generation in journalism is attempting to understand and report what happens to people without power, whose lives constitute the vast reality that lies beyond power.

This kind of active journalism involves harder choices and greater risks. In condensing the amount of time devoted to the Secretary of Defense's departure and Abbie Hoffman's press conference, editors will have to examine and act on their own values in exploring the invisible news of the society. Since good editors always have more questions than answers, those values will be reflected more in the questions they ask than the answers they find. By pursuing the questions aggressively, in response to their own consciences and under the professional disciplines of honesty and fairness, they can give us a much more useful "multitude of tongues" than that which results from massive reporting of life in the ghettos, the factory towns, the suburbs and on the campuses and the farms only when the exercise of power or violence calls them into existence.

Because they are under competitive pressure to grab attention and must live in fear of being dull or obvious, few editors have been able to concentrate sufficiently on unwrapping rather than packaging problems by giving us background and perspective rather than slick summation. But imagination and initiative can help overcome those fears and, even where the difficulties are greatest — on television news, in the newsmagazines and largest newspapers — there are signs that the best editors are, to some extent, abandoning the safety of the herd to explore the reality behind the surface of pseudo-events. "Telling it like it is" is being redefined to allow the CBS, NBC and ABC evening news, *Time, Newsweek* and the *New York Times* to send their reporters and cameras into the villages of Vietnam and the streets of American cities and towns to show how war, racism, drugs, inflation and the abuse of the environment are affecting people's lives beyond the scenes that are staged by the politicians and the protesters.

The alternative to power-oriented reporting is not simply the kind of journalistic anarchy often practiced by the underground press. Both approaches have their uses in reflecting facets of reality — hard facts from the surface of society and impressions of how life feels below that surface.

But what we need most are journalists who will not limit themselves to any preconceived approach; who will use the popular clichés as starting points for investigation rather than shorthand to cut off debate; who will not be satisfied to accept uncritically the self-serving statements of official spokesmen or to put words into the mouths of bewildered bystanders; who, in approaching complex subjects, will use the resources of social science without embracing its pretensions; who, knowing there is no absolute truth to be discovered in any situation, will nevertheless persist until they have all the facts and clues available; who will see their work, not as producing plausible little packages of words and images, but as observing and responding to the world as human beings and conveying what they see and feel to other human beings.

The critics notwithstanding, journalists are going to have to rely on their own values more rather than less, not only in interpreting the news but in deciding what it is. Otherwise, news will remain a sterile enterprise — faceless people reporting to other faceless people. A journalist's perception is his — and our — most precious possession. It has to be protected from manipulation by politicians and theorists of all kinds, from the pressures of the organization he serves and, most of all, from his own needs for comfort and approval. He has undertaken to look at the world on our behalf as clearly and honestly as he can. Nothing less is worth doing.

DISCARDED

DATE DUE

301.161 St345 1972
Stein, Robert, 1924 Mar. 4-
Media power; who is shaping
 your picture of the   144115

WAKE FOREST HIGH SCHOOL
MEDIA CENTER
WEST STADIUM ROAD
WAKE FOREST, N.C. 27587